Rebuilding Trust in Banking:

Regulation, Corporate Governance

And Ethics in Banking

Professor Ray Kinsella

'Rebuilding Trust in Banking: Regulation, Corporate Governance and Ethics in Banking'

©Ray Kinsella, Vonier Press, Dublin 2009

Dedication

To the Holy Spirit, third Person of the Most Holy Trinity.

And to Ita and my family.

Acknowledgements

I would like to acknowledge, with gratitude, the assistance and support of a number of individuals and institutions, without whose help this volume of essays could not have been published. The main inspiration for the book has come from teaching, and reflecting with, my students – particularly those who have studied with me in the module 'Regulation Corporate Governance and Ethics in Financial Services', which I established what seems like a very long time ago.

Thanks are due to a number of individuals whom I am privileged to call friends, and whose insights and friendship have sustained me and taught me over the years.

I am grateful also to my former colleagues in the Central Bank of Ireland, as well as in University College Dublin, in the University of Ulster and other researchers with whom I have been privilege to work. A particular thanks is due to Fr. John McNerney for the insights which he shared with myself and my students on the whole issue of ethics.

Many individuals from banks and financial institutions have shared their wisdom – both professional and personal – with my students. I am especially grateful to them for giving up their time and sharing their lived experience with my students and with myself. I have also received very helpful input over the years from librarians – whose professionalism and skills could hardly be over-exaggerated. The ideas expressed in these pages were the subject of discussions I have had over the years with individuals whom I am privileged to call friends. How can you thank sufficiently for friendship?

The papers included in this volume include presentations and lectures to domestic and EU forum as well as one or two research papers. The great majority are articles which were, however, published in the media *well before* the present banking, and related economic crisis – with all of the associated political strains – became apparent.

The majority of these essays were published through The Irish Times, I would like to thank them not only for the hospitality of their pages, but for their invaluable editorial expertise. Similarly, I would like to thank the Irish Examiner, as well as the Irish Independent, the Sunday Business Post, Finance Magazine and Business & Finance, for allowing me permission to publish these essays as a thematic collection, dating back over some 15 years. I am very grateful to them. I have learned a great deal in recent times from the insights and instincts of editors about not alone the economy but also the fact that it operate within a democracy with fundamental fundamental rights which should not be taken for granted.

I am also very appreciative of the support of the Irish Bankers Federation (IBF) together with the Irish Bank Officials Association (IBOA).

A major theme running through the papers relates to the impact of the short-term Shareholder Value model which incentivised greed to almost total detriment of 'The Common Good' – with catastrophic consequences on the lives of Individuals, whole economies and of the Global economy. Nonetheless, it needs to be said – and said again – that the financial services industry includes many hardworking, highly ethical and professional individuals who are, in effect, 'hostage' to a malign business model and outdated corporate mind-set. In Ireland, I have been privileged to know and learn from many of these Individuals.

To all of these, and to any person or institution whom I have inadvertently neglected to mention, my very sincere thanks.

Most importantly of all, my sincere thanks to Ita, to Maurice and Michael Kinsella for their invaluable help in preparing this book and to all of our children for their themselves and their great gifts, and to Sr. Consilio Fitzgerald SM, who founded Cuan Mhuire as a gift from Our Blessed Lady, and a microcosm of how God intended things to be.

About the Author

Ray Kinsella was born in Dublin and he received a B.Sc. and M.Sc. (Econ.) from the University of Hull, where he was awarded the Fenner Research Scholarship. He completed further Post–Graduate work at Trinity College Dublin (TCD), where he was awarded his PhD for his thesis on Structure, Conduct and Performance in Irish Banking.

Ray worked as an Economist in the Central Bank of Ireland, and was nominated to attend the IMF Institute in Washington D.C., where he received a Diploma in Financial Analysis and Policy. He was appointed Economic Advisor to the Department of Industry and Commerce. He was subsequently appointed Professor of Banking and Financial Services at the University of Ulster. He was appointed visiting Professor to University College Dublin (UCD) and was subsequently Joint-Professor of Banking and Financial Services. He is now Professor of Banking and Financial Services at the UCD Smurfit School of Business and Law. He is Visiting Professor at the School of Banking, Accountancy and Finance at the University of Wales Bangor, on the Faculty of the Management Institute of Paris, and is adjunct Professor at the University of Bryansk

Ray served as the first Chairman of the Board at the Dublin Institute of Technology (DIT), and has served on the Northern Ireland Economic Council and the Irish Bishop's Conference for Justice and Peace. He has published extensively in the field Banking, Financial Services, as well as Healthcare Economics including 'New Issues in Financial Services' (Basle Blackwell, Oxford), 'Internal Controls in Banking' (London, Wiley), 'Ireland and the Knowledge Economy'(with Professor Vincent McBriety) (Oaktree Press, Dublin), and 'Acute Healthcare in Ireland' (Oaktree Press, Dublin). He has written, researched and broadcast extensively in financial services and healthcare.

Ray is married to Ita and they have 10 children and they live in Co. Wicklow.

Table of Contents

Dedication

Acknowledgements

About the Author

Introduction...10

Section One:

Ethics and Financial Stability

1. 'The Fatal Distraction of the Minimum Wage'...54

2. 'Time for The Common Good to be Key Economic Reference'...58

3. 'Resolving the Economic Crisis in Ireland: The Need for a New Political Governance'...61

4. 'Bid to Impress Markets Will not Make for Good Budget'...65

5. 'Regulation a Weak Sibling of Ethics and Sin'...68

6. 'The Compendium on Social Teaching, The Family, Markets and Work'...70

7. 'Holding out for Hope'...89

8. 'Bank Profits Built on Real Relationships and Public Trust'...92

9. 'Catharsis in Irish Banking 2004/2005: Corporate Values and Ethics' IBOA Annual Conference 2004...96

10. 'Changing Mindsets, Behaviour and a Whole Way of Thinking at AIB'...103

11. 'Irish Banks Need to Win Back the Trust of Their Staff if They are to Succeed'...106

12. 'Banks Face a Long Haul to Regain the Public's Confidence'...110

13. 'Banks Must Recover Confidence and Market Credibility in Order to Survive'...114

14. 'US Fraud a Product of Sickness at Heart of Corporatism'...118

Section Two:

The Limits of Corporate Governance

1. 'Time for Imagination in Framing Corporate Governance Legislation'...121

1. 'Fragmentation of International Regulatory Governance and the Case for a Single Global Financial Regulator': Presentation, Basle Geneva Association...123

2. 'Ireland Inc's Policeman Needs Practical Support'...142

3. 'Banks Must Rely on Ethical and Innovative Policies to Retain its Independence AIB's Place in Ireland Matters'...145

Section Three:

Regulation: National and International Perspectives

1. 'Changed Landscape for Financial Service Providers, Consumers and Ombudsmen'...149

2. 'Putting the Pieces Together: Rebuilding the Banks and the Irish Economy'...154

3. 'Is Nationalisation of the Banking System Now Inevitable?'...163

4. 'Recapitalisation will not Lead to Business as Usual for Banks'...166

5. 'Northern Bank: from Liquidity Crisis to Solvency Crisis – A Case Study'...169

6. 'EU-Wide Approach Needed'...173

7. 'AIB's Place in Ireland Matters'...176

8. 'Changing Mindsets, Behaviour and a Whole way of Thinking at AIB'...179

9. 'Prevention of System Errors is the Key Issue'...182

10. 'Regulatory Regime Changed Beyond Recognition'...185

11. 'EU Initiative Needed to Solve Regulatory Gap in Indemnity Insurance'...188

12. 'IFSRA Bill Should be Withdrawn'...193

13. 'Ludwig Analysis Provides Opportunity to Scrutinise Plans for Single Regulator'...193

14. 'Fraud Shows Banks' Controls Playing Catch-up and Regulators Arriving Late'...200

15. 'Scrap the Single Regulator and make way for European Supervision'...202

16. 'No Bank can Afford to be "Complacent" after Barings Debacle'...209

Section Four:

The Global Financial Crises: The Meltdown of Trust and its Consequences

1. 'Alternative Vision of "Spirit of Ireland" Offers Hope'...213

2. 'The Global Economic Crisis and its Effect on Ireland: Only Transformational Change Can Bring us Back from the Brink'...216

3. 'We've Screwed Up – That's the Truth of It'...219

4. 'Irish Banking System and the Global Credit Crisis'...222

5. 'Causes and Effects of Worldwide Financial Turmoil'...226

6. 'US Fiscal Bailout a Missed Chance'...230

7. 'How Should Ireland Respond to the Global Economic Turmoil?'...233

8. 'Why this Global Financial Crisis is Different'...238

9. 'Global Central Bank is Needed'...243

10. 'Heading off Global Financial Collapse – Lessons from the 2007 Credit Crunch'...247

11. 'Developments in Hedge Funds and Global Systemic Stability: The Case for Regulation'...251

12. 'New Insurance Behemoths Scoop up Business Globally'...257

Introduction

Introduction[1]

What began as a financial crisis and metastasised into the deepest and most protracted global economic crisis[2] of the modern era was generated within the most prescriptive regulatory regime in the history of financial services. There were gaps – notably in Hedge Funds which, by their nature, exert enormous leverage – but the general statement remains true. Regulation failed to anticipate, or to firewall, the crisis. Similarly, standards of Corporate Governance by Boards of major institutions – which, after all, had evolved rapidly in the decade preceding the crisis – proved no defence against the fundamental weakness of the prevailing orthodoxy of corporate capitalism. Regulation is vital because of the nature of financial services – and there was a great deal of theory underpinning the fabric of both national regulatory and supervisory policies, as well as of international cooperation. Theory is now being debated and rewritten, and the deficiencies arising from reliance on a fragmented set of international cooperative arrangements are all the more apparent.

There is also an extensive debate around the key parameters of Corporate Governance. Standards are, for the most part, non-statutory, but they are binding. The issue is whether, or not, these standards are substantive, relevant and enforceable. The perverse effects of focusing on the short-term in relation to performance-driven remuneration, as well as the absolute levels of remuneration for entities that have pursued a fundamentally flawed business model, are among the issues that are being re-shaped.

More generally, the Boards of individual institutions, together, in some instances, with key Committees of the Boards, failed in a number of key institutions both to ask the right questions, and to provide the kind of leadership necessary to lead their institutions through

---

[1] There is a growing literature in this field see, for example, Sen Amarytha *'Capitalism Beyond the Crisis'* New York Review of Books Volume 56 Number 5 March 2009, Coleman M. *'The Death of American Capitalism'* Studies Issue 389, Vol.98, Spring 2009, and Gerry O'Hanlon's *'The Recession and God: Reading the signs of the times'* Messenger Publications 2009, as well as Kinsella R. *'The Markets and Morality'* in 'A Companion to the Compendium of the Social Teaching Of the Church' Dublin, Veritas Publishers, 2007.

[2] For an account of the main characteristics of periodic financial crisis, see, for example, Kenneth S. & Carmen M. Reinhart *'What Other Financial Crises Tell Us'*, 2009 (http://online.wsj.com/article/SB123362438683541945.html).

the global financial crisis. Perhaps too much was asked of them. At the same time, the crisis occurred in the *post*-SOX era: there had been adequate time to understand what was necessary and to put the appropriate standards in place, and to ensure that the Board had the relevant spread of expertise and access to the necessary information to meet what were, it must be acknowledged, unprecedented challenges.

More fundamentally, what is now glaringly apparent is that the primary cause of the global financial crisis and all of its consequences, both at the level of government regulators and institutions, has been an 'ethical gap'. We have begun to acknowledge the distinction between what is legal and what is ethical: we have (re)discovered that the letter of the law is not necessarily a robust platform for a *sustainable* financial system.

This is the theme of this book of readings. Effective and proportionate regulation is a necessary, but not a sufficient condition, for Financial Stability. The same can be said for Corporate Governance, properly defined and implemented. To rebuild Trust in banking and financial markets what is imperative is Ethics –'obedience to the *unenforceable*', in the words of one authority.

The papers in this book chart the journey that was envisaged when the Module 'Regulation, Corporate Governance and Ethics' was first taught, back at the beginning of the decade. The key premises behind the Module were that a crisis was inevitable and foreseeable.

The data on which the Models were based were inadequate and, in any event, the theoretical framework of applied financial economics was demonstrably deficient.[3] Moral and ethical issues are at the heart of market dysfunctionality and corporate behaviour *albeit* manifesting themselves through secondary channels. And further to this, there was not a global Financial Regulator endowed with the mandate and resources and policy instruments, available to address fear and uncertainty in global markets. This led to coordination problems among different national regulators, with inevitably different priorities. When the crisis finally manifested itself, neither the markets nor the mind-set of policy makers were prepared. And there was no Global Regulator. Policy lost credibility, contagion metastasized, inducing a paradigm shift in the functioning and in the psychology of markets. We are still lost – still in denial – still in search of a new paradigm.

Section II

Ethical Roots of the Global Crisis and 'The Common Good'

The argument at the heart of these papers is this: the global financial crisis is *primarily* a crisis in Ethics. It is the lack of an understanding of Ethics, as a sub-set of a moral

---

[3] See, for example Jean-Philip Bouchaud's *'Economics needs a Scientific Revolution'* Nature Vol.455 30th October 2008.

philosophy[4] that is rooted in a clear differentiation – accessible to, and understandable by, all of right and wrong that is at the heart of the present crisis in corporate capitalism. Such an understanding is a necessary condition for a return to stability and sustainability across our financial institutions and markets. That is the paradigm: Regulation, Corporate Governance and Ethics.[5]

Crucially, Ethics cannot be confined to the purely financial or economic domain. It begins in the Individual, in the Family, in the Community, in the governance of society. It encompasses markets and market-based enterprises, as well as statutory and voluntary institutions. It binds all of these together in an environment of Trust[6] based on an *objective* moral order, to which society and all of its constituent parts aspire, even if they do not always succeed.

Corporate capitalism, encompassed in the short-term Shareholder Value model[7], created a near-impossible dilemma for management – who were incentivized to eschew sustainability for the 'search for yield' *aka* a 'do-the-deal-and-move-on' mind set; as well as for employees who, all too often, were required to live out practises behind their office doors that were wholly alien to the values they try to live by behind their hall doors.

The global financial crisis – and its economic and its political counter-parts – represents a catastrophic failure in a system of corporate capitalism which had no regard to the dignity of the Individual, or to 'The Common Good'[8], at the heart of which is the Human Person. That is why it failed – and in the causes, and consequences, of its failure, it is entirely similar to Communism, which also subverted markets and private property, as well as idolising the proletariat while discarding the transcendence of the Person.

It follows from all this that the present catharsis in financial markets and in the economy can only be finally resolved within an ethical framework based on the 'The Common Good', such that it informs the manner in which financial transactions occur, how individuals and businesses relate to each other, and how institutions – including governments and regulators – function in practise.

---

[4] See, in particular, Alasdair McIntyre 'After Virtue: A Study in Moral Theory' University of Notre Dame Press, Notre Dame, 1984, who draws on the virtue ethics of the Greek Schools, and which is a theme running through the lectures on which this book is based.
[5] This is the title of a Module that I have taught since the early years of the decade. I am grateful once again to the students who participated in the module, and all of the wise and experienced practitioners and thinkers who have contributed to the development of this paradigm
[6] See Onora O'Neill's series of BBC Reith Lectures 'A Question of Trust' 2002.
[7] For a formal statement of the Shareholder Value model see
http://dictionary.bnet.com/definition/shareholder+value.html and, in particular 'Banking on Shareholder Value: An Interview with Sir Brian Pitman, Chairman of Lloyds TSB' by Partha Bose and Alan Morgan, The McKinsey Quarterly, No. 2, 1998. It is important to note that there are a number of very positive elements to the Shareholder Value model, as implemented by Sir Brian Pitman.
[8] See Compendium of the Social Doctrine of the Catholic Church for an insightful analysis of 'The Common Good', and which is drawn on extensively later in this chapter.
(http://www.vatican.va/roman_curia/pontifical_councils/justpeace/documents/rc_pc_justpeace_doc_20060526_ compendio-dott-soc_en.html)

The Rebuilding of Trust in Banking requires an acknowledgement of objectively-based standards of right and wrong, and these are at the heart of Ethics. This does not, in any way, relieve all stake-holders of the challenge of rebuilding contractual arrangements, engaging in institution-building, including wholly new structures, including a Global Financial Regulator.

It is simply to argue that, just as the global financial crisis had many *secondary*, but only one *primary* cause so, too, the restoration of Trust in a new and more globally inclusive financial system, and in a future that is yet to be determined, rests fundamentally on Ethics. That is to say, on a proper understanding of the centrality of ethics in relation to the manner in which institutions behave and cooperate with each other. Such an understanding can be derived from the whole Judeo-Christian culture, as well as from the insights of Islam in regard to such issues as, for example, risk sharing and the imperative of an ethical 'screening' in regard to the admissibility of financial transactions. There are some things you don't do – some transactions you don't undertake – and some obligations that are overriding and which transcend individualistic wealth-driven, and usually short-term, incentives.

It can also be seen in the Credit Union movement, which is based on voluntarism, a high level of commitment to local communities-increasingly beset by indebtedness and vulnerable to 'loan sharks' – and which strikes a balance of interests among savers and borrowers and other stakeholders. It has a very different focus to mainstream banking. It is an important both in itself-but also in holding up a different ethos to demonstrate that it is possible to be focussed on the Person/Family in their difficulties, and supportive of the community, while also demonstrating financial stability.

As far back as 2000, the mainstream orthodoxy in Banking and Financial Markets – as well as deficiencies and fragmentation in regulation – were impelling financial markets and institutions in developed countries towards an implosion – one which will certainly be seen as an inflection point in the development of modern monetized economies. Arguably, the roots can be traced back to the earlier deregulation of institutions and the subsequent exponential expansion of complex opaque instruments, all of it driven by a transactions-based 'performance' culture – and which was not effectively overseen, much less regulated, by a fragmented system of nationally-delineated regulatory governance.

Truth and Trust are the fabric out of which all ethical systems are woven. The first casualty of the global financial crisis was Truth. 'Truth' is not only necessary to market efficiency; it is universally accepted as central to an objective ethical perspective on the world. This is important because it demonstrates the overlap between, on the one hand, an efficient, profitable and stable banking system and, on the other hand, the necessity for an 'ethical benchmark'.

The argument made in this book is that the global financial crisis arises primarily from the fact that the process of financial intermediation, developed over many centuries, was infected by a lie. A return to stability – one that is believable by Individuals and markets alike –

requires a universally acceptable ethical template. Such a template must bring together all that we know, and instinctively understand, go to make up a properly functioning society – one that embraces open markets, including financial markets, as well as the institutions which 'mediate' within these markets. This template is 'The Common Good', which brings together all the elements that go to make up a national and international order that is underpinned by ethical principles focussed, in the last analysis, on the centrality of the Human Person. It is the Person that loses their job and all that goes with it: their dignity and self-esteem, their home and, not infrequently, financial protection against exigencies such as the need for health insurance.

The principle of 'The Common Good', stemming from the dignity, unity and equality of all people[9] attempts to both articulate and achieve "the sum total of social conditions which allow people, either as groups or as individuals, to reach their fulfilment more fully and more easily". The argument is, quite simply, that the Human Person cannot find fulfilment purely in *themselves*; that is, separate from the fact that they exist "with" others and "for" others.

Banking lost sight of its constitutive purpose, which is grounded in the real world and not in some quasi-virtual world of notional money and esoteric instruments which serve no purpose other than private gain irrespective of the wider effects on lives and markets and whole economies – it is what gave us, first misconceived sub-prime mortgages and then an unprecedented full-blown global crisis.

Banks, no more than individuals, do not exist by, or for, themselves. They are first and foremost a 'utility' – they provide a 'Public Good' in the form of credit and also payments services that are essential for the functioning of a modern economy. The fact that they take the form of private limited companies and require an appropriate return on capital in the form of profit makes no difference. Their importance to Society is reflected in the regulatory system, including the willingness of Society, through the Central Bank and the Regulatory Authorities, to intervene to sustain them – not for their own sake but because of the effects of a financial crisis on the lives of people.

'The Common Good' is not some abstruse construct with little immediate relevance to the practicalities of trading or strategy – the kinds of things banks do. On the contrary – rooted in basic universal Truths – it is the best objective guarantor of the sustainability of any 'Business Model'. Its rigor and relevance reflect an intellectual pedigree that long predates, but is directly applicable to, modern banking.

A key point with respect to the attainability of 'The Common Good' is that it should be seen in action in the way society goes about its business. To take this one stage further: banks and money and markets have an intrinsic or constitutive purpose. So, too, do Individuals and

---

[9] Pontifical Council for Justice and Peace 'Compendium of the Social Doctrine of the Catholic Church' Chapter IV Section 164

Families. The two have to be aligned. 'The Common Good', as a goal of society, transcends purely temporal, and therefore ephemeral, social constructs, being a teleological imperative at once both distinctly relevant to its social context, yet wholly metaphysical with respect to the embedded value of, for example, financial institutions and markets.

'The Common Good' can therefore be defined as being, in effect, the Universal Moral order within a particular society, being articulated through societal institutions, such as Banks and Government Departments. 'The Common Good' of society is not an end in itself; its value arises from the fact that it is focused specifically on the Individual Person – working in the world – and their capacity to attain their ultimate purpose.[10] It was, after all, one of the great classical economists – Alfred Marshall – who noted that: "The Economist, like everyone else, must concern himself with the ultimate aims of man".[11]

"For theistic faiths, God is the ultimate end of his creatures and for no reason may 'The Common Good' be deprived of its transcendent dimension, which moves beyond the historical dimension while at the same time fulfilling it...A purely historical and materialistic vision would result in transforming The Common Good into a simple socio-economic well-being, without any transcendental goal, that is, without its most intimate reason for existing."[12]

If the first casualty was Truth, then the next, and inevitable, casualty was Trust. Banking is based, first and last, on Trust.[13] The short-term Shareholder Value Business Model, and the perverse management incentives which it generated, subverted banks – and then subverted the markets within which they operated. The catastrophic fall in stock markets and the 'freezing-over' of inter-bank markets, on which the financial system had come to depend, tell their own story.

That is why, as noted, the global financial and economic crisis is fundamentally an ethical crisis. There will be no final resolution – no restoration of Trust or return to stability – until this reality is acknowledged and the financial *and political* systems transformed so as to engender empathy. In Ireland – and the example could be transposed to most countries – people, especially young people, would not alone know but almost lie down and die for *their* sports team. These same individuals feel little empathy with the 'corporate' identity of the banking system and almost wholly alienated from their political system.

---

[10] Pontifical Council for Justice and Peace 'Compendium of the Social Doctrine of the Church' Chapter IV Section 170
[11] Cited in Pat Collins' 'Gifts of the Spirit and the New Evangilisation' Veritas, Dublin 2008
[12] Pontifical Council for Justice and Peace 'Compendium of the Social Doctrine of the Church' Chapter IV Section 170
[13] Op. cit O'Neill

Section III

Trust, the Global Crisis and the Human Person

The great illusion which binds both policy and markets in their response to the crisis is essentially this: all that is really required is more regulation (a matter of negotiation and give-and-take) and, of course, curbs on such issues of governance as 'unethical' bonuses – which can never really be effective.

It goes deeper – much deeper – than that. No amount of regulation, no new forms of corporate governance, can resuscitate a system that has brought the global economy to its knees, destroyed tens of thousands of sound enterprises and savaged the lives of millions of families and individuals.

Nor can the political 'system' remain aloof – as if, somehow, responsibility lay solely with 'the banks'. Not so. The political system in developed countries failed to anticipate, and then to respond instinctively, to the crisis; there was a period of denial which arises from the short-term horizon of politics[14] – a characteristic it shares with mainstream banking. The net effect was that, just as the corporate culture of mainstream banking focused on the short-term, so too, were politicians, in general, slow to respond to the magnitude of the crisis. Neither were capable of acting solely in the public interest – each had their own particular agendas[15] that limited their perspectives to the short-term. In the case of banking, this reflected the Shareholder Value model and the management incentives arising from it. In the case of politics, it reflected the constraints which are well explained by the theory of Public Choice. In both instances, what was missing – and what was needed – was an alignment of their actions with 'The Common Good'. The authorities were continuously 'behind the curve' – reacting to a crisis instead of leading the way out of a crisis. In doing so, their joint response jeopardised Public Trust in markets and in democracy – which it is their responsibility to defend and uphold.

We can put this another way. James Buchanan, one of the founders of the 'Theory of Public Choice' argues that 'Public Choice' is really "politics without romance".[16] The same kind of 'romance' that the corporatist view of mainstream banking has in mind when it talks about 'we are customer focused' and that 'our greatest asset is our people'. Not so. Everyone has their own agenda so that, without an explicit commitment to 'The Common Good' which is transparent and measurable, it will be crowded-out by these agendas.

At one level or another we are all screwed up[17]. Politics, as much as financial markets, reflect – and can also 'culture' – the prevailing social value-system.' But Society *does* exist. 'Greed' is *not* good. A 'new' banking system (and economy) cannot, therefore, be built on an 'old'

---

[14] See, for a brief explanation, William F. Shughart II's 'Public Choice Theory' The Concise Encyclopaedia of Economics http://www.econlib.org/library/Enc/PublicChoice.html

[15] Leonard Cohen, in his song 'Everybody Knows' comes closest to capturing just what is going on within this dynamic.

[16] Ibid.

[17] The insight is attributable to others wiser than I.

politics which is, in its own way, every bit as dysfunctional and semi-detached from people's lives, as the short-term Shareholder Value Model is from the requirements of an ethical and sustainable banking system.

It is, perhaps, unfair to be too critical of the political response in developed countries to the crisis. There were no rule books and no doubt many sleepless nights. But the process of rebuilding Trust in banking cannot be driven by a political mind-set that is itself broken-backed and obsolete. It, too, must change – and this change must, by necessity, precede the rebuilding of Trust in an ethically-based 21st Century banking system.

To develop effective policy responses to a malign crisis that continued to morph in real time presented unique challenges to the political system. Even so, it became evident, certainly by early 2009, that unprecedented financial interventions[18] by governments and central banks – on a scale that threatens future financial stability and the credibility of fiscal policy – were being used primarily to shore-up a fundamentally flawed model. This model – and the ideology on which it is based – has demonstrably put at risk the Trust of depositors and of business; of employees and, ironically, investors – and especially the Public.

The contingent liabilities represented by these interventions now present a clear and present threat to 'The Common Good'. And still the presumption is that the same model can 'recover'; can be put back together and resume 'business as usual' – with some differences in regulation and all the rest of it. It is important, in this regard, to keep in mind the quote attributed to Albert Einstein: "We can't solve problems by using the same kind of thinking we used when we created them".

Through the latter part of the decade, Governments, directly and indirectly, continued to intervene to provide money they didn't have – including resort to the printing presses – in order to support private financial institutions. This has skewed monetary policy, impacting in particular on expectations of future inflation and raising the issue of what happens to the edifice being built when interest rates begin to rise from their present historic lows across the globe. They also failed to understand the reality that, beyond a certain point, it was ethically and economically indefensible not to redirect such resources to individuals, families and businesses which banks – essentially utilities – are intended to serve.

The present system cannot be put back together. Its demise was inevitable – and as will be argued later – foreseeable. In reality, it does not have to be rebuilt in the manner in which it has evolved. The Judaeo-Christian traditions, and that of Islam – which encompass four millennia of insights into money and markets, trade and transactions – point to a better way; to a more effective and sustainable framework for facilitating the commercialisation of human creativity. The Torah and the Talmud[19] provide a highly practical guide to the Jewish moral imperative of honesty in business. There has not been a crisis of Trust in Islamic

---

[18] See communiqué of the London G-20 Summit, 2009.
[19] A particularly interesting and relevant resource can be found at http://www.jlaw.com.

banking, not least because there is risk-sharing and an effective ethical screening of lending practises and also of financial instruments.

Commerce is an integral aspect of our human experience. The insights in the Old Testament Wisdom Books provide an unequalled template for the alignment of commerce including finance, and the wider political system that shapes its goals and governance, with 'The Common Good', which is an ethical system based on universals. This is even more the case with the New Testament of Jesus Christ, which is the fulfilment of everything that came before it and in every domain of the Human Person – not excluding commerce and politics.

'Ethics' is the 'Word' animating the moral philosophy of the great Theist religions: it is by its nature (since it is aligned to our final end) common-sense; it is predicated on the integrity of all of our relationships not excluding commerce. The crucial point here is that in each of the Theistic faith traditions 'work', 'money' and 'trade' are all imbued with an ethical sense, which is the ultimate basis of Trust. The great Thomist scholar, Dom Vonier[20], writes that 'Christ could not be the living power he is without deeply modifying the ethical sense of the nations that worship him. There are certain precepts that we all speak of as precepts of the Gospel, because they are so strongly emphasised in the New Testament. But precepts alone would not be enough to create a new and universal ethical sense. Precepts, in order to be living things, must be expressions of the hidden ethical sense of a man; they do not cross his aspirations, they merely elevate them. Now, the lessons of history are that wherever the name of Christ is alive, there we find profound ethical assurance and certainty – all of which results in great ethical peace. But Christ drew a sharp distinction between the legitimacy in principle of the tax collectors and the antics of the 'money changers' in the Temple.

So, too, does our *lived experience* of this particular financial crisis. It was generated by the all too human failings of greed –'a few basis points more...an increase in the target rate of quarterly returns...stock options...bonuses' – and lies – which go to the heart of the collapse of Trust in our institutions. Nothing short of a transformation of our business models, and of our political and societal institutions, can provide a route-map back to stability.

The post-2007 financial crisis was birthed in the uniquely lax monetary environment of the post-9/11 shock, facilitated by the umbilical cord connecting an abnormally low US savings rate and the equally abnormally high Chinese financial surpluses. There were, as argued in the text, other secondary factors.

Concurrently with the gathering momentum of the crisis, a war lacking international legitimacy perpetrated by the US and it's 'a coalition of the willing' on an evil regime, contaminated not alone economics and business but the very basis of what was legitimate. Most importantly, this war both contaminated national economies as well as distracting the attention of policy-makers from what was happening 'in the long grass'- until the crisis was almost upon them. There are resonances here of the Vietnam War, the conduct and funding of

---

[20] See 'The Collected Works of Abbot Vonier: Volume One' Burns Oates and Washburne, London, 1952. This great and gentle genius – the second Abbot of Buckfast Abbey in the UK – is an inspirational source. A number of Abbot Vonier's publications are still in print and can be accessed at http://www.bookdepository.co.uk.

which contributed to the collapse, in 1972, of the Bretton-Woods system, on which the post-World War II international expansion of trade and finance had been based.

There was also the inherent weakness of economic axioms – including the assumed capacity of the financial system to 'self-correct' – the folly of which has since been acknowledged by Former US Fed Chairman, Dr. Alan Greenspan.[21] It is not too much to say that economics needs to be fundamentally reconsidered in the light of the failures of theory as well as of practice. Its theoretical constructs failed to reflect the reality of the things that constitute 'the real world', as we know it to be, and 'orthodoxy' failed to understand that the coping stone of theory and practise of the social sciences – including economics and finance – is the transcendence of the Human Person.

Global markets and the global economy were in expansionary mode – not least in Ireland's small open economy, where it was fuelled by convergence with German interest and inflation rates, a uniquely attractive demographic/educational nexus and an innovative use of one of its few policy levers, tax.

It was the terrain of self-delusion, across which the siren calls of the invincibility of government policy and a secularist paean to wealth could be heard. Happiness was something – anything – that was bigger, larger, and more exclusive. The rise in house prices was the definitive barometer of well-being. The ratio of indebtedness to household disposable income rose to unsustainable levels.

Galbraith, in his era-defining 'The Affluent Society'[22] had highlighted the distinction between 'Needs' and 'Wants' some fifty years earlier, and how the latter were driven by emulation *aka* 'Keeping up with the Murphys' advertising – and indebtedness. The corporate mind-set of banking – seemingly incapable of learning – and trapped within a model that was seemingly incapable of thinking beyond next quarter's earnings – were only too happy to seduce a whole generation.

In Ireland, the excesses of corporate capitalism were reflected in lending at levels clearly signalled as excessive by the Central Bank but which the Boards of many credit institutions were unwilling to constrain, the Regulator unable to call to order, and the Government – with access to the data from clearly excessive housing completions and unprecedented Exchequer receipts – unwilling to acknowledge, much less intervene to stop. The excesses were reflected in breaches of accepted standards of corporate governance that exacerbated the impact of misconceived levels of lending. Combined with what was happening globally, the effect was a calamitous collapse in the share price of the main domestic banks, especially in the case of Anglo-Irish Bank – beset by a vulnerable funding model dependent on now 'frozen' wholesale markets, a collapse in the value of property and deep flaws in corporate governance.

---

[21] See, for example, Dr. Alan Greenspan's retraction of his belief in the self-correcting capabilities of financial markets.
[22] See John Kenneth Galbraith's 'The Affluent Society' Mariner Books, USA, 1998.

The Irish banking system is a sub-set of a global set of markets. The main Irish banks were well capitalised benchmarked against the Bank for International Settlements (BIS) Capital Adequacy standards. In October 2008 the global financial system was, in the view of the IMF Managing Director, on the brink of collapse, following the toppling of Lehman Brothers. Irish banks were vulnerable, not so much from excessive lending against toxic securities but from a generalised lack of Trust in banks and across financial markets. The decision by the Irish Government to raise the Deposit Protection level, together with a €400 billion near-blanket guarantee for retail and wholesale deposits – was a response to these developments and one which triggered emulation across the EU.

The Irish banks did not, however, move to take advantage of this brief 'window of opportunity' to raise capital. Notwithstanding the extensive powers reserved to the Government in the Credit Institutions (Deposit Protection) Act 2008, there was a measureable contraction of lending to businesses and households already impacted by severe recessionary impulses.

The inevitable effect was to put increasing pressures on the availability of credit; leading to a continuing progression of 'worse than expected' impaired loans. Still the Banks did not change their basic banking model: and priority was given by Government – in Ireland as well as in other countries – to the recapitalisation of institutions instead of to maintaining the level of demand in the economy and, more specifically, over employment sustaining/creating initiatives. These institutions remained committed to the interests of shareholders; even as an informal credit squeeze among businesses reinforced the pressures on cash flow arising from reduced levels of lending by institutions whose viability had been underwritten by the public. It has to be recognized that, by this stage, early 2009, banks were operating in a higher risk environment – *albeit* one to which their policies had contributed. They had responsibilities. A Loan Guarantee scheme would have reduced the 'Risk Premium' which in part acted as a brake on lending. The Banks did not raise the issue and the Government did not propose such an initiative.

There were indications of the subversion of Financial Stability, right across the markets, and, indeed, the wider corporate sector served by these markets. It wasn't primarily about failures in Internal Controls or Fraud, or even more general failures in Risk Management – though they were certainly evident within the financial sector. The point was that such failures, while indicative of corporate weaknesses, did not really impact on the centuries-old Trust invested by the public in Banks and Banking. The subversion of financial markets in the interests of a malign 'Business Model', based on the incentives for such institutions to maximize short-term Shareholder Value, was altogether a different matter.

It was about an Ethical failure. Communism had been driven by a production-based historical determinism which subjugated the Human Person to the role of a unit in the 'proletariat'. Denying God, they denied the transcendence of the Person. That meant the customer and the employee – it meant the 'mug'.

Section 1V

The failure of Corporate Capitalism

The collapse of Communism in 1989 did not lead to 'the end of history'.[23] Instead, the latent weaknesses and contradictions in corporate capitalism became more evident – and its arrogance more apparent. It was, in many of its manifestations, a legacy of Nietzsche's philosophy, just as Communism was the outcome of Marx.[24] Both rejected the reality of an objective moral order, encompassing, and giving substantive meaning to, economic political and social institutions, predicated on the innate and unrepeatable dignity of each individual – an exaltation of the 'I' to the exclusion of 'God' and the 'Other'.

Both denied the transcendence of the Human Person. As a consequence, neither had any external reference point outside of (ephemeral) Power and (short-term) Profit. One attempted to abolish markets, the other to idolise them. The effect was the same – both imploded. Communism was, of course, economically inefficient and utterly soulless: the Gulags, as much as the madness of Maoism, were an expression of the howling wasteland of nihilism at the heart of their philosophy.

And yet the failures of corporate capitalism were in some respects as great. They had good reason – from their tradition critiqued by, among others, Pope Leo XIII, Paul VI, Pope John Paul II in their groundbreaking Social Encyclicals[25], to know better. The benefits of a 'free' society, open and well-functioning markets, private property as well as profit-driven innovation were evident to all.

There was a well-developed critique demonstrating the intrinsic common sense and moral worth of placing the fruits of this model at the disposal, not alone of entrepreneurs, but also of the Person, the Family, and those who for whatever reason were marginalised. It was not just about shareholders and the maximization of their 'wealth', in the framework of a quarterly 'treadmill' that, for a brief time, generated meaningless amounts of wealth for the few, at the ultimate expense of the welfare of a generation. The concept of 'The Common Good' had been around a long time.

Instead, capitalism was 'captured'. Markets were subverted by opaque and exotic instruments, many of which were not effectively priced for actual and latent risk. They were separated from their constitutive purpose, to be manipulated, conflicted by often competing interests, and by lure of greed and power to which all human nature is susceptible.

---

[23] Fukuyama F. *"The End of History?"* The National Interest, Summer 1989.
[24] See Raymond Guess' Paper *'What Happened in and to Moral Philosophy in the Twentieth Century?'* Guess' Paper was presented at a colloquium organised by the School of Philosophy, University College Dublin 2009 to celebrate the 80th birthday of Alasdair McIntyre. Those interested in accessing the papers presented at this colloquium should contact the School of Philosophy University College Dublin.
[25] Particular mention may be made of *'Revrum Novarum'* (Leo XIII, 1891) and *'Centesimus Annus'* (John Paul II, 1991).

The Human Person was reduced to the status of a 'Human Resource' and a 'Consumer', serving a market based on servicing – for it can never truly satisfy – an exponentially expanding set of 'Wants' – instead of being directed towards 'Needs' – to use Galbraith's incisive distinction. All of this stymied the possibilities of harnessing its creativity in the interests of the Person and 'The Common Good'. It was a dead man walking.

Nowhere was this subversion more evident than in banking and financial services – which was, of course, particularly ironic since the functioning of institutions and markets have always been predicated on Trust and professionalism. In the words of one eminent banker in the early 1990's: 'I joined a profession and I've ended up working for an Industry'.

The whole structure of regulation and standards is, at least in principle, directed towards underpinning public Trust. There is a good reason for this. Beyond their status of facilitators of individual and corporate transactions – of economic growth and development – banks are 'special'. That is, a weakness in, or even more so the failure of, a bank could bring low the wider economy within which it was embedded and whose interests it was presumed to serve.

The subversion of banks by a pernicious 'Business Culture' could, because of the leverage which banks employed – a leverage based on Trust – cause 'contagion'. A whole generation has learned – very quickly – the reality behind what was until then just another esoteric term in textbooks on Banking. 'Contagion' is a virus-like process, infecting good and bad banks alike – within, and across – banking systems bound-up in an inextricably interconnected set of globalised markets that never rest and respond, in real-time, to systemic disturbances. 'Contagion' has exposed the lies and the culture of 'Power' and of 'Wealth' which are at the heart of both Corporate capitalism and Communism – and it has done so from within: the 'trigger' in both instances, has been a breakdown in Trust: people – and markets – stopped believing.

So, a dysfunctional ideology that 'crowded-out' the Human Person spawned a 'Business Model' that played to, and exploited, this weakness. This was, as noted, the short-term Shareholder Value 'Business Model'. The essential nature of the model involved the separation of ownership (shareholders) from control (corporate management). It bred a culture of incentives that aligned the interests of the supposed stewards of the banks with maximizing the short-term shareholder 'wealth', reflected in the share price and market capitalisation. It generated an increasingly frenetic transaction-based, wealth-fixated culture encompassed in the aphorism 'greed is good'.

This Model seduced, ensnared and ultimately betrayed those whom it was ostensibly there to serve: the depositor, the borrower, the employee, the lives and the businesses in its hinterland.

Section V

'Contagion' and the breakdown of Markets and Institutions

The first shudders of extreme volatility began to spook the markets by mid 2006, triggered by the meltdown in the value of asset (initially mortgage)-backed securities. It should not have come as any surprise. These were engineered not only to disperse risk but, more importantly, to squeeze out those extra few basis points for institutions 'chasing yield' in a low interest environment. The volatility in the markets was extraordinary by any standards, like the pre-tremors before the Quake. It wasn't long in coming. In 2007, with the near failure of US Investment Bank Bears Stern stock markets collapsed, gripped by uncertainty and then by fear as the 'unknown' – the scale of potential losses embedded in opaque, mispriced financial products now warehoused on balance-sheets – opened up at their very feet. Interbank markets stalled, and then 'froze'.

Large institutions began to confront precisely how greed, esoteric 'investments' and the pressure to generate earnings had corrupted their earnings and balance-sheets. Share prices – and therefore valuations, collapsed. The contagion spread. In the UK, the first 'run' on a bank for over a century was triggered – granted that the funding model of Northern Rock, dependent as it was on the wholesale markets – was inherently vulnerable and should have been picked-up by the regulatory authorities. But the real significance of Northern Rock was that it reflected a major fissure in the Public's Trust in the State. The people stopped believing in an intrinsically flawed model, based on deception – they still don't.

The financial titans that bestrode the global system began to implode – slowly. The rescue of Bears Stern and then the failure later that year of Lehman Brothers – the 'line in sand' that wasn't. Then came the bailouts – Fanny Mae and Freddy Mac – the 'shotgun mergers' and the slow haemorrhage of smaller regional banks – all well documented; and AIG, a metaphor for the 'hollowing out' that had been allowed to occur .

It is important to highlight the fact that not all institutions were impacted: more financial service providers than is generally acknowledged remained at a distance from what was happening across the sector as a whole. Equally, the overwhelming majority of employees were ethical and highly professional – and were appalled at the culture of short-termism which embedded itself deep in the bowels of the industry. It could neither be stopped nor 'firewalled'.

In the space of a year, 'a little local difficulty' that the US Fed initially thought might cost $50 to $100 million was turning into a rout, pushing the financial services industry – and the auto-industry – into the embrace of *de facto* state control. Such an ideological rout could only be ascribed to a complete misdiagnosis of the primary cause of the crisis and the consequent inability to perceive, or undertake, the kind of transformational financial, economic – and political – transformation essential to engage with the problem.

Governments have spent trillions seeking to buy 'confidence'. They have failed – because the markets know – everybody knows – that the whole edifice is built on sand: only a new paradigm will begin the rebuilding of Trust. Projections of 'recovery' miss the point: unless the underlying of the collapsed is address, any 'recovery' is little more than a reprieve. Meanwhile, a failed system will gratefully swallow the savings of today and the promises mortgaged on a tomorrow of which we cannot be sure.

Reflecting the inherent weaknesses in the global and European regulatory architecture, governments dithered, regulators charged with preserving systemic stability were – and still are – playing 'catch-up', creating ever-larger contingent liabilities that will come back to haunt them.

The crisis metastasised from what was first seen as an essentially financial problem – and quite manageable at that – to an unprecedented global economic catharsis that could neither be firewalled nor contained. Governments and banks – regulators and political institutions – are still in denial: still believe that all it will take is just more regulation and it will be 'Business as Usual'. Growth and a consumerist economy will take up where they left off.

But this is to ignore the ongoing morphing of a crisis that is now beginning to exert seeming irresistible pressures on political institutions.

This has been compounded by the financial – as well as the opportunity – costs of intervening to support what are deemed to be systemically important banks. These interventions have been set-out, at length, in, for example, the *Financial Stability Reviews* of different national authorities as well as multinational financial institutions: unprecedented liquidity support, injections of different forms of equity participations, the creation of different forms of 'Toxic Banks', as well as, in the case of Ireland, one of the first Deposit Protection schemes. Banks have – as in some previous crises – been nationalised. There have been hybrid nationalisations.

The net effect has been to bring institutions, and by extension markets, within the embrace of the State. This begs the question of how a failed politics which has proved itself unable to promote 'The Common Good' could hope to save a failed banking system.

At another level, the effect of the fracturing of credit and capital markets has been to drive developed economies into deflation. Growth has stalled – and contracted sharply. There has been a precipitous rise in unemployment. In these circumstances, the fiscal position of states has been compromised by massive injections of 'fiscal stimuli'. To date, they have not succeeded – and even if some stabilization is achieved it will be at a cost impossible to estimate and without any assurance that it will not reoccur.

What is more, the extent of contingent liabilities on the public sector's balance-sheets, are rising at precisely the same time that personal and household indebtedness is creating massive exposures – and pain. For some smaller countries, including Ireland, indicators of strain increased in 2008 and early 2009: sovereign debt ratings declined *albeit* from robust levels and credit default 'spreads' on banks widened.

The crisis will almost inevitably morph into a political crisis. Mainstream political models facilitated, and they bought into, the ideology of illusory 'wealth', failing to learn the lessons of the fall of both communism and corporate capitalism and to provide a vision for their people based on objective values, configured to 'The Common Good'. This phase of the crisis is only just beginning – reflecting the misconceived notion that 'the old politics' could regulate everyone else out of their 'wicked ways' – but were themselves immune from the imperative of fundamental change.

There is ample evidence of the extent of political anger – and incipient strain on political institutions – as a result of the slow collapse of the short-term Shareholder Value Model of corporate capitalism. It has been well documented and was evident in the scale of protests on the streets of capital cities, notably during the G-20 protests in London in March 2009.

The political disenchantment has been exacerbated by the fundamentally misconceived attempts by some countries to correct the yawning gap in their fiscal positions. In the EU, the Stability and Growth Pact constraints have been wholly swamped (not unlike Basle II), leaving the EU Commission and National Governments, including Ireland, clutching at 'ambitious' commitments to restore the general government deficit to the equivalent to 3 per cent of GDP. In the vortex of the deflation, such commitments have lost relevance as a realistic benchmark. The priority of national economies is survival and, whatever they say in public or in the rarefied atmosphere of Ministerial Council meetings, they will do what it takes to attempt to contain political pressures on their own economies, and on public finances – and by extension, public services which are being scaled back to levels hardly conceivable in the mid-2000s. There is a danger however that Governments, in pursuit of fiscal orthodoxy that now lacks any realistic context because of the burgeoning costs of the economic crisis, will seek to push through 'cuts' in public expenditure that are not alone counter-productive, but leave them vulnerable to criticism that they are becoming semi-detached from the pulse-beat of their own economies – and their people.

In the case of Ireland, three successive 'Budgets' in 2008/9 have not made any appreciable progress towards fiscal stabilisation. They have, instead, exacerbated the effects of an economic crisis, with the lack of demand driving the economy deeper into depression.

What was required, in an environment of escalating unemployment, falling costs and spare capacity, was a Budget written in factories, and on farms; in family homes and in hospitals; a Budget driven by a vision of using Ireland's natural resources – its farms and fisheries and its natural energy – as a means of employing its greatest capability; namely, its people living in a 'golden demographic' era. Making minimal progress towards fiscal stabilisation, the Government has, through a whole series of taxation increases and 'levies'– including measures that strike directly at the heart of Ireland as a Community – drained the economy of demand and confidence; of morale and direction.

This fiscal 'orthodoxy' is simultaneously undermining the domestic economy and political stability. Political stability is increasingly vulnerable to the pressures associated with mass unemployment, pressures on public services – and the effects of the implementation of potentially politically repressive measures that have been legislated and which could be used to constrain legitimate protest arising from such instability.

A theme running through the papers in this book is that this is no 'ordinary' crisis – a point highlighted in a paper to a Conference in the European Parliament in early 2008.[26] The amount of assistance provided to support this failed banking paradigm – at the cost of supporting households and businesses – has generated widespread opposition. No State even considered consulting it's people – even though it was the political establishment world-wide that presided over the crisis while it is the people who are already paying the price. In these circumstances, there is a robust argument to be made for two propositions.

The first is that interventions – such as recapitalisations that are continually chasing an upward spiral of 'impaired' loans, Asset Management Companies that transfer 'bad' bank loans from the balance sheets of banks to the public balance sheet and the backs of families and businesses – are misconceived and that banks should not – and cannot – be rescued. This argument is predicated on the fact that banks are essentially a public 'utility' – which is the basis of their systemic importance. The welfare objectives of this 'utility' has, in effect, held hostage to the interests of shareholders (very many of who have seen the value of their wealth decimated).

One alternative is some form of 'Narrow Bank' – that is, an institution serving the 'core' needs, domestic and international, of the retail, corporate and international sectors, but whose governance and strategy is not-for-profit, focused unequivocally on 'The Common Good'. There is, therefore, an argument to be made that Government assistance and support should be switched to this 'Narrow', bank, thereby ensuring that in a possible future crisis, of some kind or other, the process of intermediation will continue to function in the wider interests of the economy, employees and society. We return to this below.

There is a second argument to be made. It is this: Governments, including Monetary Authorities have – as they move through the portals of this crisis – failed to understand the paradox embedded in their policies and in the process got their priorities wholly wrong. Unimaginable amounts of money have been channelled into supporting a terminally failed banking model. By re-diverting these resources – *which no one thought were actually available to Government* – towards supporting and strengthening businesses and households – which are the ultimate supports of any functioning economy – there is the prospect of measurable progress towards economic stabilisation.

---

[26] See 'Why this Global Financial Crisis is Different' in Section Four of this Book.

Moreover – and this is the key point – it is precisely such stabilisation that can most effectively contribute to supporting the balance-sheets of banks, some of whom may be technically insolvent, so opaque are the accounting standards which now apply. Households are deleveraging under the simultaneous impact of an increase in unemployment and the beginnings of a radical shift in mindset away from a brand-driven consumerism. This same adjustment involves a reduction in costs and therefore an increase in competitiveness. In other words, save the businesses, support the households, and go with the grain of a downward adjustment in living standards that is already underway and *that does not need* to be further ratcheted-up – and the long-term interests of the banks will also be best served.

Section VI

The Global Crisis: a 'Wants'-based culture and the emasculation of the Family

The Family is the ultimate 'shock absorber' of an economy traumatised by the scale and suddenness of economic recession and at the sharp end of a breakdown of Trust underlying this collapse. It is the community within which all of the values which contribute to an outward, inclusive and responsible society are absorbed. The consequences of a breakdown in the family reverberate across all of society: there is not one Government Department – not one line of Public Expenditure – that is not impacted.

In his classic 'The Affluent Society', referred to earlier, J.K. Galbraith dissects the cancer at the heart of a 'consumerist' society. He distinguishes between 'Needs' and 'Wants', and highlights the fact that the fixation of an increasingly secularist and consumerist society on 'Wants' was driven primarily by the forces of marketing, jealousy and the inculcation by financial institutions of a culture of indebtedness.

The data on household indebtedness, to take just one example, plainly bear out just how right Galbraith was and, equally, just how catastrophic have been the consequences of the rise in this indebtedness for Individuals – who are alienated from their dignity as Human Persons – they are simply sold-short by a consumerist culture as 'want-fodder' – and for a society wholly alienated from any 'Common Good'. Galbraith's analysis casts a prophetic shadow over Ireland as we come to the end of the first decade of this millennium. He was right then, and he is still right.

Nowhere is the displacement of fundamental freedoms by a 'Wants'-based culture, spurred on by financial institutions, more evident than in the case of the Family. The Family has been commoditised and emasculated by the 'consumerist culture' at the heart of corporate capitalism. The concept of 'Family' is quite useful as a marketing ploy, but its substantive and transcendent value has been emptied of all support and affirmation by the state which has effectively forced parents out to work and stood by while prospective parents were seduced into the dependence of 40 year mortgages and the insidious enslavement of the ubiquitous 'charge/credit card'. What we are looking at here is, effectively, trans-generational indebtedness with all that it implies in terms of a legacy of pressure on public services and on households: it is the obverse of intergenerational solidarity and considered fundamentally unethical.

In a developed world where dependency rates are rising, with all this implies for the fiscal costs of such dependency, the demographics arguments supportive of families are so evidence-based and so obvious that it must be regarded as surprising that this anti-family culture has taken root in Ireland. But it has, and, unless fiercely resisted and overturned, the basis for a platform on which to build a society based on the pillars of 'The Common Good', a Leadership based on service to the Person, as well as the core principles of subsidiary and social solidarity, will have been eroded.

This generation will rediscover the intrinsic and indispensable value of the Family – not least at a time of major social stress. It is within families that children first experience unconditional love and acceptance. They learn to respect the 'Other', as well as the centrality of responsibility and the boundaries of their rights. They learn the indispensable value of prayer as the key to their transcendence as a Person. It is to Family that young couples, threatened with the pressures of 'negative equity' and unemployment, revert to regroup and to find again their innate self-worth. It is within Families that the true worth of the nurturing of young children, across all the domains of their Personhood, becomes evident.

It is within families that Trust in our own capabilities to heal and overcome the self-inflicted wounds that have exacerbated the effects of the global banking and economic crisis will be rebuilt.

In Ireland, to take just one example, at the height of the 'Celtic Tiger', pressurised parents – incentivized by the taxation code not to commit to marriage – could attempt to compensate through expenditures on 'Wants', funded by ever-higher levels of household indebtedness. Now these same families are confronted by a shortage of 'Needs'. It wasn't just bad economics – it was a betrayal.

The victims of this neglect by successive Governments both of their Constitutional responsibilities and of the abundance of data in support of the Family – supported by the traditions encompassing all of the Theistic faiths – are children. Their unique gifts are stunted and often stymied by the prevailing political orthodoxy, which has no democratic mandate. This malign process is being intensified under the shadow of escalating unemployment and cuts in Education as the impact of 'corrective' measures for a crisis which we, and our political and financial establishments, watched develop – up close and personal.

The consequences of this deliberate erosion of the Family are evident across a swath of economic and social data: the breakdown of marriage, delinquency, including addiction-related problems that present in GP surgeries and Emergency Department, a swamping of social services, of Courts and Prison and Probation services. Taxation policies incentivize two individuals living on social welfare not to marry. Neither is there any acknowledgement in the tax code – although given the very specific provisions of the Constitutions one might have expected this – that one of the parents of children might wish to be with their child, especially in the early special years. There is strong evidence that, not alone is this enormously enriching for the child, but that it contributes immeasurably to social stability. Instead, both parents have been forced out to work – many now finding themselves and their relationship ransomed to fiscal and banking models as malign and indefensible as is their 'policies' on families.

This whole process is not, of course, confined to Ireland: in 2007 *Financial Times* columnist Martin Woolf highlighted 'The War on the Traditional Family', citing UK research[27] relating to the effects of this very real 'war'. Ireland has reason to know better – it has seen the effects of misconceived anti-family policies in the US and the UK. And the UK does not have a Constitution, much less one that upholds the importance of Family, of belonging, of acceptance and of autonomy from the 'reach' of the State which has failed so disastrously across so many domains of its own legitimate responsibilities. It should not be forgotten that some of the most important services are excluded from National Accounts and GNP – and these included family-related services. This 'social capital' is the essential foundation for financial, economic and social transformation.

The end point is this: the economic crisis now rolling across the landscape is threatening to swamp families, debilitated and weakened by a culpable failure of political parties and institutions to discharge their constitutional responsibilities. Meanwhile, the State, bereft of the resources to support the victims of its own misconceived anti-family policies, is in fact diverting resources to support financial institutions driven by an equally untenable mindset.

The victims of 'the scourge of unemployment' – and increasingly those impacted by pressures on maintain their homes – were evident in the March 2009 Budget, left without even the traditional additional welfare resources to exist through Christmas. This is a painful reality – and an appropriate metaphor for the 'old politic' that is grappling futilely with the greatest crisis in modern Ireland.

Section VII

The Global Crisis and the Transition to a New Paradigm

There is no going back to where we were. It was the rejection of the indispensability of 'The Common Good' to a sustainable economy and a civilized society that is the root-cause of the present crisis. Until that is acknowledged and our mind-set and institutions transformed to a wholly new paradigm, there will be no permanent 'recovery' – only the probability of a slide towards political totalitarianism to try to cope with the inevitable economic and political consequence of an ethical failure which continues to be denied.

---

[27] Research carried out by the UK Institute for Economic Affairs.

A number of countries have undertaken the most convoluted intellectual somersaults – from regulatory 'band aid' right through the spectrum to nationalisation and State control: all in the space of two years. It is worth dissecting the flaws in this model – if only to indicate the need for a wholly new and transformed set of banking and political institutions.

In Ireland, the Pensions of a generation – being built up in the National Pension Reserve Fund – which has spent its life working and the future of a generation that is being denied the opportunity to use their gifts and talents were used to part-fund the 'rescue' of a perverse banking 'model' and a 'hollowed-out' philosophy that still denies the centrality of 'The Common Good' as the essential basis of stability and sustainability in all that speaks to the dignity and rights of the Human Person.

It was short-term in nature. Overriding precedence was given to Shareholders who were, however, just one of a wider set of stake-holders who contributed as much, and arguably more, to the embedded value of banks and financial markets in highly monetised economies.

This was the Shareholder Value (SV) maximisation model. It was main-stream. It was also deeply flawed. Banks cannot function – as is now all too apparent – without a stable base of depositor's funds. Banks cannot generate profits in the absence of borrowers who can put these deposits to productive market-determined productive uses. They certainly cannot engineer innovative products and services for their customers – both depositors and borrowers – without talented individuals imbued with both professionalism and integrity.

When a company – however large – fails, it is a tragedy for employees, shareholders, and suppliers. There is a loss of welfare because of the reduction in consumer choice.

However, when a bank – and particularly a large bank – is perceived to be in danger of failing, there is, in the existing model of banking – a tearing of the fabric on which the whole economy is based. The erosion, first of confidence, and then of the credibility of policy, and finally of Trust, can trigger systemic disturbances across global markets that metastasise into crises within the wider economic and also political system

The flaws in the short-term Shareholder Value based approach to financial intermediation are threefold. The first is that the model is obsolete in a world where capital is no longer the scarce factor of production that it was when modern banking was established. Secondly, the model isn't balanced, therefore, in giving precedence to shareholders over the legitimate claims of other stakeholders, including the Community.

Thirdly, it created a whole set of target-based incentives for 'top management' to pursue to the interests of shareholders – and this was to be expected since it was the accepted model which none would reimage – at the expense of other stakeholders. It also exacerbated the classic 'Principal and Agent' problem: management were able to, in effect, capture much of the 'gains' arising from increases in Shareholder Value in the form of a wide range of remuneration packages that were, in many instances, both disproportionate that co-existed alongside the notion that the results of this malign philosophy – enormous losses – could be 'socialised' – transferred to the very stakeholders which banks were ostensibly there to serve.

Then again, this model had, by its nature, a short-term time-horizon. The monster had to be continually fed. And so, instead of focusing on sustainability and stability, there was a fixation on next quarters' earnings. It was this which drove markets. But it also drove the internal dynamics, *and organizational politics*, of banks because next quarters' earnings could only be that little bit higher by continually 'raising the bar'; upping the targets imposed on those who worked within the organization, whether interfacing with the markets, or dealing with customers, or in backroom activities. But it was inherently unstable. It was bound to collapse.

The Regulatory system simply could not simply cope with the latent strains which this pernicious model demonstrated. At one level, there was the all too evident fragmentation of international regulation. Institutions and markets had gone global. Regulation remained obdurately national and, to a large extent, institutionally-based, in nature. The exception was the EU financial market, where a genuine single market shaped by Directives, which were near universally applied, did create something approaching a common 'regulatory space'. Even here, however, the European Central Bank (ECB) was established without any substantive regulatory mandate for financial stability, that role evolved – and is still evolving, within the context of national central banks.

The fragility of this arrangement was fully exposed in early and mid-2008, with divergent approaches to ensuring the solvency and liquidity of banks. In October 2008, even the most sober assessment of the volatility, and fear, evident in the Markets, could not but conclude that the financial systems and payments arrangement of western liberal democracies, were on the brink of imploding.

This, it should be noted, was within the EU. The fragmentation of regulatory governance was significantly more acute at a global level. The central banks of the major countries – notably the US Fed., the ECB, The Bank of England, and those of the other major countries, all had different mandates. Cooperation and coordination is a poor substitute for what was, and remains, manifestly absent: namely, a global Financial Regulator which could respond pro-actively and with a wide range of policy instruments to emerging strains within global markets.

It is worth reiterating the fact that the issue of reform of the international monetary system never went away, following its collapse in the 1970's. There were extensive discussions on changes in the 'international financial architecture' in the 1990's. And it would be wrong not to acknowledge what was achieved – especially in the EU – but also in specific sub-sets of the markets such as clearing and settlements arrangements. But on the issue of regulation *per se* the locus of policy remained strictly national – and all of the talk was of 'enhanced cooperation' and the like. Everyone missed – or avoided raising the issue of – 'the big picture'; namely, the need for a Global Regulator[28] not alone because the degree of integration had become so great – but also because of the prospectively catastrophic impact of a 'Black Swan' event. It is to precisely the financial markets that one instinctively look to anticipate a 'low frequency/high impact' shock such as one might expect to incubate in globalised 24/7 markets of unimaginatively large nominal, as well as real, financial flows.

A Global Financial Regulator would certainly have picked up on the extraordinary volatility which was evident in 2006. Some individual Central banks did – but to little effect, since they had neither the mandate nor resources to anticipate and to intervene decisively. Central banks were continually playing 'catch up' – just one or two steps behind a global crises that continued to gather momentum.

The periodic coordinated interventions – for example the interest-rate cuts initiated by the US, China, the EU and other Central Banks in November 2008 – simply served to highlight the glaring regulatory deficiencies in global financial architecture. They didn't cause the problem. But they didn't pick up on it early enough, or in a coordinated manner. Then again, a major theme running through these essays, relates to the limits of regulation.·

There is a strong message in the fact that the global financial crises was spawned within, and transmitted across, the most prescriptive regulatory regime ever devised. The Basle II Capital Adequacy Directive – which was developed over a period of a decade or so, and is *still* being implemented within banks, at a cost of hundreds of millions of dollars – was simply swept away in the form which was being implemented. In an environment where Trust has melted away and the credibility of policy interventions strained to breaking point, the markets have reasserted their role as *de facto* regulators of what exactly is meant by capital adequacy.

Basle II, and its counter-part in Insurance markets, was envisaged as the coping stone of a new risk-based regulatory regime. What we are learning is that Regulation, of itself, is no guarantor of Financial Stability. It has failed to protect institutions from fraud perpetrated from both within and without. More significantly, it has failed to protect the stability of the mainstream model on which financial intermediation is currently based.

This is not simply because regulation can never be guaranteed to catch the 'bad guy', intent on getting round the rules. Neither can – and this is equally important – Corporate Governance. We have learned over the last decade that the manner in which a Board operates is important to the integrity and sustainability of individual organisations. A whole swath of requirements has been put in place. Some are useful. Some less so. Even with all the innovations that have been introduced, they have failed to protect stake-holders in the largest most supposedly transparent and accountable institutions from bad decision making catastrophic losses.

---

[28] See 'Fragmentation of International Regulatory Governance and the Case for a Single Global Financial Regulator', in Section Two of this Book.

Auditors are a part of the Regulatory process; their role is central to ensuring financial stability. It hasn't, for whatever reason, worked as one might have expected it to work.[29] There is now a case for stripping out a pure 'audit function', distinct from the provision of one which encompasses non-audit service, and whose sole-focus is ensuring the integrity, transparency and accessibility in plain English of all of the information necessary for Regulators, Boards, and the Markets, to make informed decisions.

What all of this suggests is that, while there are problems with Regulation, the solution to the global financial crises does not reside in *more* regulation. Regulation has its place – and one of the contributions in this volume, dating from mid 2006, argued strongly for greater Regulation of Hedge Funds. Neither will it be found in yet more detailed requirements regarding Corporate Governance.

The challenge is Ethics – the reality that all investment should be directed towards, and certainly not contrary to, 'The Common Good'. By contrast, the present mainstream banking model is inherently immoral. It incentivises skewed and self-serving behaviour. It marginalises the interests of other stakeholders. If indeed it is the case that 'by their fruits you shall know them', then the calamitous damage that is being wrought on the global economy, the destruction of companies, and the loss of jobs: the foreclosure on homes, and the devastating cuts in Public Services arising from a collapse in Public Finances right across developed countries, points unambiguously to a wholly unethical business model which no amount of Regulation or Governance could sustain. Why demand sacrifices from your people to rehabilitate a banking model while leaving the root causes of their sacrifices in place?

The transition to a different banking Model, as well as to a truly global system of regulation, is perfectly feasible. The insights and common sense which underpin this argument go back well over 3000 years. Rebuilding the banking and financial systems at a national, let alone an international level, may take a generation to achieve, and even then, only if the lessons have been learned and internalised in the value systems, mind-set and behaviour of financial institutions. It has taken that long to understand that the Basle II Capital Adequacy regime is no guarantor of stability within the present orthodoxy.

In the short-term, the markets will require higher levels of capital and the authorities will have to be vigilant to ensure that this process is not second-guessed by 'innovative' ways around this imperative. The amount of capital is a function of economic fundamentals, the source of capital-specifically whether or not it is provided by the State – because capital requirements are inevitably bound up with Trust.

It may indeed take longer because the restoration of the financial stability is inextricably bound-up not alone with economic stability, but also stability within western political institutions. These are now threatened by the consequences of a failure in ethical standards within financial market which has brought a generation to its knees, and compounded the

---

[29] See Malcolm S. Salter's monumental 'Enron: Innovation Corrupted' Harvard University Press, 2008.

misery of developing countries, whose financial markets are subjugated to those of developed countries.

There will still be periodic crises – the product of entrepreneurialism, innovation – and bad moral choices – and most likely continued unexpected 'shocks' generated by changes in expectations within the economic system. What would, however, be different is that there would be an external reference point – outside of the system itself, against which strategy and behaviour can be measured, and which will animate, in a manner not possible or present, regulation and corporate governance.

A failure to make this transition to what is in effect a wholly new paradigm, threatens our economic system, and political stability, in a way that could hardly be conceived outside of war. The perceived costs and complexity of this undertaking have to be measured against the catastrophic effects of the failure of the present paradigm. The paradigm is being – and will continue to be – ferociously defended by banks themselves, by governments, as well as by regulatory authorities.

Section VII

Some Aspects of State Intervention in Financial Markets

In Ireland, intervention has taken the form of the nationalisation in January 2009 of Anglo-Irish Bank; the recapitalisation of the two systemically important banks, Bank of Ireland and Allied Irish Bank; and, more recently, proposals to establish a National Asset Management Agency (NAMA).[30]

Draft proposals for a Bill to establish NAMA were published in August 2009 with the aim of producing a Bill in September 2009 which would provide the legal basis for this proposed agency. There are examples of similar institutions ('Asset Management Companies') that have been set-up by governments in order to assist banks restructure their balance sheets in the wake of financial crisis. In the case of Ireland, NAMA – as one such asset-management company – was established in order to acquire property-related impaired loans swamping the balance-sheets of banks and impeding them functioning normally.

At the heart of the NAMA initiative is a mechanism whereby it will acquire impaired property and construction-related loans in exchange for bonds backed by the Government. Such bonds could then be exchanged with the European Central Bank (ECB) who would supply the banks with liquidity, enabling them, in principle, to begin functioning 'normally'. The price for which the impaired loans would be acquired by NAMA from the banks would involve a significant discount (haircut) reflecting the belief, that, since there is no affective market for the property on which the loans are secured, some form of discounting to an

---

[30] The relevant draft legislation 'Proposal for National Asset Management Agency Bill 2009' is available at http://www.nama.ie/

estimated value is necessary. NAMA would, the Government propose, acquire up to €90 billion of such impaired loans.

NAMA dwarfs all of the other forms of intervention. It is essentially an Asset Management Company (AMC), the general aim of which is to acquire 'impaired' property/construction-related loans from credit institutions and, in this way, rehabilitate the (discounted) assets of the banks. In the case of NAMA, what is at issue is an agency empowered to absorb €90 billion in property/construction-related assets, which are the 'black-hole' at the heart of Ireland's enfeebled credit markets.[31]

The 'logic' of NAMA[32] is to help repair the balance-sheets of credit institutions damaged by impaired property and construction-related loans. These are to be acquired, at a discount ('hair-cut '), in exchange for Government-backed bonds which can be exchanged for liquidity by the banks via the European Central Bank. By exchanging non-marketable assets which have no market valuation, but must have a value assigned to them, for liquidity, the Credit Institutions can thereby liquidate its impaired loans allowing it to resume lending and facilitating capital-raising by creating greater certainty in relation to the assets-side of its balance sheet.

The orthodox view is that unless, and until, this is done, banks will not be able to resume their role of intermediating between depositors and borrowers. To put this another way, the orthodox view is that the failure of systemically important banks – which is possible given the magnitude of the 'impaired loans' being carried at face value on balance sheets as well as other prospective losses – cannot fully 'internalise' the costs of such failure. Directly and indirectly, these costs impact on the wider economy and on society. This is deemed to merit the establishment of NAMA, which – very generally – would absorb the bad loans in exchange for liquidity which can be used to stabilise their balance sheets and to strengthen their capacity for lending.

However, before accepting all of this as a sufficient justification for establishing an institution whose net-effect may be to write-off upwards of €30 billion in bad-loans made by banks, there is the most compelling case for challenging this sort of orthodoxy.

It is worth, firstly, reflecting on the power of the prevailing orthodoxy. The British economist John Maynard Keynes once made the argument that every politician whether they knew is or not, was 'slave to some defunct economist', in this regard, the global financial and economic crisis has tested much of modern economic theory – and found it wanting – this is hardly surprising. An eminent scientist-turned-financier has argued that:

---

[31] There are other mechanisms which have the same general objective, such as the insurance-based scheme in the UK.
[32] For details of proposed arrangements relating to the establishment and operation of NAMA, see http://www.finfacts.ie/irishfinancenews/article_1017303.shtml

"The supposed omniscience and perfect efficiency of a free market stems from economic work done in the 1950's and 60's, which with hindsight looks more like propaganda against communism than plausible science. In reality, markets are not efficient, humans tend to be over-focused in the short-term and blind in the long-term, and errors get amplified, ultimately leading to collective irrationality, panic and crashes...classical economics has no framework through which to understand 'wild markets' even though their existence is so obvious to the layman. Physics, on the other hand, has developed several models that explain how small perturbations can lead to wild effects."[33]

This strengthens the argument for challenging the orthodoxy. It is very much larger than initially seemed to be the case; its funding requirements – and the 'opportunity cost' – of such funding greater; and the scale of other losses larger than had been the case when the initiative was first mooted.

The establishment of NAMA also needs to be looked at in a broader context. Rebuilding Trust in Banking requires a wide-spread acceptance of the integrity of Credit Institutions across all corporate management and operational domains. It also requires that Regulation will be market-sensitive, even-handed and proportionate and, also, that the costs of whatever form will be proportionate to the putative benefits. In such circumstances, markets will emerge, innovate and develop, thereby creating efficiencies and enhancing the welfare of society.

Where these conditions are not met – where Trust is no longer a given, and where regulation is not affective – then at some point a 'chain reaction' will be set in motion. This will subvert markets, destabilise institutions and undermine the Public Trust which is essential if banks are to perform their core function of intermediation.

There is little support for diverting billions of Euros into NAMA for three reasons. Firstly, it is not remotely clear 'how much will be enough'. No one knows – and no one knows how to go about knowing. Secondly, despite the protestations of the State and of the banks, this does amount to a further and open-ended 'bailout' – because NAMA will leave the basic 'Business Model' untouched. Thirdly, establishing NAMA, its operational costs and, most of all, its funding have a quite literally incalculable 'opportunity cost' to individuals, families and businesses – and to society. There is no sense of proportionality between unknown and unknowable costs and putative benefits.

It is important to bear in mind that it is not difficult, with prudence and effective risk management – both of which bankers learn at their mother's' knee, to earn a competitive rate of return from their franchise. It takes a very great deal to preside over total losses which, according to IMF estimates, are now approaching $4 trillion.

---

[33] Bouchaud Op.cit

At a broader level, there are no indications that the State is prepared to approach this issue from an unorthodox – human rather than purely banking – perspective. There are, as pointed out by those working in the field of homelessness – such as the Simon Community[34] and Peter McVerry[35] – many homeless people and families coexisting alongside boarded-up houses and empty apartments. This does not make economic sense, and reflects an impoverished thinking and an inability to see what is staring us in the face.

This land provides an extraordinary opportunity for the State to invest in whole range of amenities which are desperately needed. This is not about the National Development Plan – this is about common sense. We do need more sporting facilities – we do need facilities that can bring communities together. We do need land both on which our young companies develop and which, when we get on top of this problem, can provide the foundation for projects attracting multi-national investment. If we allow ourselves to be hypnotised by present difficulties, we will simply never be able to see the opportunities in these difficulties to begin to reshape our future.

The reality is that housing assets are available at a price which could not have been conceived of by Government two or three years ago. The difference is this; the driving force behind the utilization of at least some of these housing assets could be 'The Common Good' of the people of Ireland. We need to think big, as well as responsibly, if we are to grow our way out of deflation.

Housing, *by itself*, will not alleviate the plight of many of those who are homeless. They need, as Sr. Consilio Fitzgerald, Founder of Cuan Mhuire which is the largest provider of Residential Rehabilitation services for individuals suffering from addiction and its effects including homelessness in Ireland, has pointed-out, not alone to be loved, but to be encouraged to understand that they are themselves of inestimable and eternal value. Housing is, however, a necessary condition without which other interventions cannot be developed. A proper *understanding* of this reality – a redirection of, for example, at least part of the surplus Housing fuelled by an excessive growth in Credit for Housing by the banks – to individuals and families without homes, could help make sense of an intervention such as NAMA. It would not necessarily justify NAMA but it would demonstrate to people that something good might come out of such an intervention.

The issue of state interventions merits further analysis. The perverse incentives generated by the present orthodoxy undermine 'The Common Good' at two levels. Firstly, in the 'good times' – the 'Celtic Tiger' years – one of a number of stakeholders – investors (which is a pretty heterogeneous term encompassing everything from Pension Funds to 'Short Sellers') benefit disproportionally at the expense of other stakeholder. They 'internalise' the games from an environment which is largely under their control. Secondly, in the really bad times – such as the present crisis – when the cost of negative externalities arising from a collapse of

---

[34] http://www.simon.ie
[35] http://www.pmvtrust.ie

Trust from these same institutions and markets are almost incalculable, they 'socialise' all or a part of the losses which are the inevitable consequences of their decisions.

The erosion of Public Trust in financial institutions and in our societal institutions – which is perhaps the most striking characteristic of the present crisis – inevitably brings institutions and markets crashing down on society; on the heads of those not responsible for such failures, on those least equipped to bear the costs. This is profoundly unethical and inequitable. The 'Special' nature of banking[36] and the regulation and supervision of financial institutions and markets, are indicative of the reality that they are, first and foremost, a public utility – the central nervous system of the wider economy. The management are, in effect, the trustees of this utility. Banks are granted a franchise because their mindset and activities are presumed to be a 'Public Good' as well as a private enterprise; the former takes precedence.

It follows from this that the costs of a crisis which arises directly , as well as indirectly, from the exploitation of their franchise should not be 'socialised' by society, which provides the opportunities for profitably in exchange for the prudent management, as Trustees, of their franchise.

It is, of course, the case that 'Cycles' and even periodic 'Asset Bubbles' are endemic within capitalism, they reflect changes in the economic, and political, environment, leading to changes in expectations and triggering a reallocation of resources. The history of banking is a very long one. Banks, and regulators, have a great deal of experience in the causes, and effects, of such crisis, including how best to anticipate them and to mitigate their costs. That is why the present crisis was both inevitable and foreseeable.

'Reasonable people' were therefore, justified in assuming the institutional integrity of banks and markets, and the robustness of the regulatory and supervisory structure which oversees their activities. They were justified in taking for granted that any insipient speculative bubbles would be identified in good time and would be properly managed; that is, in the words of one former chairman of the US Federal Reserve 'the punch-bowl would be taken away before the party was in full swing'. The global financial and economic crisis has laid waste to all such assumptions. Equally, 'reasonable people' are entitled to assume that, where catastrophic failures occur which can be directly traced to the prevailing business-model, as well as to political and regulatory failures, they should not be required to bear the costs of such failures.

Intervention on the scale envisaged by NAMA, coming as it does on top of the costs to society of recapitalisation and nationalisation, raises serious questions which cannot be addressed within the current political and financial orthodoxy. These costs for warehousing 'impaired loans', for writing-off bad loans, do not take account of those relating to estimated future losses on the non-property/construction related loan book which ultimately have to be absorbed by the Individual, the Family, and more generally, the Community as a whole.

---

[36] See Eugene Fama's *"What's Different About Banks?"* Journal of Monetary Economics, January 1985.

The prospective burden of NAMA, if in fact it is established, and of the unprecedented write-offs now envisaged by the banks, is without precedent. The burden on this generation and the next is vast whether measured in terms of the additional tax-burden or the impact of 'cuts' in public services, or the jobs which have been lost, or the devastation of individual lives. They are of such a magnitude that they can only be justified on the basis of two prior conditions.

The first is the endorsement of the people through the democratic process. An administration is empowered by the Constitution so long it commands a majority, however slender, in the Dáil. But it is an open question whether, or not, the initiatives taken so far and in particular the establishment of NAMA should be legislated for without consulting the community which must bear the costs.

The second is transformational change in the business model and in the mindset that led to the crisis in the first place. A resumption of 'Business as usual' by institutions responsible for such catastrophic mistakes – mistakes which are embedded within its mind set – cannot be justified.

It may, or may not, be the case therefore that NAMA coming on top of previous and likely future interventions, may be 'justified' on the basis of the political criteria. But the case for transformational change in the 'Business Model' as the necessary corollary of such intervention cannot be reasonably argued against. Indeed, it could be argued that the proposed restructuring of financial regulation, involving the establishment of a new Central Bank Commission, provides an ideal opportunity within which to introduce radical changes to achieve a more equitable and stable banking system.

There has also been in Ireland, as well as in other countries, a new awareness of the fragility of seemingly robust Corporate Governance arrangements. It doesn't matter. The theme of this book, which has been born out of developments worldwide as well as in Ireland, is that while regulation may be a necessary condition for financial stability and strong corporate governance arrangements highly desirable, neither of these is a sufficient condition for an ethical and sustainable banking system. It's the model and the mindset which has to change. There is little evidence that this is happening. Neither NAMA nor further recapitalisation can, therefore, be justified unless and until such transformational change is made.

Section VIII

Rebuilding from the Global Financial and Economic Crisis: Lessons from Ireland

Ireland is now at a defining point in its modern history. In three key domains – employment, education and health – which impact on every man woman and child – the indications of a fracturing of stability arising from the financial and economic crisis and which have ominous implications for individuals and families and indeed whole communities, are evident. The global financial crisis – as it has manifested itself in Ireland – is at the heart of this historical catharsis.

There is now a compelling case for rethinking the Irish financial sector – in its governance and regulation. The inherent flaws in the present system, combined with the misconceived response by the authorities to these flaws, are threatening in effect to pull the roof down over the head of the Irish economy. Pretty well every domestic economic indicator as at mid 2009 foreshadows the sharpest decline in jobs, living standards and public services in modern history. That is just the economy.[37]

There is a whiff of fear, which resonates with a centralisation of political power that Ireland has not seen before. In a paper to the OSCE, in June 2009, the author posed a series of questions which essentially asked why our political institutions should regard themselves as immune from the brutal impact of the global crisis on our financial markets and on our economy.

There has been no transformational change in our political mind-set and behaviour commensurate with sheer scale of the challenge which Ireland faces. A culture of 'Power' appears to predominate.

A failure to engage in transformational political change as the essential basis for beginning to grow the economy out of the deepening recession and beginning the process of re-engaging with the public and rebuilding Trust in institutions that *serve* all of the people runs a triple risk.

Firstly, a fracturing of political stability accompanying a full-blown economic crisis as the country is impacted by an un-fundable debt crisis; a shrinking employed workforce begins to wilt under the pressures of misconceived fiscal policies and the consequences of a failure to 'leverage' the innate entrepreneurial capabilities encapsulated by, for example, the *'Spirit of Ireland'* Initiative.

Secondly, were this to happen, there is a danger of a 'political contagion' beginning in Ireland and transmitting itself across a wider EU, which is already under considerable systemic, fiscal and organisational strains. Ireland's resilience, its spiritual and cultural traditions, and a capacity for our institutions to understand and internalize the key pillars of any civilised society – democracy, the transcendence of the Human Person and, 'the Public Good' need to be brought to the forefront of political dialogue on transformation.

A 'new capitalism' cannot be built on an 'old politics' or on an 'ethical' sense emasculated of *true* Christian values. A political orthodoxy that not only failed to challenge, but actively exploited, a self-serving banking paradigm the better to consolidate its hold on power, is incapable of building a 'new' Capitalism. What (almost) passes belief is that, at this stage of the crisis, there has been so little change in the nature of our political mind-set and structures.

Thirdly, it is apparent that the rebuilding Trust in Irish banking institutions and in our political system – as much in the financial sector – will require first a values-based leadership. There has been no significant change in political values or even institutions in

---

[37] http://www.finance.gov.ie

Ireland or world-wide: it is as though the existing mind-set and structures could, quite simply, accommodate the global financial crisis and its consequences as just another *albeit* large-scale economic.

Restoring Trust in our political as well as our financial institutions will require not so much reform, as transformation. It is certainly the case that such transformation will be exceedingly challenging. It will, for example, require a leadership based on 'Service to the Person' – be they in a bank or on a trolley in an A&E Department.

What we are looking at here is the need for a wholly new 'politics' far removed from the increasingly irrelevant pattern on the now hollowed 'our civil war' politics and devoid of the values which once animated them.

Such a transformation is a necessary but not a sufficient condition for changing the trajectory of Ireland's fractured economy and a societal mind-set – evident across health and social welfare – that is almost wholly emasculated of values that are enshrined in the constitution and which are a cornerstone of 'The Common Good': itself the coping stone for remaking Ireland's history.

Challenging it may well be, but the alternatives are even more daunting. The misconceived response to the economic crisis outlined above – and set-out in successive chapters – threatens Ireland with a political catharsis. But – and this is the 'good news' – we as a nation have been here before. It is part of our history. Equally, at an EU level, there is a yawning gap between, on the one hand, the political establishment, now bounded by a culture of 'managerialism' and interventionism and, on the other hand, lacking in the kind of vision that animated the original concept of European Solidarity.

A failure to *believe* that we can achieve this leaves us vulnerable to a Keynesian-type deflationary trap. This will result in a crisis, the magnitude of which depends on the root causes, on the degree of integration of institutions and markets, and on whether, or not, the 'authorities' have the mandate and the capacity to realign a system which has turned rogue to the objective ethical standards embedded in 'the Public Good'. Achieving this realignment is made all the more difficult by the fact that the prevailing political orthodoxy is impacted, at least in part, as predicted by the theory of 'Public Choice' – by its own self-interest. In effect, 'The Public Good' is caught in a trap between on the one hand, Shareholder Value driven banks and, on the other hand, by the 'politics' of the next Election.

The key point is this. A transformation in Ireland's political institutions, its financial system and the kind of economy that it underpins, is necessary *as an end in itself.* Even with such a transformation, the unwinding of contingent liabilities incurred by the State in the recapitalisation of banks and, prospectively NAMA, as well as a rolling back of a growing Statist legislation, will take the best part of a generation.

However, such a 'new politic' would provide the impetus for a new set of policies which leveraged the embedded strengths of the Irish people and economy.

Trust-rebuilding aligned to 'The Common Good', social solidarity including a real appreciation of voluntarism and subsidiary, could provide a benchmark for the wider EU. What is needed is a wholly new start. However, in a country whose civilisation dates back 5000 years BC, there have been many fresh starts.

Ireland can only transform that small part of a much wider global regulatory catharsis for which it is responsible. But that, in itself, is important. And, if we get it right, we can help restore Ireland's reputation for resilience, innovation and a values-based society.

Global markets weighing up the risk of funding a government deficit, bloated by liabilities generated by rescuing banks and multi-national companies weighing up their strategic options in terms of location, would opt for deploying such funding into resource-based development aimed at growing the economy out of an otherwise insoluble economic problem.

What is important is political consensus built around *growing* the economy – and a 'Needs'-based rather than a 'Wants'-based society. It is a conviction on the part of Ireland that it can reconnect with the values that until recently underpinned its international standing as a location for inward investment, and which also challenges the capabilities, and harnesses the gifts, of a young and now pluralist population. The opportunities are there.

Focussing on these opportunities, rather than diverting the savings of one generation and the living standards of the next, into supporting a failed system offers a way out of the way out of the present *cul de sac*. There is, for example, the prospect for the development of the International Medical Services Centre (IMSC). The case for a project on this scale was put forward in Croke Park a number of years ago. Firstly, Ireland already has major multinational companies – leaders in pharmaceutical and medical devices – and we need to anchor these here. It has outstanding researchers in its under-funded universities. We are at the threshold of a whole new knowledge revolution in medical services. The scope for developing technologies – from ethically-based genetic technologies, to nano-technology – is virtually limitless. Innovation continues even during the most protracted cycle. An IMSC, based in the West of Ireland – and Westport is an obvious 'hub' – would not only be a viable project in its own right, it would serve as a clear signal that Ireland Inc. was in the business of transformation. The International Financial Services Centre (IFSC) was launched in 1987 – at the nadir of that depressing decade – and succeeded beyond all expectations. The main driver of success was the leadership and vision and quality of the value proposition that Ireland put together. The template is there.

There is an even more compelling case for a massive national programme to harness natural wind and hydro electrical power on the scale put forward by 'Spirit of Ireland'. This research-based initiative has the potential to transform Ireland from a net importer of energy – to the extent of some three billion Euros per year – to being a net exporter of the single most economically and strategically important resource driving European economies. It has the capacity to create a whole new generation of technologies – and jobs. In the process, it could reverse the deterioration in Ireland's energy competitiveness, which has seen both industrial and household energy costs fall from being one of the least expensive to the second most expensive in the space of a decade.

If Ireland were to focus on a vision to engage hearts, minds and talents it could move on from its neurosis with fixing a failed banking model – at an incalculable cost. It could transform its future: on the lessons for contemporary 70th anniversary of the Shannon power scheme, which itself was utterly transformational, it could retain the thousands who are now emigrating with little possibility of work and offer some hope to a generation of students now seeking shelter – instead of using their gifts-in our third-level colleges.

Section IX

Reforming Ireland's Regulatory System

Ireland, in some respects, stands as a microcosm of the wider globalised financial system. It has a highly-open economy, driven by trade and foreign direct investment. It has also developed in the period since 1987, one of the most impressive and robust international financial services centres. The IFSC, in addition to attracting some of the world's largest financial institutions, together with a wide spectrum of specialised financial service providers and back-office functions, has generated high value-added employment in expert-based global financial services operations. It has also transformed the economic, social and cultural environment of inner-city Dublin, touching the lives of, and impacting on the opportunities accessible to, many thousands of young people.

The important point here is this: this transformational change is an example of 'good' decision-making which focused not simply on creating a profitable environment for financial institutions, but, equally, of pro-active transformational changes in the lives of those who work in and within the penumbra of the IFSC. It wasn't just about profit; it was also about ethical investment in the fullest meaning of the term.

Ireland entered into the financial, and subsequent economic, crisis in the latter part of 2008, with both of its systemically important banks strongly capitalised and with lower levels of exposure to toxic sub-prime related securities than was the case in many EU countries. On the other hand, both had high levels of exposure to excessive levels of lending across the property-related sectors. The Government had both the data at its disposal as well as the means of intervening to mitigate self-inflicted wounds. It failed to do so; having said that, the final responsibility for the effects of such levels of exposure lies with the boards of the banks.

The impact of these mistakes on depositors and borrowers, on employees and the wider economy, have been catastrophic. The initial precipitous decline in the share price of the banks, together with the high level of credit default spreads, indicated the market's judgement. In these circumstances, and because the State at present lacks the resources and the credibility to afford successive recapitalisations on a scale necessary to appease markets that have no longer any interest in 'the Celtic Tiger', nationalisation must be seen as a possible element in the stabilisation of the financial sector and the economy.

Both Bank of Ireland and Allied Irish Bank missed a vital 'window of opportunity' to recapitalise in the immediate aftermath of the introduction of the Deposit Protection Initiative Scheme 2008. Neither institution (nor the wider domestically-headquartered system) changed its 'Business Model' in the wake of recapitalisation.

At the same time, even nationalization could not be expected to function properly in the absence of transformational change within Government and Ireland's wider political institutions. Both AIB and Bank of Ireland, now under a significant *albeit* temporary degree of public ownership, could operate alongside a new 'Narrow Bank' – as a permanent feature of the Government's financial and economic infrastructure and which would operate on a not-for-profit basis and be focused exclusively on 'The Common Good' and on 'firewalling' the banking system against the threat of ever becoming vulnerable to the prospective effects of a failure of systemically important commercial banks.

It is difficult to understand why the state, having recapitalised both institutions, did not use its 'leverage' sufficiently to ensure that priority was given to underpinning national recovery over the rebuilding of the bank's balance sheet. There are strong indications of a restriction on the availability of credit, particularly to smaller businesses, in the period preceding the 2009 Budget which drained an already anaemic economy of demand and confidence.

Nationalisation is cannot be ruled out in the light of developments in 2009/2010; consolidation of credit institutions is almost inevitable. The possibility of one or more of the systemically important banks being taken over cannot be discounted. Such developments, in conjunction with reforms of the 2004 Act, point towards a new regulatory landscape. The issue facing Ireland is whether such a conjunction of factors will be a platform – or a *cul de sac*.

Regulation is, almost always, a second-best response to actual, or incipient, instability. What is more important, by an order of magnitude, is the quality of leadership and standard of ethics within the boardrooms operating within a wholly new business model aligned to 'The Common Good'. A strengthening of bank's capital 'cushioning' (including dynamic provisioning to counter the pro-cyclicality of the Basle II rules) and curbs on remuneration, do not amount to much when benchmarked against embedded ethical flaws of the mainstream Model

The existing financial regulatory system was the outcome of an inter-departmental hiatus in the early parts of the decade. It left the Central Bank, which is responsible for monetary policy, semi-detached from responsibility for the stability of the banks and the markets through which monetary policy is transmitted. This never made sense. Consumer Protection has been transformed out of recognition. But the synergies between Financial Stability, whose domain is global and which operates in real time, and Consumer Protection, which is essentially domestic and is not time-sensitive, are weak. The Government's proposals for a

Central Banking Commission which reintegrates responsibility for central banking with Financial Stability provide a platform for financial reforms including rationalisation as well as stability.

This will require access to a much wider pool of expertise so that the proposed Central Banking Commission is not permanently in 'catch-up mode' in relation to both systemic risk and the spectrum of interventions necessary to mitigate such risks. In this context, the new Central Banking Commission will be operating within a wider framework of regulation, including the Office of the Director of Corporate Enforcement and the Criminal Assets Bureau – both of which encompass highly innovative institutional features. Leveraging the potential synergy of what is an interlocking set of regulatory arrangements will be central to the effectiveness of the Financial Stability Mandate of the Central Banking Commission.

The Central Banking Commission's most urgent challenge will be to rebuild the credibility of Ireland's banking and financial sector, including its regulatory regime. Equally important will be the capacity to contribute to, and indeed to lead, the debate for parallel reforms to the regulatory architecture both within the EU, and globally.

The kind of regulatory change now being proposed in the US, the EU as well as in Ireland simply side-step this ethical challenge. The nature of the 'Business Model' which has laid waste to the global economy has simply been put into intensive care, and all of the indications – from the nature of the regulatory changes being proposed, right across to the resurgence of arrogance within global financial markets – point unambiguously to the fact that lessons have not been learned. History teaches that there can be a negative inter-dependence between political power and the power of global financial markets lacking both a core set of universal moral values and an inclusive global financial architecture: an architecture that could at least mitigate the damage that this would periodically inflict on poorer countries as well as communities, businesses and families.

The reality is that the Irish Regulatory regime will be operating within a wholly new set of international regulatory arrangements. It would, in the light of recent experience, be facile to assume that more regulation, *per se,* is an appropriate response to this.

Section X

Political Transformation: A Leadership based on Service to the Person

Ireland's capacity to respond to the global crisis also reflects structural problems to do, for example, with the size and cost of the State. The burden of the State is still growing. These structural difficulties exacerbate the consequences of the crisis whilst also impeding then Government's political will to engage in the transformation. The latter involves, above all moving from a Power-based view of politics to one based on one of *leadership of Service to the Person.* A failure to do so erodes the State's legitimacy and its moral right to criticize financial institutions fixated by their own form of power.

Government is too big. This has bred a culture of power and an interventionism that has been enormously damaging. In the ten years up to 2008, the total population grew by a very robust 10 per cent. Total employment in the Public Sector (including health but excluding commercial semi-state bodies), rose by almost 30 per cent, from 234,000 to 332,000.[38] This extraordinary growth in the size of the public sector, representing as it does a fixed over-head that has to be funded by business, left the economy highly vulnerable to the full force of the economic crisis.

Between 2003 and 2008, Government Revenue remained constant at 34 per cent of GDP. Government Expenditure, by contrast, rose from 33 per cent to 41 per cent. In fact, expressed as a percentage of GNP, Government expenditure rose from 40 per cent to almost 50 per cent.[39] Since then, there has been an implosion in the Public Finances characterized, above all, by a collapse in Revenue. This has left the economy vulnerable to the pressures of adjustment arising both from the global crisis and its domestic counterpart.

The 'burden of adjustment' is not falling on Government or the Public sector. It is the labour market and business - which generates incomes for families and revenues for the Public Services - which is taking the impact. Business is suffocated by an administrative mind-set seemingly incapable of understanding either the nature of capitalism or, at a micro-level, and the pressures on businesses in recession and on whose viability Public Services ultimately depend.

There is an obvious need for a realignment of party politics in Ireland – we need democratic choices that mean something to contemporary society. We need a whole new political ethic premised on a leadership based, not on power but on *Service to the Person*. This is at the heart of the kind Leadership on which Christ laid such emphasis in His Ministry and with unambiguous and emphatic purpose at the Last Supper. It is a Leadership alien to political power and shareholder value.

Given the nature of the present trajectory of the Irish economy, the Government needs to have the humility – and common-sense – to co-opt expertise from outside to serve in a decision-making capacity: 'Advisory' positions provide a 'let-out' clause for the old failed paradigm. To take a few examples; Scientists and Technologists – as well as entrepreneurs and nurses – may have to be brought in from outside of the world of politics.

Political leadership needs to engage individuals who have little interest in power as such, but who have a commitment, as well as a widely acknowledged expertise, that is capable of restoring Trust, confidence and a sense of direction. The protection of Ireland's economic autonomy - and even our democracy – requires a leadership that embraces 'the Public Good'; a holistic and substantive support for the Family in its strategy for addressing the financial and economic crisis. This is the essential construct for the kind of transformation without which there can be no sustainable recovery – whether in Ireland or globally.

---

[38] Based on CSO Data (http://www.cso.ie)
[39] Ibid.

Ireland requires a Cabinet capable of correctly diagnosing the underlying nature of the problem as well as how best to address its economic consequences. In a classic study on Leadership (1998) the Harvard Business Review defined 'Leadership' as 'Humility with fierce resolve'. It is an evidence-based definition which speaks powerfully to the catastrophic effects of poor leadership as well as one driven by Power and short-term Shareholder Value. Humility is also a strong ethical virtue – one specifically embraced by Christ.

It is all too easy to downplay the integrity and commitment of Individual politicians and their commitment to 'The Common Good'. There is a problem of *perception* and equally the real difficulty that they are functioning within a 'politic' that is in real need of transformation. Ireland's political Institutions and its system of governance run the risk of alienation from individuals who have lost their jobs, businesses which are tethering on the brink of failure, and families that are literally crushed by the twin-burdens of debt and deflation. Addressing the crisis requires a deconstruction of Ireland's political culture. Ireland has a political system largely rooted in obsolete divisions and, in the view of many, emasculated of the values which once animated them. This is not to say that there are not highly committed professional and ethical politicians. There are. The tragedy is the defining characteristics of the system as a whole is a culture of 'Power' instead of 'Service to the Person'.

Ireland's essentially adversarial political institutions have demonstrated little understanding of the imperative of restoring Trust in financial institutions, and providing a sense of direction to the economy, at a time of unprecedented stress in modern Irish history.

Politics in Ireland is still largely dominated by an 'apprenticeship system', which favours those who have served their time over those who can contribute most to addressing the problems now confronting the country. Importantly, the system of Ministerial appointments makes little or no sense. All too frequently, it is geographically-based. Even more fundamentally, they commonly lack the relevant expertise to direct, with a sure and experienced hand, policy in the Departments to which they are appointed.

There is no formal training required from Ministers from their first day in Office. This simply makes no sense. It would not happen for a moment in any other profession or vocation. Our political landscape is littered by 'silos', each driven by their own agenda and political dynamic.

There is the ambiguity of the relationship between, on the one hand, the legislature, and, on the other hand, the executive. This ambiguity leaves itself open to the 'capture' of policy; it leaves itself open to the *de facto* delegation of key areas of policy. This can tend to subvert democracy.

Conversely, it can also inhibit those within the Public Sector who have a real capacity to contribute, from putting their head above the parapet. The old political canard of the first priority on getting power being to retain it corrodes and demeans the very nature of what politics should be about. Political parties have allowed themselves to be defined primarily in terms of opposition to the status quo. Opposition is, of course, part of what an alternative administration is about. But it is only a part. It has to go much deeper if "change", "fresh starts" and "new beginnings" are to have new meaning. It must mean something new.

All of this is exacerbated by the paradox of coalition government. The electorate votes only to find, when the dust has settled, a coalition government cobbled together is in charge. This means that an administration then governs the country without having been endorsed by the electorate. The people – at this critical time – have no way of knowing, having cast their votes, the values of those who will subsequently be appointed to lead the country. It is, of course, the case that any administration confronted by a crisis must take unpalatable decisions. What is different this time is the sheer scale of these decisions which could have a make-or-break impact on the Irish economy.

The only power that has the capacity for transformation is a Leadership of Service to the Person. A Leadership of Service becomes all the more important at a time of uncertainty and fear – an emergency. Ireland is now in a national emergency.

Whether, or not, the existing order is capable of such a dispassionate process of self-reflection, is an open question. But we should be clear that, economic stabilization, much less recovery, will be stymied by any such alienation of the people from our political system, by fragmentation of political support, and by the very real prospect of a rise in disenchantment and extremism among the tens of thousands who have joined the Live Register which is heading remorselessly for half a million individuals. History teaches us that political change and the growth in extremism are marked by fracture and discontinuity. The fire suddenly breaks out.

It is not just a matter of the deficiencies in the political system. It is the failure to contemplate new and awful questions:

- What is the *political* counterpart to the global financial crisis?

- *Do the present political systems have immunity from the meltdown* that has happened in finance and economies?

- How do our political institutions deal with the *social consequences* of the crisis and how can we prevent a *political contagion* that could subvert political stability when the jobless exceed more than half a million people?

The scale and consequences of Ireland's evolving financial and economic crisis is such that we need to move away, while there is still the time, and the capacity embedded in our entrepreneurs, technologists and scientists, to re-imagine the Irish economy.

This will require a reference point outside of political power and Shareholder Value. That reference point is 'The Common Good'. This dictates that the maintenance of employment should take precedence over subsidising share-holder based banks with borrowed funds. It points to the case for the community, which underwrites the viability of banks – especially in times of stress – being the decisive reference point for credit creation, consistent of course with financial stability. It points to the importance of re-sensitising our institutions and mind-set to the overriding importance of the Human Person as the measure of public policy. It highlights the importance of the natural Family unit to society, especially in times of economic crisis and political dislocation. If our politicians lack the courage to break with the current paradigm, then it will break our economic autonomy and our solidarity as a nation.

'The Common Good' is the only ethical and political construct within which to undertake the transformational changes to the Irish economy that provide an alternative to an unprecedented period of austerity, the loss of Ireland's economic sovereignty in policy making and a 'political contagion' that could trigger an unravelling of the EU.

Section XII

Some Conclusions

Among the core issues on which transformational change depends on – but are not restricted to – include the following:

- An understanding by the state and by the regulatory authorities that domestically headquartered banks in which there has been public investment are, first and foremost, a public utility. Their capacity to function effectively depends on rebuilding Trust with their key stakeholders. The best – the most robust and equitable – basis for achieving this is by means of a new corporate business model. Such a model should be specifically aligned to 'The Common Good', as a template for ensuring financial stability, sustainability and a balance among the complementary interests of all stakeholders. If Social Partnership is to mean anything in the troubled and problematic economic, social and political environment confronting this generation – and the next – it should mean striving precisely towards this objective.

- A national debate on the transition from a 'Business Model' based on short-term Shareholder Value, with all of the perverse incentives which it generates, to one based on 'The Common Good' which can deliver stability within banking – and the wider economy within which functions.

- New regulatory arrangements encompassed within the proposed Central Banking Commission. Such arrangements should have as a priority strong international and domestic expertise at a technical as well as policy level and, also, should include representation of the key sister regulatory bodies and agencies, so as to ensure that there is an integrated and effective Board. There is also a compelling case for ensuring that there is a strong and informed social voice. In this context, it would make a great deal of sense to have the Irish Bank Officials Association (IBOA) as well as the Irish Banking Federation (IBF) and, importantly, representation from the Irish League of Credit Unions – which is the closest Ireland has to a vocationally-driven banking system whose focus is unambiguously community-based. If the present crisis has taught us anything it is that there should be a strong and informed 'social banking' voice within the regulatory arrangements, thereby providing a domestic counter-part to the international, market-sensitive technical expertise that is necessary. This would take the Central Banking Commission into a whole new domain in terms of governance arrangements. A two-tier Regulatory Board could best meet the needs of informed oversight and authorative and pro-active formulation of policy, wholly independent of political involvement.

- Changes in the structure of financial markets, including consolidation of domestically-headquartered credit institutions and the establishment of a state-capitalised/guaranteed 'Narrow Bank' to reduce the vulnerability of the public interest in any future 'shock' to the system.

- The stability of banks is inextricably bound up with the health of economy of which it is the 'central nervous system'. Domestic credit institutions have a role helping to restore confidence to the domestic economy by adopting a medium-term perspective focussed on maintaining existing businesses, supporting growth and promoting entrepreneurialism especially in natural-resource based activities. Promoting the exploiting of Ireland's natural energy resources, including the transition to the kind of transformational model envisaged in the 'Spirit of Ireland' Initiative is a natural starting point.

- Supporting an adjustment *already under way* in households and business, including farms/fisheries and agri-business. Farming is perhaps the best indication of how a resource that is also an integral part of Ireland's culture has been allowed to contract: this limits our economic autonomy, which has already been subverted by the economic crisis and our immediate response to its effects on employment and public services. It makes no sense for a nation that is uniquely rich in natural resources to allow such resources to progressively atrophy in terms of employment and innovation in maximizing their value to the economy – and to the wider nation. Banks rise and fall under the present form of corporate capitalism – the land endures.

- A significant reduction in the size and cost-burden of the State. This burden is now wholly disproportionate to our size as a country, and represents a claim on scarce – and in fact borrowed – resources, which are being diverted from social goods such as healthcare, education and the protection and support of the marginalized.

- Reductions in state expenditure to relieve the 'burden' of the state overhead, reflected in the relative increase in the size and cost of the public sector, are essential to create 'room' for maintaining public services and focussing on growth and the private sector.

- At the same time, it is essential for mainstream politics to acknowledge the reality that Ireland cannot 'cut' its way out of the worst recession in its recent history. 'Cuts' are frequently short-term and counter-productive. Ireland has a uniquely favourable demographic profile at present. Within twenty years, this 'golden demographic' advantage will have melted away. This provides a compelling argument for investment in entrepreneurship and education and, also, in ensuring that this 'knowledge equity'[40] animates the private traded-goods sector.

- More generally, there is need for a consensus on how best to achieve a significant reduction in the size and cost-burden of the State without at the same time reducing vital investment in health and education and social solidarity. The burden of State interventionism is now wholly disproportionate to our size as a country, and represents a claim on scarce – and indeed borrowed – resources, which are being diverted from social capital in order to support credit institutions without ensuring fundamental reform.

- In this context, there is an urgent need to address the imbalance in the prevalence of third-level qualifications in the public, compared with the private sector, identified in the CSO National Employment Survey (2007).

- Implementing a medium-term fiscal strategy which gives priority to supporting domestically-based companies and households over the recapitalisation of financial institutions for whom rebuilding their balance sheet, in the interest of shareholders, remains an overriding priority.

- Empowering the Family and local communities in Ireland by rolling back a suffocating blanket of State interventionism and 'rent-seeking' *aka* 'red tape' semi-detached from the realities of businesses and families struggling to survive.

- A transformational change across politics involving a new form of leadership based, not on the aggregation of political Power and control vested in 'The Minister' as an end in itself, but instead a form of 'Leadership of Service to the individual Person'. In this regard, there is a compelling case for co-opting external expertise via the Seanad where the Cabinet lacks expertise specifically relevant to the imperative of addressing what is a national economic emergency.

- Acknowledging, and supporting, the role of 'voluntarism', in an environment in which the state has overreached itself, funding is not available and voluntary bodies can achieve such objectives more efficiently and cost-effectively. A particularly good example of this is the agreement in 2009 between the Credit Unions and the St. Vincent De Paul Society whereby the latter will provide guarantees for individuals and low-income families 'crowded-out' of the banking system.

- Concurrently there is a compelling case for engaging in supply-side policies that further incentivise capacity-building, instead of cutting back, within our universities and third-level institutions.

---

[40] Kinsella R. and McBriety V. 'Ireland and the Knowledge Economy: the New Techno-Academic Paradigm', Oaktree Press, Dublin,1998.

The essays in this volume are simply one set of perspectives which track the implosion of the financial system of western liberal democracies. They do not presume to be prescriptive – and if this is what comes across, it shouldn't. Equally, while one may legitimately disagree with and challenge prevailing orthodoxies, it is not less important to acknowledge the integrity of those who believe in them. That is what democracy is about. The great danger is that a failure to engage in an open debate in which the good faith of all is taken as a given, may threaten our democratic institutions. They are pretty well as originally published. They provide some form of support for the proposition that we must inwards from regulation, through corporate governance, to a proper understanding of the indispensible importance of Ethics as the essential reference point for preserving the integrity, stability, and sustainability of our financial institutions and markets.

Section One:

Ethics and Financial Stability

The Fatal Distraction of the Minimum Wage

The debate on the minimum wage is a classic example of *political* economy. The background to the debate is both simple and, for about 85,000 who are on the minimum wage or close to it, traumatic.

The economy is now at a point where the burden of a fragmented and dysfunctional fiscal regime is beginning to cannibalise its capacity to maintain, jobs. This has been aggravated by the disconnect between, on the one hand, the funding that has is being diverted by society to rescue 'covered institutions' and, on the other hand, the reality that the interests of society take second place to restoring shareholder value of these same institutions. When the summer is over and children head back to school and the inexorable rise in the Live Register continues to rise towards 450,000, the real pain and pressure will be felt. It may well prove impossible to frame a Budget. Those on minimum wage are at the sharp end of all of this.

World trade will fall by 13% this year. Foreign Direct Investment (FDI) in the EU is declining. The economic condition of our major export markets remain parlous: in the UK for example, per capita income is forecast not to return to its 2008 levels until 2014. These are key external drivers of growth and jobs in the Irish economy.

Meanwhile, the domestic economy continues to contract – by up to an estimated 10% in 2009. This is, in part, because of a series of reactive budgets policies that are draining whatever demand, and confidence, remains in the domestic economy. And coming down the line are proposals for a Property tax (we've been here before) and Carbon-related taxes – both of which seem strangely disassociated from the grim realities of where the Irish economy is now mired.

What is euphemistically called the 'Burden of Adjustment' – aka the pain and grief of adapting to these conditions- is falling squarely on the labour market.

This is the context of a seemingly appalling dilemma: should the Minimum Wage Act, 2000 be set aside? The Trade Unions are vehemently opposed to any such move. There is, they argue, a 'threshold of decency' below which wages should not be allowed to fall. David Begg has described the proposal as 'toxic'. That is fair enough. The imperative of a 'Just Wage' has a long pedigree.

At the same time, as matters now stand, simply to hold onto a job people are working fewer hours, shorter weeks and, as the Central Bank points out in its recent 2008 Annual Report: 'many firms in the private sector have negotiated reduction in the wage rates.' The Central Bank goes on to argue "The decline in wage rates, while undoubtedly painful for those concerned...will mitigate the decline in unemployment in the short-term and contribute to an improvement in competitiveness." It would be hard to find a better statement of the mainstream orthodoxy.

But it is more complicated than that. Flexibility in *overall* labour costs can contribute to competitiveness. But it is difficult to sustain the argument that the removal of the *minimum* wage requirement can make any kind of a decisive contribution to national competitiveness. The 85,000 or so workers on, or about, the minimum wage, account for about 5% of total current orthodoxy employed. They are not, for the most part, working in high value-added activities central to a turn-around in the economy. So, at the level of the Individual, the Family, and the Firm, the issue of a minimum wage matters. But at the Macro level – i.e. turning the economy around-it is distracting attention from what really needs to be done.

There are really two issues underlying the debate on 'labour market flexibility', competitiveness and, in this context, the Minimum Wage. The first is whether, or not, it is right to stop people who are prepared to take less than the minimum wage of €8.65 per hour. There is an argument that individuals should have the freedom to work at whatever rate they choose. This is reinforced by, firstly, the fact that **all** work has an intrinsic value, over and above the actual level of remuneration. The significant increase in current numbers of individuals suffering psycho-social stress presenting at G.P.'s and Clinics would seem to confirm this and to reinforce the argument that individuals should have the freedom to work at whatever rate they choose.

A difficulty here, however, is the very real danger that some unscrupulous employers will-exploit the recession and the plight of individual's desperation for work. Trade Unions – and governments – are there to protect workers against such exploitation. The elimination of a statutory minimum wage would make the task of Trade Unions more difficult. A key point here is that the Minimum Wage is set at a low level: the CSO's Survey of Employment (2007) cites average hourly earnings of €18.07 for private sector workers and €21.07 for all workers.

The issue of incentives is central. Too high a rate will deter some employers from holding on to/employing workers, when they themselves are under pressure. Too low a rate will deter workers or encourage them to default into the social security system.

The problem here is reconciling an individual's right to work-with all that this implies-with the prevention of exploitation. At the heart of this problem is the lack of Trust in Ireland: we are no longer a 'High-Trust' society. This is a problem that merits debate.

The second issue is whether, in any event, removing the minimum wage would make a material difference to "mitigating the decline in unemployment in the short-term and contributing to an improvement in competitiveness". For individuals in the Minimum Wage zone, it is difficult to sustain the argument that a reduction would make a decisive contribution to national competitiveness. It would, however, affect incentives facing both firms and individual workers. It is, however, almost certainly the case that for individual firms the suffocating impact of 'red tape' has a greater deterrent impact than the minimum wage.

In fact, the division between those who argue that the removal of a minimum wage would be morally reprehensible and those who believe that individuals should be free to seek work at less than the minimum wage is a false dichotomy. This is where the *political* economy comes in. The Government's 'rule nothing out' approach distracts attention from the only sustainable way forward – one in which the issue of reducing the minimum wage as a potential important factor in national competitiveness fades into insignificance.

The only way out of the growth and competitiveness *cul de sac* into which the economy has been driven is a strategy for growing the economy. The Government doesn't have one. Firstly, it is losing – or has already lost – whatever leverage it had over 'covered institutions' putting national recovery ahead of restructuring their balance sheets. Secondly, its 'core' fiscal projections are the stuff of fantasy. Its commitment to the EU that the Government deficit will be reduced to 3 per cent of GDP is not tenable. Thirdly, the scope for implementing the 'Smart Economy' is stymied by a lack of scientific and technological competence within Government and – largely – within the banks. All of these are more important in terms of competitiveness and flexibility than reducing the Minimum Wage. Indeed, the whole rationale for developing Ireland's Knowledge-based 'Smart Economy' is at variance with seeking national competitive advantage from amending minimum wage legislation.

The Government needs a tenable strategy for growing the domestic economy while reducing the size of the State. By listening to the siren voices calling for a Lenten Fast for an already emaciated economy in the interests of 'fiscal sustainability', we have lost time, credibility, revenue and jobs. We have impressed no one- least of all the rating agencies.

We have got things the wrong way round – and this continues to be the problem. Restoring the Public Finances will require, first and foremost, maintaining employment, giving priority to entrepreneurship and maintaining domestic demand. The most striking feature of the IMF's summary data on Ireland is the precipitous decline in the real economy compared with the Government sector. Equally, while reducing the burden of the state is essential to reducing borrowing, the remit of 'An Bord Snip' should have been extended to cutting back 'rent-seeking' State interventionism that stultifies entrepreneurial risk-taking and the rebuilding of competitiveness in Ireland. It could still be done. A combination of the rigour of Colm McCarty, the ruthlessness of Michael O'Leary and the vision of Graham O'Donnell (the entrepreneur behind 'Spirit of Ireland' initiative – which really does have the capacity to transform Ireland's competitiveness) should take about three weeks to report on what needs to be done.

To the response 'That will mean more borrowing', the answer is "yes- and it will require even more (expensive) borrowing if there is not a shift towards upsizing domestic industry and downsizing Government. The most telling indication of just how far we have to go was the inclusion of an 'Enterprise Stabilization Fund' of €100 million – over two years and knee deep in caveats – in the last Budget – at a time when the Government was diverting €7 billion to banks.

This takes us back to the *Political* Economy of the Minimum Wage. Too much Politics, too much kite-flying – too little real economics. It things don't change – and soon – it will be time for the boys at the IMF in Washington DC to begin making travel arrangements before a once proud, now broken-backed economy triggers a contagion across the EU.

This Article was published in the Irish Examiner and The Irish Times, August 2009.

Time for 'The Common Good' to be Key Economic Reference Point

We are fast running out of time to get to grips with the economic crisis – can our current political system manage?

We entered the second half of 2009 as one of the most debilitated and vulnerable economies within the Organisation for Economic Co-operation and Development.

Nothing short of a political transformation is going to get Ireland out of the vicious circle in which we are now and which is drawing us into a vortex of political contagion.

Government expenditure for 2009 is estimated to come in at about €60 billion. Revenue is projected at about €34 billion. We have to borrow some €26 billion to keep the show on the road; and this adds to our stock of debt. It pushes our debt-gross domestic product (GDP) ratio northwards.

Now assume that existing trends will continue by, say, five years which is the normal term of office of a government. Assume Government expenditure rises by 5 per cent (compounded) over the next five years. That is conservative; it leaves out, for example, the escalating costs of social welfare payments and rising debt service commitments as well as "rolling recapitalisation" related costs. By year five, expenditure would amount to €77 billion.

Now let's examine revenue, which has collapsed over the last two years. Let's assume that it will grow by 2 per cent on average for the next five years. That's pretty generous for an economy dependent on international recovery and a domestic economy that is running on empty. This would result in revenue of about €38 billion after five years. Crucially, our stock of debt would still rise by €167 billion over this five-year period.

Let's be generous and assume that revenues will rise, not by 2 per cent but by 10 per cent per year over this period. This would still mean that our stock of outstanding debt would be about €120 billion higher than it is today. The interest payments on the increase of about 6 per cent would mean that we would have to find another €7 billion per year in servicing costs – just for the increase in debt.

Interest rates are not going to stay at their present historic lows – they will rise. Even with spare capacity in the major economies, there are latent inflationary pressures on the horizon. The European Central Bank, especially, and the US Federal Reserve, will respond by increasing interest rates over the next year. The resultant increase in rates for sovereign borrowers will be significant, particularly for those countries which have a credibility problem – including Ireland.

This simple model can be made as complicated as you like. The point is still clear. A defining political issue of the next five years will be how to address the correction of the public finances. The finances have been holed below the water line by a crisis in banking. The banking business model remains essentially unchanged. We need a new model of government if we are to preserve democracy.

This will require cuts in public expenditure, not the kind of counter-productive and socially insensitive cuts which we have had to date. Somebody is going to have to ask the elephant, very politely, to leave the room. For elephant, read size of public sector.

Equally, reversing the implosion in revenue will not come from the kind of levies, increases in excise on fuel and VAT that have debilitated the domestic economy. We need to grow our way out of this trap. This means listening and responding to real businesses: removing constraints on them and incentivising them to maintain, or even increase, employment. The scale of the task can be seen from the figures above. We need to more than double the size of the economy to make ends meet based on our current spending trajectory. That is a measure of what it will take to return to sustainability and to relieve pressure on political, let alone, economic, stability.

Misconceived fiscal policies, conformed to a failed and humbled economic orthodoxy, are part of the problem. The last three budgets have bled the economy of domestic demand at a time when international trade and foreign direct investment are contracting. Equally, the costs of recapitalising financial institutions, whose business model and corporate modus operandi precipitated the crisis in the first place, is now equivalent to half of the costs of funding the health system.

There is no longer an optimal or even reasonable set of options: there are only least bad options. We are running out of time – and balance-sheet – to make these options.

A failure to support what is intrinsically an innovative economy, and to demonstrate a values-based politics, raises the spectre of sovereign default. It's not pleasant to name, but it's priced into the financial markets' forward-looking evaluation of Ireland. This could incubate a political contagion – the counterpart of the virus-like financial contagion which has infected the global financial system – across the wider EU. If our political parties and institutions do not respond with courage, then responsibility will pass out of our hands – to external agencies and to market forces.

Government is too big. In the 10 years up to 2008, the total population grew by a very robust 10 per cent. Total employment in the public sector (including health but excluding commercial semi-state bodies) rose by almost 30 per cent, from 234,000 to 332,000. This extraordinary growth in the size of the public sector, representing as it does a fixed overhead that has to be funded by business, has left the economy vulnerable to the full force of the economic crisis.

Political parties have allowed themselves to be defined primarily in terms of opposition to the status quo. Opposition is, of course, part of what an alternative administration is about. But it is only a part. It has to go much deeper if "change", "fresh starts" and "new beginnings" are to have new meaning. It must mean something new.

All of this is exacerbated by the paradox of coalition government. The electorate votes only to find, when the dust has settled, a coalition government cobbled together is in charge. This means that an administration then governs the country without having been endorsed by the electorate. The people – at this critical time – have no way of knowing, having cast their votes, the values of those who will subsequently be appointed to lead the country.

It is, of course, the case that any administration confronted by a crisis must take unpalatable decisions. What is different this time is the sheer scale of these decisions which could have a make-or-break impact on the Irish economy.

The protection of our economic autonomy – and democracy – requires rethinking such fundamental concepts as legitimacy, competence and leadership. Political leadership that requires the humility to appoint some sorely needed expertise from outside to serve in a decision-making capacity.

It is not just a matter of the deficiencies in the system. It is the failure to contemplate new and awful questions:

- What is the political counterpart to the global financial crisis?

- Do the present political systems have immunity from the meltdown that has happened in finance and economies?

- How do our political institutions deal with the social consequences of the crisis and how can we prevent a political contagion that could subvert political stability when the jobless exceed more than half a million people?

We need to move away, while there is still the time, and the capacity embedded in our entrepreneurs, technologists and scientists, to re-imagine the Irish economy. This will require a reference point outside of power and shareholder value. That reference point is The Common Good.

It is difficult to step back from power. It is equally difficult to step back from seizing the long-awaited moment of power, certain that we have the right solutions. Ireland is now in a national emergency.

This Article appeared in the Irish Times, June 2009.

Resolving the Economic Crisis in Ireland: The Need for A New Political Governance

The Global Economic Crisis, as it is manifest in the wasteland of what was once the 'Celtic Tiger', is now entering a final and arguably devastating phase. Our political institutions and systems of governance are now coming under inexorable pressure in the face of inadequate policy responses to the rise in unemployment, the decimation of the domestic economy, and a palpable feeling of 'quiet desperation' among individuals and families and businesses.

The most recent IMF assessment of the Global Economy – and its evaluation of Ireland's financial sector – makes sombre but not unexpected reading. The most recent CSO data for the final quarter of 2008 show a sharp decline in investment. Meanwhile, the live register is now escalating and is set to reach new levels before the end of this year.

This would strain the most robust and inclusive political system. In the case of Ireland, which faces both local elections and a contentious Referendum, there is every possibility that what has happened will test the limits of tolerance of a population that is not without experience of the pains of unemployment and emigration. We are looking at a fracturing and realignment of political institutions which do not speak to the sensibilities of a young generation that they have beggared, nor to the needs of those who felt themselves entitled to something better having contributed much of their lives to the development of the Irish economy.

The roots of this latent political crisis are – like those of the global financial crisis – starkly ethical in nature. We have a political system largely rooted in obsolete divisions and, in the view of many, emasculated of the values which once animated them. This is not to say that there are not highly committed professional and ethical politicians; there are, and many will be, not without some courage, knocking on doors. The tragedy is that, they are a 'dead man walking'. The defining characteristics of the system as a whole, is a culture of power instead of service to the Person. Our essentially adversarial political institutions have demonstrated little relevance to the imperative to restoring hope, and a sense of direction, at a time of unprecedented stress in modern Irish history.

It cannot be right that, for our legislature and political systems, it continues to be 'business as usual' while, in virtually other every domain of our national life, the most painful adjustments are being made without consolation or consensus.

We have screwed-up – that's the truth of it. We cannot build a 'new capitalism' on 'old politics'. Rebuilding Trust in our institutions and in our political system – as much in the financial sector – requires a values-based leadership. The time for political rhetoric and the old fashioned Ard Fheis-based nonsense is long past.

Political Institutions and the system of governance are semi-detached from the pulse-beat of individuals who've lost their jobs, businesses tethering on the brink of failure, and families that are literally crushed by the circumstances in which they have suddenly found themselves.

They are still dominated by an 'apprenticeship system', which favours those who have served their time over those who can contribute most to addressing the problems now confronting the country. The system of Ministerial appointments makes little or no sense. All too frequently, it is geographically-based. Even more fundamentally, they commonly lack the relevant expertise to direct, with a sure and experienced hand, policy in the Departments to which they are appointed. There is no formal training required from Ministers from their first day in Office. This simply makes no sense. It would not happen for a moment in any other profession or vocation.

Our political landscape is littered by 'silos', each driven by their own agenda and political dynamic. There is the ambiguity of the relationship between, on the one hand, the legislature, and, on the other hand, the executive. This ambiguity leaves itself open to the 'capture' of policy; it leaves itself open to the de facto delegation of key areas of responsibility to quangos of different kinds. Conversely, it can, and does, inhibit those within the public sector who have a real capacity to contribute, from putting their head above the parapet. The old political canard of the first priority on getting power being to retain it, corrodes and demeans the very nature of what politics should be about.

The contradictions, ambiguities and inefficiencies in all of this, are all too evident in the manner in which we have responded to the economic crisis that continues to gather momentum across the entire economic landscape. The resources generated during the years of the (healthy) Celtic Tiger were, in substantial part, dissipated in a process of political largess. The legacy of the last 10 or 15 years can be stylised as being represented by interminable Tribunals, Legislation, much of which has served only to increase the burden on basic freedoms as well as on basic businesses, and Regulation, which has turned to dust under the stress of recent events.

These deficiencies raise the question, for example, of why it is only in an unprecedented deflationary period, we have appointed 'An Bord Snip' to seek out inefficiencies in public expenditure. It is difficult to explain this either through a lack of political leadership and foresight. Equally, we have a Commission of Taxation – one that is expert and one that will produce an excellent report – side-by-side with ad hoc responses to a crisis that continues to gather momentum. The anomalies and contradictions that riddle our taxation system have been evident for well over a decade. Neither markets, nor the lives of people, can await the production of reports. We have had too many Reports. Paradoxically, government will commission external agencies to prepare detailed reports when all the knowledge necessary is already within their own Departments. There is an acute lack of confidence in our own expertise and in our own resources.

The three 'Budgets' that have followed in rapid succession as government failed to keep up with events, are a mess of additional levees and ad hoc taxes which result in a totally fragmented funding system. All of the time, the landmine of unfunded pension liabilities remains deep in the long grass and a clear a present threat not only to those who are presently employed, but even to those who have recently, or will in the near future, lose their jobs. It makes no sense to prioritise the allocation of resources, written as IOUs on our future, to financial institutions over businesses whose survival is essential not alone to individual families, but to the wider economy – and by extension to the banking system. We have our priorities all wrong. We are spending undreamt of sums of money – which we do not have – to support utilities which are skewed in favour of Shareholders (and that is the supreme irony, since their interests have been entirely subverted by a malign business model) – while we continue to have a fragmented, unfair and multi-tiered healthcare system. That too does not make sense.

The recent Budget was seriously misconceived. As argued in these pages, what was needed was a budget written in our factories and on our farms; in our hospitals and in our homes. What we got was a malign orthodoxy that impressed no one – least of all overseas investors – but will do great harm. The test of a good Budget, particularly in this critical time, is whether or not the economic and fiscal dynamic is likely to sustain jobs, incomes and public services over the medium-term; whether it will restore confidence and a sense of Trust and, thirdly, whether it promotes those institutions that underpin social solidarity in the face of unprecedented social strain. The Budget fails these tests. The window of opportunity has shut and we face a period of grave economic, social and political strain and instability.

It failed to acknowledge the adjustments that were already underway within Households which are deleveraging their indebtedness and Domestic Businesses which are clinging to viability in an ever tightening credit crisis. Equally, it is clear that the domestic banking system is under-capitalised, as well as being in need of consolidation.

All of this is reflected in the Credit Default spreads, both in relation to the banks, and even more so in relation to sovereign debt. Ireland's reputation and standing is being interrogated not alone by markets, but by informed and dispassionate critics.

We will not get through this crisis if our political institutions and system of governance do not change radically. Whether, or not, the existing order is capable of such a dispassionate process of self-reflection, is best left to the people of Ireland. But we should be clear that, economic stabilisation, much less recovery, will be stymied by alienation from our political system, by fragmentation of political support, and by the very real prospect of a rise in disenchantment and extremism among the tens of thousands who have joined the dole queue. It is an incredible affront to the dignity of the Person that we should be so desensitised by what has happened so far. But history teaches us that political change and the growth in extremism are marked by fracture and discontinuity. The fire suddenly breaks out.

We need a realignment of politics in Ireland – we need democratic choices that mean something to contemporary society. We need a sense of right and wrong. We need a whole new political ethic premised on values-based leadership. We need to engage individuals who have little interest in power as such, but who have a commitment as well as a widely acknowledged expertise, that is capable of restoring trust, confidence and a sense of direction.

This Article appeared in the Irish Times, May 2009.

Bid to Impress Markets Will Not Make for Good Budget

The budget provides a window of opportunity that will have closed by tomorrow evening.

Confidence has been drained by the failure of three successive budgets to keep pace with the increase in the Live Register and with the burgeoning Government deficit.

The recent, albeit marginal, downgrading of Ireland's sovereign debt rating by Standard & Poor's has further dented confidence. The biggest drain, however, is the new reality among domestic companies, particularly small to medium-sized firms, that in the absence of decisive action by the Government they too will disappear. When such firms fail, they are gone. It is immeasurably more difficult to bring new start-ups to the same stage.

There is an obvious temptation on the part of the Government to frame a budget intended to impress or appease the financial markets. This would be misconceived.

Further expenditure cuts and tax increases will make little difference to the overall size of the borrowing requirement. But they will drive the economy – whose trading partners are also mired in economic crises – deeper into recession, eroding confidence and undermining the capacity of a stressed and debilitated business sector to stabilise, let alone recover. Ireland needs a budget that is written, not in the Department of Finance, but in factories and on farms, in small businesses clinging to viability, and in family homes and hospitals.

Financial markets, whatever about their immediate reaction, will be more impressed by a country that holds its nerve and demonstrates a capacity to transform its mindset as well as its financial and regulatory system than one which rolls over.

There is an adjustment process well under way in the corporate and the household sectors which is not yet reflected in the Central Statistics Office (CSO) and finance data. Trade unions have a responsibility to maintain social solidarity. Many companies are talking to staff about how to mitigate the effects of an escalating recession on jobs.

Some companies will exploit this. Even more importantly, however, there is a new flexibility that can only be understood by individuals who have seen their friends and colleagues let go. There is a deep tide of empathy running throughout the country.

This adjustment is being stymied by the effects of a triple squeeze on Irish companies.

Firstly, there is a steep decline in demand, reinforced by uncertainty. Secondly, there is a ferocious pressure on cash flow as credit facilities tighten and companies are forced to act as creditors to one another. This pressure is breaking companies. There is a real risk of a vicious circle of cash-starved companies failing, leading to more bad loans and further credit tightening.

This much is clear. Successive recapitalisations of credit institutions which are at the epicentre of Ireland's economic crisis are neither feasible nor defensible. The provision of support to businesses should take priority over the allocation of costly and scarce resources to credit institutions that have already benefited from the deposit protection initiative and have had a capital transfusion of €7 billion into their balance sheet. Bringing companies back from the brink helps to strengthen banks balance sheets by reducing the probability of default.

Thirdly, by far the most important contribution that the budget can make to the survival of Irish companies and incomes is to reduce the administrative burden that is suffocating businesses.

It would cost nothing. Companies can no longer afford the kind of meaningless red tape that made no sense even in better times than now. This administrative "rent-seeking" is being driven by a mindset that is semi-detached from the lived experience of companies.

The banking system needs to be fundamentally changed. This could involve anything along a spectrum from an exchequer-capitalised "narrow bank" with a focus, not on shareholders (whose interests have been devastated by a malign corporate mindset that remains unchanged), but rather on the interests of depositors and businesses, employees and the public interest. Nationalisation may become inevitable.

In any event, the present structure needs to be changed to reflect the fact that systemically important banks are a utility whose stability is underwritten by the wider community whom they serve. The Government's proposed "toxic" vehicle intended to strip out selected bad loans, underpinned by some form of insurance, is a necessary part of restructuring of balance sheets.

The household sector, too, is undergoing an adjustment process. The budget can either go with the grain of this process, or strain it to breaking point. A key driver of the crises is the secular rise in household indebtedness as a percentage of disposable income. This is now being reversed, both because of rising unemployment and the reality check brought about by the scale and suddenness of the recession.

John Kenneth Galbraith, in his iconic The Affluent Society, explored it best. He highlighted the distinction between "Needs" and "Wants"; how wants are driven by advertising and futile efforts to keep up with the Joneses; all of which is fuelled by indebtedness – until the whole process implodes. His analysis resonates powerfully with what we are experiencing.

In these circumstances, excessive cuts in productive ("Needs") spending and increases in taxes are counterproductive. The adjustment is already under way. It makes no sense to, in effect, take money from businesses and households, which have a higher propensity to spend and invest than do banks intent on rebuilding their balance sheets. Equally, further ad hoc cuts in service provision in healthcare and in education are indefensible, both in terms of economics and The Common Good. The effects of the health cuts of the early 1990s have never been exorcised.

The "old politics" which still dominate the political landscape – emasculated of their original values – make no sense to a new generation. The legislature cannot legitimately, and without consultation, push through unprecedented severe cuts without re-examining itself and how far it too has failed the country. There is much about the public sector and political institutions that makes no sense.

Tomorrow's budget provides a window of opportunity that will have closed by tomorrow evening. The markets are more likely to give albeit grudging respect to a country whose fiscal policy facilitates on an adjustment process already under way – one reinforced by social and political transformation, including financial restructuring – than one which is transfixed in the headlights of the consequences of its past excesses.

This Article appeared in the Irish Times, April 2009.

Regulation a Weak Sibling of Ethics and Sin

Crimes against the moral order have fuelled the financial crisis. A philosopher talking in Dublin tomorrow will cast light on our lurking belief that regulation can prevent such crimes.

This weekend, one of the great moral philosophers of this century, Alasdair MacIntyre, visits Ireland to be feted by UCD's school of philosophy on the occasion of his 80th birthday. His visit – and his public lecture tomorrow evening – provides a catalyst for a debate that could shape Ireland's response to the economic crisis.

Unless – and until – the unfolding global crisis is seen as primarily the result of a seismic failure in the ethical order, it will neither be firewalled nor reversed. The scale of interventions by developed countries – aimed at stabilising banking institutions and markets, restoring confidence and trust and mitigating the economic consequences – are without precedent in peacetime.

They are not working. Contingent liabilities of enormous proportions now stretch into the future in the United States, the European Union and Ireland. At some stage this will, in itself, become a source of instability as the markets stall in the face of the cold reality that the "lender/capital-provider" of last resort is running out of balance-sheet and credibility.

Parallel to this process, it is now evident that what appeared initially to be an esoteric financial crisis has, in less than two years, metastasised into worldwide economic reversal that could neither be predicted nor modelled by the institutions it has devastated.

There are financial, economic and political factors that have exacerbated the crisis, giving it a fresh momentum. Ireland, like other countries, has its own self-inflicted wounds. But these are secondary to a deeper dynamic. This is about making wrong choices, misusing human freedom and a denial of the demands of a moral order that "modernity" had presumed to cast off. History – with the rise and fall of civilisations – provides support for this argument. One such example is Marxism.

Bernard Lonergan once observed that "a civilisation in decline digs its own grave with relentless consistency. It cannot be argued out of its destructive way."

The West has subverted the very markets which, as a key utility, support the generation of wealth and its distribution, as well as international trade and welfare. It has become desensitised to any objective understanding of morality.

The sense of "right" and "wrong" at the heart of ethics, resonates the public's perception of an intrinsic "unfairness" with various aspects of the economic crisis and its consequences.

Regulation, to take one example, is a necessary but not sufficient condition, for a restoration of financial stability.

Individuals, no less than corporations or countries, cannot be regulated to do the "right" or "moral" thing. Ethics is, by its nature "obedience to the unenforceable" and the ultimate guarantor of trust. This fact is at the heart of the seeming dichotomy. "It may be legal, but surely it can't be right..."

We are talking about "sin" here. A type of behaviour or mindset may not be a crime; it may not be prohibited by rules or regulation, but instinctively we recognise it for what it is – an offence against the moral order.

Ireland is inextricably bound-up within a moral catharsis just as real as that which brought about the fall of Marxism, and of which the global financial crisis is the most immediate manifestation.

This is why Alasdair MacIntyre's critique of moral philosophy is of such importance. MacIntyre's stature and the authority of his critique make this a very public and prophetic event

This Article appeared in The Irish Times, March 2009.

The Compendium on Social Teaching, The Family, Markets and Work

1.1 Introduction

The Compendium is a landmark contribution to our understanding of the root causes of global imbalances in wealth and political governance as well as exploitation-driven environmental degradation. It sets-out the consequences of these realities, in particular for the individual Person and for the Family. These are, the Compendium argues, the cornerstones of society which should, therefore, be free from subjugation in any form, by State and/or Corporate sectors. More positively, the Compendium sets out a Values and Principles-based framework, within which <u>sustainable</u> global development can be achieved.

The Compendium is, at one level, a rigorous synthesis of the Social teaching of the Catholic Church. These teachings embrace the whole social, economic and scientific order. The Compendium draws on the great Papal Encyclicals, notably in the period since Leo XIII's Reverum Novarum. It is also informed by a wide range of addresses, by successive Popes, to specialised audiences. The unique philosophical insight of Pope John Paul II – focused on the innate dignity of the Human Person – permeates the whole analysis. The roots of the synthesis, however, go deeper. They encompass, and build on, the whole Judaeo-Christian tradition.

At another level, the Compendium is timely, to the point of being prophetic. It addresses the Nihilism which is at the heart of much of western mainstream thinking on the Person, especially within the context of work, and which has infected market-based economic and political systems. Most importantly of all, the Compendium provides an alternative Values-based vision of the future of the new *Globalised* economic and environmental paradigm.

It sets-out the case that a sustainable politico-economic system – or, at the micro–level, 'Business Model' – can only be built on a set of 'Universal' values. At the heart of this perspective is the transcendent value of the individual Human Person, made in the image of, and redeemed by, God.

This reality, by definition, requires a decision-making process, based on Values, which are aligned to the dignity of the Person. These Values apply equally to the employee and the employer – to the small company and to the internationally mobile multinational company operating in vulnerable, indebted developing countries.

The Compendium is not prescriptive in regard to specific 'Business Models' or organisational systems. But is emphatic that any such models, or systems must, in their mind-set and operation, be values-based, in their regard to the Human Person.

1.2

This contribution is focused on the narrower issue of the Compendiums analysis of Markets and Morality. The connection between the two is crucial to its wider analysis. This is for two reasons. The first is this. The fall of Soviet Communism, with its Statist economy, in the late 1980s, and the more recent development of Communist China's *economy*, have contributed to the pre-eminence of the Western free-markets-based paradigm. There is compelling evidence that this system is in crises. The symptoms are many. They range from the Nihilism of Western consumerism through to a total asymmetry in political power, uninformed by any understanding of substantive principles such as 'Common Good' or 'Social Solidarity'.

The system is in crisis precisely because it has become detached from any *lived* experience of Morality and Order. It is important to be clear about what is meant by 'Order'. The final end of the Person is to be open to the love of God. It follows that the different domains within which they work out and affirm this end on earth must be so *ordered* as to facilitate this end. This means, in practice, respect within the workplace. It means corporate leadership, characterised by Humility. It means that the wealth produced within economics is intended not just to meet the needs of the privileged few but, rather, that there is a 'universal' destination of wealth, which takes precedence. This must be reflected in the ethos of the company as well as in national and International laws and governance.

The near global financial crises of the late 1980s – notably the Asian Banking contagion and the near-implosion of the Long Term Capital Management (LTCM) – provided a glimpse of this. The corporate failures of the mid 1990s to the early 2000s, disclosed notably in the US but not restricted to there, a *moral* malaise that generated enormous human, as well as economic costs.

The ascendency of the Short-term Shareholder Value Maximization 'Business Model' infected the market-based economy and "crowded-out" any acknowledgement of the dignity of the Person. Market information was distorted, and corporate balance-sheets manipulated, in order to inflate earnings and, therefore, the Market-based value of the Company. It would be more accurate to say that the concept of 'Person' simply did not exist within this construct. Individuals were there as 'Resources'; they were commodities to be used, exploited, coerced, bullied – and disposed of – without any regard to their innate dignity and their final end. This was serious disorder.

Within Western mainstream Markets, formerly "High-Trust market institutions were drawn into an ethical 'Black Hole'. These ranged from Banks through Institutional Investors – as well as Accountancy firms and Auditors who had quasi-guardianship of the markets-based model and on whose integrity the whole Corporate-Markets axis rested. Not all, by many means – moreover and the overwhelming majority of individuals working in these institutions were undoubtedly highly moral.[41] But enough to subvert morality, order, and the value of the Person.

The consequences of this disorder, stemming from the lack of any Values or Principles based system of governance or management were visited on employees of wealth-fixated Corporates, on small investors misled by false information, on Pensioners and most evidently on senior Management of these companies, seduced by the lie on which the model was based.

Major Companies were destroyed, tens of thousands of jobs lost, fines of hundreds of millions of dollars were imposed by the US regulatory authorities on swathes of institutions, Executives in manacles, families shredded – this was all a part of the Collateral damage of the absence of Morality within a Business Model that subverted the role of Markets. Against this backdrop, the case for a Values-based system, focused on the dignity of the Person and the unique role of the Family, looks less like an aspiration and more like an imperative for Markets to be able to function at all, let alone fulfil their role within an economic context.

The dominant mind-set –"Greed is good"[42]– had this effect: the values by which individual Persons attempt to order their lives behind their hall doors were increasingly (and violently) put at odds with the 'values' that drove corporate activity behind their office door.

The emptiness, the lie, should have been evident from the coffee time chatter and clichés: "Move up or Move out", "If you can't turn up on Saturday, don't bother coming in on Sunday", "Least Value Employee (LVE)". It was, of course, nonsense, but it shaped the corporate environment. It devalued and 'commoditised' the Person and was intensely destructive of relationships – especially of the Family – within the wider society underpinned by the economy.

It was doomed commercially – *precisely* because it was unethical and immoral. Being unethical, it systematically undermined the operation of the market-based economic system; – not least, incidentally, in the regulatory overkill (including the Sarbannes Oxley Act in the US) that ensued.

Trust is what individuals (and, it is no coincidence, banking institutions) seek out most in any relationship. Trust is imperative for the functioning of Markets. Trust was the first casualty of the mainstream adoption of a "Business Models" that was obsessed, above all else, with maximizing wealth for privileged elites within the Corporate Sector.

This takes us back to the paradox as noted above; on the one hand, the near contemporaneous triumph of Western Market-based economic systems and, on the other hand, the deep crises in this same system. It is within this space that the Compendium makes its prophetic case for change.

---

[41] This point is well made by Liam O'Reilly (then) Chief Executive of the Financial Regulator (Ireland) in his first Report on the AIB Investigation (Irish Financial Services Regulatory Authority [IFSRA],) Dublin, 2004
[42] This maxim, from the film 'Wall Street', became a perfect aphorism for a generation – as well as providing an insight into the basic reason for its implosion

In the wake of the corporate crises Governments have, of course, legislated for reforms to financial regulation, strengthened accounting and auditing standards as well as implementing changes in Corporate Governance. They have, incidentally, done so without seeing the beam in their own eye.

Reforms are a necessary, but not a sufficient, response to the emergence of a systemic crises, slowly gathering momentum across three fronts; Global poverty, in particular the Aids pandemic; Corporate Nihilism in the wealth-fixated market-based western "Democracies", and an unprecedented threat to the global Environment, which is largely induced by the excesses of these latter countries.

In terms of responding to these threats, the Compendium upholds the dignity of the Person and, also, of the Family as the corner stone of society. Any real understanding of the <u>Nature</u> of these threats – in other words, just what is being threatened, starts from here. So, too, does a response to these same threats. The Compendium deals in 'Universals'– not platitudes, it must be said; but realities that can be <u>instinctively</u> understood and acted upon as being 'good' and 'right', by all persons open to Truth. It steadfastly avoids criticism of individual countries and/or regimes. Instead, it sets out the fundamental Values and Principles by which such countries – and we, as individuals – stand condemned, and challenged.

1.3 A perspective on markets

Economic agents – from the small farmer to the multinational corporate – operate within an extraordinary range of economic systems, social constraints (e.g. Social Partnership) and 'Business Models'. The products and services generated by economic agents are, for the most part, traded through markets. These 'markets' range from the informal stalls on which farmers in less developed countries sell vegetables or crafts, through to high octane I.T.-based, 24/7 global financial markets.

Organized Markets are the central nervous systems of National economies, as well of the increasingly open and interdependent Global economy. They generate significant benefits or, more formally, 'welfare gains' to the individual, the family and the wider community which is underpinned by economies functioning through Markets of different kinds.

These benefits arise primarily because Markets reduce the costs of acquiring the *information* necessary to allow producers (savers) and purchasers (investors) to meet on common ground. Note the absolutely central role of information, and, by extension, of the <u>integrity</u> and timeliness of such information. This information allows markets to generate (relative) prices based on the demand for, and the supply of, assets. Such assets range from goods and services which are directly consumed at the point of production, through to *tradable* services, and on to highly complex financial assets, which have less to do with production and are more related to managing/transferring risk, speculation and arbitrage.

In other words, information is what markets are based on. Equally, efficient markets generate information that would be impossible or highly costly, to produce. Importantly, just as the existence of markets are predicated on certain human freedoms, the operation of markets requires honesty, transparency and "fair dealing", in order to encourage individuals to participate in such markets.

The greater the degree of participation in such markets, the deeper, more liquid and, therefore, efficient are markets. Conversely, an erosion of Trust arising from a lack of honesty, integrity or transparency will fracture markets, leading to the possibility of default and the impossibility – except at a wholly disproportionate cost – of enforcing contracts.

Markets incentivise the production of goods and services. More specifically, they incentivise the production of a surplus, for exchange trade. This enhances the welfare of the individual and of the wider community of which they are a part – most immediately, the Family. This surplus can also, as noted, take the form of 'contracts', based on specific underlying asset.

These contracts called for Derivatives, a feature of modern, highly monetised, economies. The contract is, effectively, separated from the underlying asset. While risk is directly or indirectly, embedded in all forms of exchange, derivatives as the largest category of contacts in financial Markets are now based on the *de facto* 'Commoditization' of Risk, only tenuously connected to a underlying asset e.g. oil or other commodities set of assets. The value of trade in such 'Derivative' instruments/contracts now entirely dominate the value of 'real' transactions.

The point is this. Derivatives have been regarded by the most eminent authorities (such as, Alan Greenspan, former chairman of the US Federal Reserve) as being essentially positive. Equally, they have been criticised by market authorities (such as Warren Buffet, the greatest financial entrepreneur and fund Manager of all time) as "financial weapons of destruction". This is the point to which markets have evolved and the test of the need for public intervention and regulation is the impact of a global financial crash on people, families and communities not involved in, but highly vulnerable to, speculation in those esoteric markets.

Markets have provided the essential dynamic behind the growth of international Trade, the rise of political systems and the spread of ideologies. The advent of the Internet has given almost unimaginable leverage to markets, broadly defined.

Morality – 'right thinking' based on fundamental ethical values – is a necessary condition for the existence, and the efficient operation, of markets. Markets are predicated on certain individual freedoms which are based on morality. These include the freedom to work, and to produce, exchange and trade the 'surplus' over and above that required for subsistence. Countries that deny such freedoms lack moral, and therefore political, legitimacy. The denial of such freedoms inhibits economic specialisation and the conditions necessary for international trade and the market systems to operate effectively. There are important human needs which simply cannot be 'commoditized' and delivered through the market.

It is important to highlight the point – as indeed the Compendium does – that the most obvious example is the provision of medical or educational assistance to the poor, dispossessed and marginalised.

Subject to this caveat, markets are, nonetheless, central to the economies which underpin human societies. They embody networking, Communication. They generate relative values/prices, which underpin the whole operation of exchange and trade. They empower the individual/family are rooted. Where they are allowed to operate, the positive effects diffuse through the wider communities within which they operate. They create and sustain employment and drive innovation. Markets tell the 'Truth', based on available information. They can confound, and bring down, Governments.

This takes us back to the relationship between Markets and Morality. A 'free act' can be good or bad. 'Bad' means subversive of Truth and, therefore, destructive of Relationships. Sin, in fact. The *capacity* to sin is a uniquely human attribute and a measure of the Church's (and God's) respect for the freedom of the individual Person. To put this another way, it is not possible to speak of Love (which is at the heart of the Compendium's analysis, as in Fig 1, if the Person is not free to reject love. And the rejection of love is driven by Greed and, ultimately, Pride. Case Study after Case Study highlights these all too human deficiencies and their destructive impact on institutions, which go to make up a 'Market'.

The effective operation of Markets – their capacity for generating welfare gains – requires above all, Trust. Whatever the extent of regulation, markets will always be vulnerable to manipulation for personal or corporate gain by individuals, corporate, cartels and Government. Where this happens, first and second order consequences will be catastrophic. The damage in human terms to the Person, and to the economic system in which they function, is incalculable. In the absence of Moral Order, markets stall, fracture and even 'meltdown'– until Trust is restored.

Markets are, therefore, institutions of the highest social importance. It is no coincidence that they operate most effectively in real democracies (which can ensure basic freedoms) and within a system of governance and regulation that is 'High Trust' in nature and characterised by honesty and integrity. They can, for these very same reasons, be subverted.

This reality highlights two key points made in the Compendium. The first is what it calls "the concrete risk of an idolatry of the market". Markets are a means to a greater end. The market "cannot find in itself the Principles of its own legitimization". This, the Compendium points out, "belongs to the consciences of individuals and to the Role of the State". The consequences of a lack of morality in relation to the first point is very clear from a critique of corporate debacles in recent years which aimed at manipulating the market.

In relation to the second point, the role of the State, the key point is that, notwithstanding the State's central economic and societal role, there are limits to the scope of markets. At the limit, it is the role of the State to decide on an appropriate framework for the oversight and regulation of markets. This does not dilute the responsibility of institutions or individuals for ensuring the integrity of market transactions.

Section 2

2.1

It is important to understand the "scaffolding" on which the Compendium rests. This, in turn, demonstrates both its rigor and the manner in which it integrates a *Person*-centred vision of the economy, operating within free competitive Markets, with an *ethically*-based system of global economic and political Governance.

Figure 1 provides a schematic "Deconstruction" of the Compendium. It attempts to distil the key elements of the critique of the Compendium, the Values on which it rests and the Normative Principles which it generates. These apply across all peoples and cultures because they are aligned to the Natural Law. They resonate with the prescriptive teachings, and the insights, of the Torah and Talmud, the Old and especially, New Testament and the Qur'an; the emphasis may differ, but at the heart of each is the transcendent dignity of the Person and the application of the "Golden Rule", across all domains of human existence, including economics.

These are a number of points of particular relevance. The first is this. It immediately becomes apparent that the analysis of the Compendium is based on Values. We are into the realm of the Intellect and Free will of the individual.

In effect, these Values (Fig 1) are, in terms of their applicability, 'Universals'. All Persons – worker, entrepreneur, policy maker – have an *instinctive* understanding of such values "hard wired" into their understanding. This understanding can – and has been – subjugated by ideology; as well as by wealth and 'the idolatry of markets', as if there were not higher Values to which both the functioning and outputs of markets are subject.

The Compendium identifies, and validates, these Values as the indispensable basis of any sustainable market-based system of economics and politics. 'Markets' are, in themselves 'neutral' with respect to the concept of morality. But – and this is the point – they can only function effectively within a framework based on moral values. This argument admits of no exceptions.

These Values, as set out in the Compendium, are Truth, Freedom and Justice. The Compendium develops the scope of each of these Values. It is **insistent** on the relevance of Love, as the origin of these Values. It asserts:

"Love must be reconsidered within its authentic value as the highest and universal criteria of the whole of Social ethics."

Source: Compendium (underlining added)

This applies to the manner in which a company is managed in all its aspects. It applies to the strategy of multinational Corporates. And it applies to applications of law, regulation and 'Best Practise' by Governments in International Trade, which is mediated through markets.

A second point in this "Deconstruction" in Fig 1 follows on from the first. Values generate Principles, by which human actions, behaviour and – in "Business Speak", 'Strategy' – are directed towards the "highest and universal criteria". These Principles are 'The Common Good', Subsidiary and Social Solidarity.

The Compendium develops the argument at length. It is, however, worth stressing the point that the authority of the Compendiums argument is based upon the Life of Jesus Christ, as set out in the New Testament and, equally, in the teaching of the Church, which is His Mystical Body. This has never been more effectively stated than by St. Paul, when writing to his fellow Christians in Corinth

"Remember how generous the Lord Jesus was: he was rich, but he became poor for your sake, to make you rich out of his poverty. This does not mean that to give relief to others you ought to make things difficult for yourselves: it is a question of balancing what happens to be your surplus now against their present need, and one day they may have something to spare that will supply their own need. That is how we strike a balance: as scripture says: The man who gathered much had none too much, the man who gathered little did not go short."[43]

The 'Person' in a market-based system

The innate dignity of the individual Person is acknowledged, particularly by the great Theistic religions of Judaism, Islam and Christianity.[44] In each of these, the essential morality of transactions and entered into by individuals are explicitly acknowledged. It is Persons who enter into these transactions – and individual Persons who are impacted by them. They are, therefore, subject to Moral norms. The Torah, for example, states that when a Jew meets with God in judgement, the first question that they will be asked is whether, or not, they were honest in their business dealings. Integrity in business relationships, based on *intention* as well as word, is an integral element of both the Jewish and Islamic faiths.

Christianity is predicated on the transcendent Nature of the Person and on Relationships. This is true at two levels. Firstly, the nature of God as a Trinity of *Persons* in an infinite, eternal, procession-based *Relationship* of Love. Secondly, the Incarnation of the Second Person of the Most Holy Trinity, taking on a fully human Nature; being born in historical time of the

---

[43] Corinthians 8:7.9. 13-15

[44] It is upheld by other religions and by such great Pagan writers as Marcus Aurelius (see: 'Meditations'). It is, on the other hand, ultimately rejected by Totalitarianism, in all its forms.

Virgin Mary, interacting with other, with a world of Work, Emigration, Trade-based markets and Finance.

The Incarnation reconciled the Person with his Creator, in whose image he is created. By so doing, the Individual is restored to Relationship based on the right use of free-will – as sons and daughters of God, in Jesus.

In the Providence of God, the Incarnation was accomplished through the voluntary suffering and death ("like man, in all things, save sin") and Resurrection of Jesus. This is the ultimate expression of God's Love for the human Person and source of the Gospel imperative addressed to all Persons, in all circumstances: "Love one another, as I have loved you". This injunction encompasses all dimensions of the Person.

The Person lives, and works out their contingent (that is, driven by Intellect, Free Will and responsiveness to Grace) Relationship with God within the world of work. In this context, the centrality of the Person is always paramount.

The outcomes of work are, as noted earlier, mediated through mechanisms of exchange, including highly developed global markets in Finance and commodities. The Incarnation means that this process is touched by – and directed towards – the Divine. This is the basis of the compelling logic of the Compendium's analysis, with its interface of Values and Principles; of Love and the Human Person.

An economic system – a "Business Model" – that subjugates the Person may take the form of Totalitarianism in some form or other. Or it can be driven by substituting the *outcomes* of work – wealth creation/economic surplus – for its final *end*. This is the 'idolatry of the markets'.

Wealth, as an end in itself – or, as is frequently observable in the corporate sector, a surrogate for Power over other Persons – is wholly at variance with the 'universal criteria' of Love. This, in fact, is frequently found to be the main cause of the implosion of a major corporate, since power is the means by which Internal Controls are undermined directed towards maintaining the integrity of business process.

The centre of gravity of the 'New Economy' is Knowledge. At the heart of the global productive process is Intellectual Capital. Mans' intellectual capacity is, largely, what animates his essentially spiritual Nature. Wealth, *in isolation from Principles which direct its use and distribution,* is inevitably destructive of the human Person, whose creative genius is actually the essential source of wealth creation.

It is a fundamental error not to acknowledge that *Relationship* which shapes a Person's final destination. It should in fact permeate the environment, including work, within which this destiny is worked out.

This reality has to be relearned and acknowledged. Even in the post-Enron reform environment – with its unquestionably positive emphasis on 'Business Ethics' and 'Corporate Social Responsibility' – mainstream "Corporate speak" and "Policy speak" remain desensitised to the uniqueness of the Human Person. The almost infinite capacity of the individual for goodness is suffocated by perceptions of the Person as a "Human Resource". Such a perspective opens the door to the de facto disposability of the individual and the displacement of *relationships* by *contractual* arrangements, which is destructive of social solidarity.

The *relationship* of "I" to "the Other", having its source and fullest expression in the Person of Jesus, is essentially one of "**Giving**". Conversely, the *'Contractual'* (as opposed to Relationship-based) model of work, is predicated on "**Having**" (A 'must-have' mind set fixated on the "I" to the exclusion of all others). That is why the Short-term Shareholder Value Maximization 'Business Model' self destructed.

Figure 2 follows on from the 'Deconstruction' of the Values-based Model, around which the Compendium is built. It is, in effect, the same model, as it operates in the social institutions of market-based economies.

The Primacy of the **Person** – based on their nature, destiny and, as a consequence, their responsibilities – is at the top of Fig. 2. It is precisely the **nature** of the Person that generates the Values and Principles, by which they are called to live.

This, in turn, requires that, whatever the political or economic system within which they live and work, the Person has certain inalienable **rights**. These include the Right to work and to Private Property. These rights encompass the value of all work. It means, for example, that unemployment, especially when it is the direct outcome of State and/or corporate policies, is a moral, not just a political issue. This is why the Compendium refers to "the scourge of unemployment".

This perspective has a pervasive relevance to **Corporate Structures**: i.e. the ethos of a company and the principles (or lack of principles) by which it is managed. The Compendium is not, in any way, prescriptive regarding these structures. Based on developments in Corporate Strategy, corporate structures and "Business Models" are subject to constant, competition-driven change.

The Compendium acknowledges, and upholds, as a necessity, the need for **profitability**. At the same time, it asserts the right of employees to strike and also the legitimate and important role of **Trade Unions**. These rights are not absolute; they are bounded.

Corporate Structures, of whatever kind, can most effectively operate within **market-based** systems. This is for reasons explained earlier in this paper. It has to do with the role of markets and, also, the fact that there is a powerful synergy between, on the other hand, a Values-based sustainable "Business Model" and, on the other hand, the efficient operation of markets – which requires Trust, Honesty and Transparency.

The Compendium, as noted, observes that there are limits to "unfettered Markets". It asserts the overriding importance of the 'Universal Destination' of Economic wealth. The Torah (and Talmud) would concur with the Compendium that, in principal, wealth is good and profits are imperative. The issue is the proper use of wealth (the modest life of Warren Buffet, one of the richest men in the world, and his recent disposal of his vast wealth to charities provides am example). The issue is how profits are generated and how and by what criteria they are distributed.

This is where the Values and Principles, set down at the outset, are of crucial importance. They take precedence over purely market-determined outcomes.

In Figure 2, this iterative process takes us to the **Economy**. At one level, whatever the actual Nature of the economy, it will be shaped by the prevailing values, principles and freedoms of Society. At a deeper level, the Economy – from the Gulag through Wall Street and, in contrast, the Economy of Community developed by Ciara Lubrick – is an expression of the nature of *community*. Its mode of operation, and public policy management, determine whether or not individuals are able to be totally free – and free to work out, in Relationships (primarily in Families), their final destiny to be with God who, as St. John in his sublime writings insists, is Love.

But the Compendium argues that the Economy can only be a partial answer to the Persons' innate needs. It is constrained by the 'Universal Destination' of economic wealth. This underpins the intrinsic relationship between Morality and Economics, including the Markets, which are the essential mechanism through which economies' function.

Getting this balance right is not easy and is subject to constant pressure. Against this background, the Compendium makes the point that:

*"The objectives of a **business** must be met in economic terms and according to economic criteria but the authentic values that bring about the development of the **Person** and **Society** must not be neglected"*

The Compendium presses its case further. In doing so, it makes an enormously important contribution to our understanding of the challenges faced by Humanity. In Figure 2, this is set out as the 'plateau' of Globalization, analogous to, say, other anthropological 'inflection points' through which humanity has evolved.

The key driver of economic wealth today is not resources or location or even military power. As indicated in Figure 2, the 'Knowledge Economy', the key driver is the intellect – a unique characteristic of the Human Person. The key elements of this new stage in the development of Humanity and the Human Person, include technology, the emergence of highly mobile multinational companies aligned to the pulse of the global economy, an enormous relative increase in international Trade (and, hence, global interdependence). There are, in turn, based on the operation of global, highly innovative sets of financial markets.

This whole new construct has been both generated, and brought to the fore, the phenomenon of unprecedented global immigration and imperative of upholding Human Rights, not simply inside 'national' jurisdictions, but globally. The imperative, "My neighbour is *all* mankind" has taken on a whole new importance.

In these circumstances, the Compendium makes a prophetic case for an Ethical basis for international arrangements and governance in relation to e.g. economic immigration and, equally, the status of refugees.

In summary, the core Value is Love; the Principal is respect for the Person, and the rationale is that we are all made in the image and likeness of God, as our ultimate goal. This is the definite benchmark for evaluating the Morality not alone of Markets but of international regulation and governance across the whole sphere of economic and trade cooperation.

What emerges from a close study of the Compendium's analysis of Markets, and the market-based economic system, is this: the outcomes help to explain why corporations (and Governments) which do not respect the Person, frequently self-destruct, with enormous collateral damage to employees and other stakeholders. The evidence suggests that corporations can be highly successful in monetary terms over the shorter-term – but that their lack of lived Values and Principles will, ultimately, bring about their demise.

More positively, it helps to explain why other companies are successful. De Guis, writing in the Harvard Business Review, sets out the concept – based on over 30 years experience of senior management experience – of the <u>Living Company</u>. His analysis resonates not alone the critique set out in the Compendium but, also, the insights of the Torah and Talmud on work and what is most to be valued in business:

*"Why do so many companies die young? Mounting evidence suggests that corporations because their policies and practices are based **too heavily** on the thinking and language of **economics**...because their managers focus exclusively on producing goods and services and forget that the organisation is a **community of human beings**...'**Living Companies**' know who they are, understand how they fit into the world, <u>**value**</u> new ideas and new <u>**people**</u> and husband their money in a way that allows them govern their future."*

Conclusion

"Business Models" embedded in ideologies which deny the centrality of the Human Person – whose defining characteristic is a capacity for an authentic experience of Love – will inevitably implode. It is a short step from Red Square, or Tiananmen Square, to Wall Street circa the mid 1990s/early 2000s.

Paradoxically, the aftermath of the fall of Berlin Wall saw the rise of the "Greed is Good" philosophy. The rise of the short-term shareholder value maximization model led to the manipulation of corporate earnings and balance sheets, leading to the subversion of Markets. The consequences were visited on employees of wealth-fixated companies, on small investors and stakeholder of Pension Funds. Most evidently, it has been visited on senior management investigated and prosecuted by the U.S. regulatory authorities – the SEC and the New York Attorney General Elliot Spitzer.

Not alone that. Formerly "High Trust" organisations – from Banks through Institutional Investors as well as Accountants and Auditors – on whose integrity the whole corporate – markets axis depends – were drawn into a fundamentally flawed and Immoral 'Business Model'. Not all by any means – and the overwhelming majority of individuals working in such organizations were undoubtedly highly moral. But the dominant corporate 'mind-set' of organisations in which they worked had this effect: the values by which individuals ordered their lives behind their hall doors were at variance with those demanded of them behind their office doors.

Trust is what individuals seek above all in a Relationship. Trust is also imperative for the functioning of markets. The interrelationship between Morality (which is, above all about Relationships) and the Markets, is compelling. Public Trust was the inevitable casualty of successive corporate debacles, notably in the US, but also permeating the whole market-base economic and financial system. Regulatory reforms, changes in corporate Governance as well as in standards and in oversight of Accounting and Auditing are a necessary – but not sufficient – response to an ethical crisis in the western, market-based, economic system.

The core of the Compendium is an interface between Love and the Human Person. That is Truth. No dimension of the human experience is semi-detached from this reality. The Compendium sets out a rigorous, evidence-based case that a *sustainable* economic system can only be built upon a set of Values. At the heart of which is the respect for the Person.

Markets (i)

The outcomes of work – specifically the production of a 'surplus' over and above immediate needs – presupposes the Rights of the individual Person to private property, as well as certain basic freedoms. These rights are preconditions for the existence, and operation, of markets. They also highlight the integral relationship between, on the one hand, political freedoms, and on the other hand, market-based economic efficiency, with all that this implies for social solidarity as well as national security.

This 'surplus' is largely mediated through 'Markets': local and global, as well as physical/local and technological.

Markets enhance individual 'welfare' – 'economist-speak' for people being better off – and thereby the resources for promoting "The Common Good". They create benefits over and above the value of goods/contracts/commodities being traded through the exchange. At the most basic level this is because markets bring together individuals/economic entities with different needs and time/risk preferences. Markets generate process and, to a greater or lesser extent, provide oversight of assets/contracts being exchange, in accordance with different needs and preferences.

Some examples may make this clear. In (a highly stylised) capital market, some barriers may require short-term financing while others require medium to long-term funding and are prepared to pay a higher rate of return to compensate savers/investors deferring consumption or the alternative deployment of their funds. Such an alignment of needs and preferences might not be possible, or only at a prohibitive cost, for individuals. These costs include, typically, "search costs", "transactions costs" as well as the costs of monitoring and enforcing contracts. A market provides, in effect, a 'Quality Control' mechanism. In fact, modern markets provide highly complex technical infrastructures as well as sophisticated control and governance systems that are wholly beyond the scope of an individual. Equally, modern capital markets raise funds, provide trading-based liquidity to the claims that are the counterpart of such funds and facilitate the transfer of Risk.

Markets not alone encourage individuals to produce a 'surplus'; they also incentivize individuals/corporate, even countries, to specialise in the production of what they are good at (in other words, in those areas in which they have a comparative advantage) the 'surplus' can then be exchanged/traded for other goods thereby contributing to higher living standards – and in an environment of relative certainty.

Such contracts may be physical-like oil, which is traded on the commodities market. Or they may take the form of standardized contract, such as in foreign exchange markets. These contracts may take immediate effect ("spot") or at some future date ("future"). They may be absolute or contingent, in the sense that one or other of the parties has the option to enforce, or not, the contract. The contract may comprise one clan of commodity or contract – or, alternatively, a portfolio of such assets.

Importantly, contracts may be semi-detached from an underlying asset. What is being traded is not e.g. the commodity, but a claim on the commodity. It may in fact, be an entirely synthetic asset which mimics the characteristics of an asset. Notwithstanding, such trades – being substitutes for the underlying or primary asset – have the capacity to impact directly on such assets and trigger systemic changes throughout, and across, markets. Increasingly, markets trade the attributes of an assets or contract, which have been unbundled into components. The most important component is Risk – a concept and/or attribute which has now been commoditized. Markets have always facilitated the exchange of assets (from vegetables/crafts to metals and currencies). Now they trade Risk and synthetic 'attributes' to better meet the needs of those who need, or work, to hedge risk, to engage in arbitrage, or to speculate.

The participants in markets depend on the Nature of the market. They vary from the smallholder in a village micro-economy through to the most sophisticated stock exchange, commodities, and foreign exchange and derivatives markets. The direct participants in the latter include Governments, Institutional Investors, Pension Funds, Banks, Analysts, the treasury, Departments of large corporates right through to the individual small investor. Indeed, so central are markets and so deeply embedded within the Trade/Investment axis of modern and highly monetized economics are they, that every single individual Person is a stakeholder – second, third and forth order effects have a systemic effect that is diffused throughout the economy and impacts the well being of all individuals and families. Think mortgage rates or the price of oil.

Markets depend on, and are driven by, Information. The greater the amount of information, the more effective – "complete" – the market. They also depend on the quality of the information: its integrity, transparency and timelines. Markets require Trust. And Trust is the mirror image of Truth. Markets are, therefore, vulnerable to manipulation and subversion, to non-disclosure and the use of inside-information since markets establish relative prices and values. Where individuals or corporations or cartels or Governments perceive there to be a self–interest in such prices/values, the operations of markets will be subverted. Trust is the first casualty. The restoration of credibility and therefore confidence will ultimately be achieved – but usually at an enormous cost in human terms quite apart from the financial cost. Liquidity – which lubricates markets – as well as interest rates/exchange rates will be impacted. As these change there is a knock-on effect ("contagion") throughout what are now highly interdependent markets. Investment, employment and economic growth will all be negatively affected: the greatest impact will be felt by the most vulnerable; the indebted – whether individuals or countries – and the poor and the pensioner.

The effective operation of markets is a matter of morality, since it impacts on the Person. It is a matter of morality since the subversion of markets wreaks havoc on lives in individual people and families and countries. And it highlights the fact that the efficient operation of markets is, in the final analysis, dependent not alone on economic fundamentals, political uncertainties and the decisions of corporates: it depends on the integrity of those who have the capacity to influence market sentiment. Morality is not only a matter of individual ethics of the Person – it is imperative for a sustainable market-based system that is sensitized to the values and Principles which underpin the Compendium's critique of the social order.

Markets (ii)

This final section sets out a perspective on the markets – based in particular, on the short-termism that dominates corporatist thinking economic system. It is based primarily on research and teaching in this field. It attempts to draw out lessons and inferences by which the integrity of the market based system can be protected – and, thereby, harnessed to its proper role. The basic idea is to suggest a number of ideas that, quite independently of the Compendium, allow for the 'benchmarking' of its analysis.

It is important to make the distinction between the two perspectives: "Having" and "Giving". The former is a by-product of western consumerism which has, in reality, subjugated the market mechanism for its own purposes. It a framed on 'self': the interests, and satisfaction, of the "I" at the expense of the "Other". It is the "must have" mentality characterised by "Brand"-driven consumerism and peer-driven attitudes and behaviour. It is supported by a short-term addiction to spending, leading to high levels of indebtedness – and resultant individual/family/societal stress and frustration.

At the corporate/strategy, level an 'atomistic' corporate culture is evident, with a rights-driven contract-based approach to work and to the disposability of the individual.

By contrast, one can stylise a perspective, based on the overriding value of the Individual. This, by definition, is one in which the "I"– instead of being self-fixated – is open to the dignity as well as the needs of "the Other I". This is, as a direct consequence, a "must-share" perspective, with a longer-term propensity to save and accumulate. This is supported by a corporate 'Business Model', characterised by a participative culture and responsibility (from the 'employee as Person') to the Environment-driven wage relationship, which rates out the idea of 'Person as Commodities/Resource'. The overall perspective is stylised but is highly recognisable.

Fig 2 puts this into a wider, global perspective. It was argued, at the outset of this paper, that western market-based consumerism is confronting three major threats; Global Poverty and in particular, the AIDS Pandemic, secondly, the Nihilism of Western Consumerism, which has desensitised both the individual and country to the enormous imbalance in wealth and power and, thirdly, the Environmental, crises which is in large part, a product of Western consumerism or the "Having" mind-set outlined in the previous figure.

There are two key Models – one, the short-term Shareholder Value perspective and the second, characterised by a "High-Trust", ethically-based Corporate Culture. They have very different outcomes, in relation to both Work and to Corporate pathology. In the first, work is purely Transactions-based; in the second, Work has an intrinsic value. The first is generally characterised by an 'atomistic' structure, the second by indecisiveness. It is important to highlight the reality that, for a whole variety of reasons, companies may become uncompetitive and even fail. The important point is whether – in success or in having to lay-off employees in order to maintain commercial viability – the Person and the rights and value with which they are embedded, informs and shapes organisational structure and strategy.

The important point is this. A focus on short-term maximising of Profit for shareholders (and, simultaneously, management) – with an impoverished view of the Person as a 'Resource') – contributes to the Nihilism of western consumerism. Equally, it contributes to, while *also* failing (by its very nature) to respond to the needs of the Poor. Conversely, a 'Business Model', based on ethical principles to do with the Greek concepts of 'Virtues' and the Person-centred philosophy of Pope John Paul II, both demands (and finds within itself the resources to) respond to the threats of Global Poverty and Western Consumerism.

Finally, Figure 3 highlights how the 'Idolatry of the Markets', in the striking phrase used in the Compendium, brings to bear extraordinary pressures and stresses on homes and families, in addition to those who work in financial institutions and markets dominated by the prevailing mainstream orthodoxy – an orthodoxy which is leading us to a major crisis in the prevailing global/political paradigm: a paradigm which increasingly threadbare, bears all the hallmarks of an orthodoxy that has not alone undermined the global economy, but has, and continues to, subvert the Family, which is at the heart of society – and also, it is worth noting, the Irish Constitution.

Figure 1.

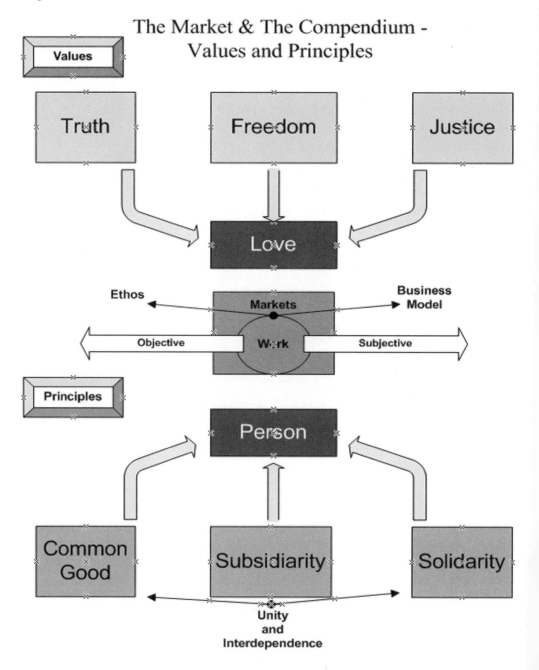

The Market & The Compendium -
Values and Principles

86

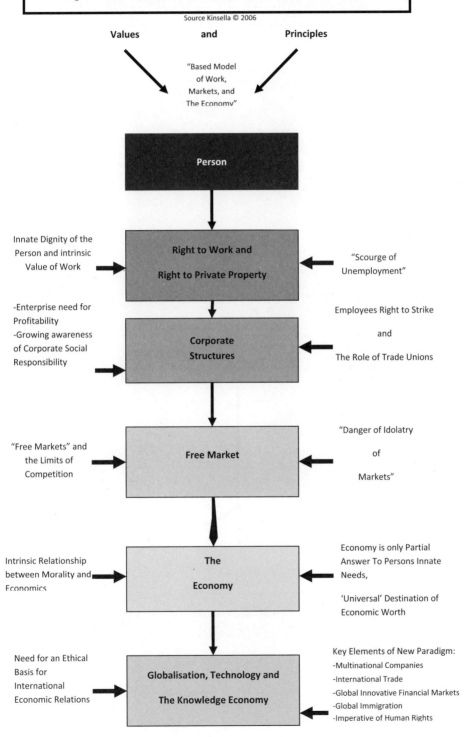

Figure 2 The Market and the Compendium Values and Principles

Source Kinsella © 2006

Values   and   Principles

"Based Model
of Work,
Markets, and
The Economy"

Person

Innate Dignity of the
Person and intrinsic
Value of Work

Right to Work and

Right to Private Property

"Scourge of
Unemployment"

-Enterprise need for
Profitability
-Growing awareness
of Corporate Social
Responsibility

**Corporate
Structures**

Employees Right to Strike

and

The Role of Trade Unions

"Free Markets" and
the Limits of
Competition

Free Market

"Danger of Idolatry
of
Markets"

Intrinsic Relationship
between Morality and
Economics

**The

Economy**

Economy is only Partial
Answer To Persons Innate
Needs,

'Universal' Destination of
Economic Worth

Need for an Ethical
Basis for
International
Economic Relations

**Globalisation, Technology and

The Knowledge Economy**

Key Elements of New Paradigm:
-Multinational Companies
-International Trade
-Global Innovative Financial Markets
-Global Immigration
-Imperative of Human Rights

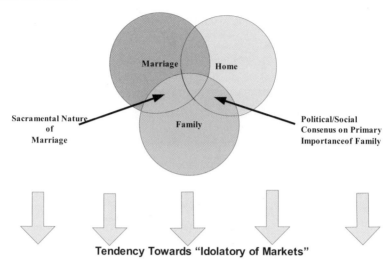

Figure 3 "Idolatory of Markets" Subverts Marriage, Home, Family

Environment of Convergence

Marriage

Home

Family

Sacramental Nature
of
Marriage

Political/Social
Consenus on Primary
Importanceof Family

Tendency Towards "Idolatory of Markets"

Environment of Divergence

Pressure

- Primacy of Profit instead of Person
- 'Business Models' based on Target-obsessed
  short-termism
- "Contractualism" displaces both Relationships, especially Family and
  Marriage, and Business as an 'Economy of Communion' (Ciara Lubick)

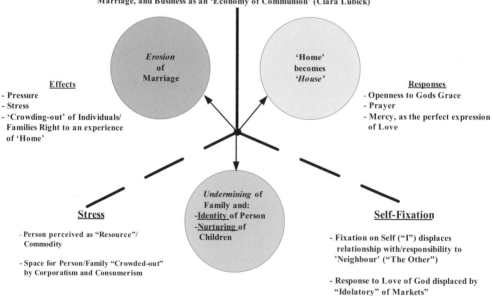

*Erosion
of
Marriage*

'Home'
becomes
'House'

Effects
- Pressure
- Stress
- 'Crowding-out' of Individuals/
  Families Right to an experience
  of 'Home'

Responses
- Openness to Gods Grace
- Prayer
- Mercy, as the perfect expression
  of Love

*Undermining of
Family and:*
-Identity of Person
-Nurturing of
Children

Stress

- Person perceived as "Resource"/
  Commodity

- Space for Person/Family "Crowded-out"
  by Corporatism and Consumerism

Self-Fixation

- Fixation on Self ("I") displaces
  relationship with/responsibility to
  'Neighbour' ("The Other")

- Response to Love of God displaced by
  "Idolatory" of Markets"

Holding Out for Hope

It is as well that Christmas is very firmly in view. We need a sense of Hope. Hope is not about wishful thinking. It is about the tenacious faith-based conviction that the hard work of our future has been accomplished – and it is also about taking responsibility for enduring that the real and tangible benefits are transmitted through our own lives into society, which means work, jobs, investment and homes. It's not much in evidence out there.

Ireland is already experiencing what is likely to be a severe and protracted recession. The consequences are being felt in negative economic growth, rising unemployment (probably upwards of 70,000 over the next year) and an unprecedented deterioration in public finances, on which the funding of our Social Services – all the investment that holds us together as a community and a nation – depend.

In these circumstances a sense of Hope is not just desperately important – it is, if we take the right steps, fully justified. What is needed is a sense of purpose and direction on the part of the Government. Ireland has lost its way. It is not at all clear what any political party stands for. Ireland needs to be, in the words of Yeats, 're-imagined'. This means not just a reactive mode of cutting expenditures, but rather investment in areas such as health. It means critiquing the moral and political vacuum at the heart of Irish Society.

It also requires sensitivity on the part of core financial institutions not alone to the damage that is being caused by misconceived strategies, and the abandonment of sound banking practices. More importantly, the banks really need to explain to the public, their customers, their employees, and to the public, precisely what they are doing, and plan to do, to shoulder their part of the burden of getting through this recession. They need to explain it now. This is more important than the PWC Report. It is more important than the strategic two-year plans they are preparing for the Financial Regulator. It's more important even than recapitalisation, which is the big issue of the moment.

Trust was the first casualty of the Global Financial Crisis. Trust within, and across, the Financial System imploded. This was for two reasons – the mainstream banking model was based on a lie. Also – and wholly inexplicably – banking globally abandoned the cornerstone of good banking practice: the management of credit risk. Credit Risk is what professional bankers learned at their mothers' knee. In the 'Search for Yield' – these days the lexicography of banking is littered with poisonous acronyms and 'bank speak' – this core principal was abandoned. Banks stopped trusting each other. There was systemic collapse of Trust in the Banking System itself.

Not surprisingly, the next casualty was Credibility – the belief on the part of the general public, and in particular bank customers, that the authorities were 'in charge'. They weren't. It was not until last month, when the IMF, the G7, and Europe collectively got its act together, that some semblance of credibility was wrenched back from the wasteland to which Global Financial markets have been reduced. This is vitally important for two reasons.

The first is that macroeconomic policy – the management of interest rates as well as of public expenditure – has been pulled all over the place. This is now exacerbating the underlying problems caused by the failures in Western mainstream banking. The second is that there is only so much that Governments and Central Banks can do – the policy instruments at their disposal are limited, and the capacity of the public finances to absorb catastrophic misjudgements on the part of private financial institutions is limited – not least by the patience of the public and their understandable reluctance to see resources that are desperately needed in areas such as Health and Education to support a sector which by its very nature – and that's an important point – should be profitable. It really is not difficult to make profits within a sound banking system: everything is in place to enable the banks to do just that. It is extraordinarily difficult to lose literally hundreds of billions of dollars of value. That tells us something about the very nature of the social as well as financial pathogen which has spawned this crisis.

As we face towards Christmas and into a new year, the problem that our financial system, and that of the Western world, faces is this: Banks are no longer performing their key role of intermediation, that is, accepting deposits (from both personal customers, and from the markets) and making loans and investments in the real economy of jobs, and trade. The nature of the crisis in Ireland is rather different from that in other and larger economies. In particular, the proportion of banks total loan book accounted for by property in one form or another has been excessive. It is a fact that Irish banks have, by what were accepted as official benchmarks until quite recently, well capitalised, and well reserved. But these benchmarks – including the landmark Basle II capital adequacy – have been swept away. What matters now is the view that the markets take of whether, or not, a bank is well capitalised. Ireland's Deposit Protection scheme was necessary and proportionate as well as being necessary for the economy. It provided a basis for the restoration of Trust and confidence. It made it easier, *at least in principle*, for Irish banks to go to the markets to recapitalise should this be necessary. It almost certainly is now necessary – but the markets have dried up.

There is now a case for recapitalisation of the banks on the part of the Government – even in the teeth of understandable opposition on the part of the public; it may be that what is required is a package of initiatives on the part of both the banks and the government. It may, for example, require disposals on the part of some of the banks. Recapitalisation is no 'magic bullet', it should be recognised recapitalisation has made very little difference in the UK. It hasn't restored trust to the international money markets and the banks willingness to lend to each other. Most important of all, what Irish households and businesses now need is not so much additional funding – because the economy is demonstrable in recession – but rather support to help them get through this recession. At the same time what the banks need to do is to invest selectively in indigenous Irish industry.

The banks are caught between a rock and a hard place: on the one hand, they are slamming on the breaks in terms of risk assessment, in an effort to restore their balance sheets and to work off their bad loans which can only increase as we go deeper into the recession. On the other hand, there is enormous pressure on them to support the Irish economy, businesses and households, through this corridor of pain; the latter has to be their priority. There has been a serious lack of balance in the distribution of lending by the banks: relative to their total loan book, there has been far too little invested in manufacturing, in services, in transport communications, in new indigenous start-ups, in university knowledge-based industries, in supporting agri-businesses and farm-based enterprises. The banks owe this to the society that has written an insurance policy for their shareholders. They owe it to their customers on whom their value ultimately depends. They owe it to their employees on whom the burden of high level strategic mistakes has been visited, and who will suffer. The government have to address this issue – possibly in the form of some Loan Guarantee Fund. But there is much more that the government need to do.

The problem is, is that there is no alignment – no sense of balance – between where the banks are still embedded and where the government want them to be. This will require not simply forensic examinations of the banks' loan books – the Financial Regulator – should have most, if not all, of the information in one form or another. It will require concrete medium term initiatives on the part of the government that are developmental in nature, and not just cutting costs. It goes far beyond reform of the Public Sector, which is threatening to become a catch-all solution to our problems, which it is not. We need to identify, very specifically, the gaps in intermediation by the banks – what they are lending, and what they *should* be lending, and to whom. The government needs to come up with a developmental strategy which generates Hope – and which says to the banks 'look here is where we want to focus'. It needs that much maligned word 'Partnership', one that is non-adversarial between the banks. It requires of the banks rising above a psychological 'silo' and re-imagining not alone their importance to the economy, but how that importance should be reflected in the manner and mindset in which they operate. Happy Christmas.

This Article appeared in The Irish Examiner, November 2008.

Bank Profits Built on Real Relationships and Public Trust

Leadership requires that banks show they are not fixated on short-term Shareholder Value, writes Ray Kinsella.

More than a year after the onset of the international credit crisis, the International Monetary Fund (IMF), in its most recent financial stability report, has warned that "global financial markets continue to be fragile, and indicators of systemic risk remain elevated". It is not only the IMF. In June, the European Central Bank (ECB) warned that "the risks to the euro area financial stability system had, on balance, increased compared with the previous six months".

This, it argued, pointed to "a protracted adjustment period within the financial system as banks seek to increase their liquidity and capital positions". They are having a hard time doing both. This unprecedented financial crisis is not going away.

There is a persuasive argument, based partly on levels of volatility, that behind the facade of "Business as Usual", the system is increasingly vulnerable to tectonic shocks with unknowable consequences for the real economy of jobs, trade and living standards.

As recently as two weeks ago, the two titans of the mortgage markets in the US – Fannie Mae and Freddie Mac – which between them hold some $6 trillion (€3.89 trillion) in mortgages, and already enjoyed privileged access to the capital markets, teetered on the brink of failure.

Had the US authorities not stepped in to provide additional guarantees, they would have effectively failed. They are not out of the water yet. In the UK, the Alliance & Leicester Building Society has been acquired by Banco Santander, as the UK mortgage sector goes deeper into crisis.

With each new collapse and/or "near miss", the credibility of the authorities is being further eroded. The next time round – and there will be a next time – neither investors nor the public may trust in the markets or the regulators to contain the implosion.

Recent data from the US on the acceleration of foreclosures on mortgages – the epicentre of the initial crisis – together with the fact that an increasing number of people are simply walking away from mortgages mired in negative equity, is a pathogen within the system that has the capacity to bring about its collapse. All of this highlights the case for a global central bank, as argued some months ago in these pages (The Irish Times, *"Global Central Bank is Needed", January* 23rd, 2008).

These developments raise important issues for Irish publicly quoted banks: AIB, Anglo-Irish, Bank of Ireland and Irish Life & Permanent and, by extension, the wider economy. The recent recovery in share prices is well–founded. Such was the extent of the decline in share prices over the last 12 months or so that, prior to the recent recovery, share prices had fallen – on average – by some 70 per cent compared to the previous 12 months. Such declines are not justified by reference to balance-sheets or recent performance, as AIB's recent results demonstrate. It is an axiom of financial theory that markets are efficient and rational. But the operation of markets over the last decade has been subverted by a business model that is flawed, rooted in greed and excess.

It is not functioning effectively. It is a rogue market, spawned by the malign sub-prime debacle to which it gave birth and the parallel universe of "structured finance". It is now beset by uncertainty and fear. The credibility of policy has dissipated.

The US and other world central banks have injected hundreds of billions of euro into global credit markets – effectively exchanging publicly funded equity for the toxic debt acquired by banks in their pursuit of short-term shareholder value. Even this hasn't succeeded in regenerating trust on the part of the financial markets.

The Irish economy is structurally stronger than it was in the 1980s. Equally, the banks, while exposed to prospective write-offs, have balance sheets fully compliant with regulatory requirements. The Financial Regulator imposes limits on the extent of exposures by banks to specific sectors. Importantly, unlike their European peers, the liquidity position of Irish banks was presciently "stress-tested" before the onset of the crisis. They also have access to liquidity from the European Central Bank (ECB).

However, higher write-offs and the fall in the demand for mortgages and loans, as well as a lack of market confidence and difficulties on the funding side experienced by all banks, have impacted on their share prices. This has been reinforced by the fact that Ireland is no longer "flavour of the month" with international institutional investors. The Celtic Tiger was always a niche play for them and, in any event, there is no longer any incentive to acquire Irish bank shares to gain indirect exposure to the Irish economy.

In the present savage bear market in global equities, financial stocks have been hammered and Irish banks shares have been a casualty. Domestic investors lack the stomach for "value investing" in institutions that would appear to be undervalued, while international investors have simply lost interest. Against this background, the recent modest strengthening is encouraging.

The four listed banks – each with a very different business model – have an importance to the Irish economy that would be difficult to overstate. It's not alone the jobs, and the quality of these jobs. It's the knowledge-base encompassed within the banks' branch network. It's also about the sensitivity of domestically-owned and headquartered banks to the pulse of the Irish economy and their informal role as a conduit for public policy directed towards The Common Good. The IFSC, to take one example, would never have happened in the absence of a commitment by Irish banks.

Compared with 12 months ago, and taking a short to medium-term view, the market value of Irish banks has contracted. Smaller banks generally find it more difficult and/or expensive to raise capital. The issue here is not that the banks need to raise capital from a regulatory perspective; rather, the market reserves to itself the right to decide on what it regards as a sufficiently robust capital base.

There are a number of options for the banks. They could seek to "sit out" the recession, on the basis of the economy's latent strength, the quality of their recent performance and, also, their balance sheets. The markets, it is reasonable to assume, have factored all of this into the existing share-levels.

This option of sitting it out, however, may leave individual banks vulnerable to takeover. It is quite certain that more than one potential predator has run the slide-rule over them – and they will almost certainly have redone their homework in recent times. An attempted takeover could, in principle, be friendly or hostile. One point is clear: the implications would be very far-reaching indeed.

Another option would be for one, or more, of the banks to initiate merger talks. This would require the consent of the Financial Regulator and the Competition Authority. The fact that the Irish banking system is now an integral part of the EU Internal Market, together with the ease of entry through new technology-based platforms, means that the implications for competition would be very different compared to the past. A merger would reduce the absolute number of competitors, particularly in retail, business and mortgage finance. But the Irish banking market would remain contestable – any attempt to exploit market dominance would attract new entrants.

The Irish financial system has been enormously enriched, in terms of consumer choice, alternative business models and competition, by the entry of overseas-based banks. This is what the EU internal market is all about. Nonetheless, if one or more of the listed banks were to be taken over, particularly through a hostile takeover, there would be a serious and lasting loss of welfare for the Irish economy.

A newly merged bank would be less vulnerable to a takeover. It would almost certainly find it easier and cheaper to raise additional capital, should this be necessary. In the mid and late 1960s Dr Ken Whitaker, the economic architect of modern Ireland, impelled the then eight Irish clearing banks to merge in order to form four larger and stronger banks, capable of competing with an influx of overseas banks. The same logic – albeit in different circumstances – applies in today's environment.

A merger would inevitably lead to job losses and the closure of some branches. It is the staff that creates value in any bank. In order for a merger to succeed, it would be imperative that management, staff and the IBOA engage in dialogue, in an environment of trust and respect. A post-merger rationalisation process has to be set against the possible consequences of an overseas acquisition of one of the core banks, at the heart of the Irish financial system. This would involve not alone job losses, but also the migration of key management, operational and technical functions abroad.

There is another perspective that needs to be factored into any attempt to understand, let alone resolve, this crisis. It began within the banking system. It was transmitted across the banking sector and credit markets. The sheer scale of the fallout from what has been a monumental failure in leadership within the global banking system is simply incalculable. The banks continue to be insulated from consequences of their actions at two different levels. Firstly, by shareholders (including pension funds – the irony!), whose investment in the banks has been diluted by capital–raising to mitigate disastrous strategic and operational decisions. Secondly, the banks have been bailed-out by governments and global central banks. The business model within which banks operate needs to change. "Business as usual" is no longer an option – not after what has happened and its cost in human terms.

It is important that banks be proactive, whichever of the options above is pursued. Leadership requires that they demonstrate they are not fixated on maximising short-term shareholder value. They have other stakeholders, whose commitment and loyalty has helped to generate shareholder value. Households are now struggling with mortgages, including those of 100 per cent on a 40-year term, on properties that have fallen sharply in value – mortgages that banks were marketing aggressively as recently as last year. Businesses are confronted with an economy at the cusp of recession while, at the same time, being subject to much stricter conditions and requirements in relation to funding.

The Irish listed banks prospered during the years of the Celtic Tiger. It is in their strategic interest, and that of the country, that they demonstrate an understanding of this reality: sustainability and profitability are built on real relationships and public trust, rather than on a fixation with shareholder value through the pursuit of a metric/targets-driven culture imposed on staff. It is in the hard times that the sincerity of such "relationships" is truly tested.

This Article appeared in The Irish Times, August 2008.

Catharsis in Irish Banking 2004/2005:

Corporate Values and Ethics

"Corporate Culture and Ethics"

The opening years of the new millennium have seen a fundamental catharsis in the morality of business, especially large multinational corporates. The catalyst for this sea change was undoubtedly the collapse of the US energy giant Enron in 2001, followed swiftly by an implosion in Worldcom. What had been thought by consumers and regulators – by staff and investors – to be robust, efficient and well-regulated businesses were found to have gaping holes in their balance sheets and to have been kept afloat by fundamentally flawed accounting procedures and management practices. In the aftermath of these, and subsequent corporate debacles, two realities have emerged.

The first is that 'High-Trust' institutions and professions – Banking as well as Auditing/Accounting – were found to have been complicit in, or to have facilitated, the kind of practices which led to the collapse of some major individual companies. In the case of banking, US Regulators, including the SEC, found a wide range of malpractice among providers to the Banking Financial Sectors. In Ireland, the deficiencies, at the heart of the Irish banking catharsis 2004, have been called 'legacy issues'. This is because on the one hand, they have their roots in the economic environment and corporate culture of the late 1980s-1990s and, on the other hand, because of the limitations of the control systems and enforcement necessary to properly address the 'fall-out' of this culture.

Collateral damage

The second was the enormous collateral damage this apparent breakdown in the governance and management of some banks and other companies has caused: damage to pensioners in companies who had knowingly inflated their profits and engaged in illegal activities leading to their collapse and the wiping out of their Pension funds, damage to staff who were laid-off in their thousands and, more importantly, whose lives and values were subverted by subversive management behaviour, stemming from the prevailing 'Business Model' and which was wholly beyond their control.

Flawed business model

This damage reflected a corporate mindset that was focused solely on maximising profitability of the company – to the exclusion of any consideration of the *manner* in which these profits were generated. In more formal term, staff were inducted into a 'Business-Model' based on maximising the market value of the company – that is, its value on the stock market quarter after quarter after…Companies who bought into this Business Model struggled to increase the 'value' of the company. This 'value' – being based on corrupt management practices, corrupt incentives for staff and dubious accounting – could be wholly different to the *real* value of the company.

Pressure on staff

The insatiable demand for higher and higher shareholder value was transmitted into pressure on employees – which, in turn, generated extraordinary stress as they attempted to deliver on frequently unrealistic targets.

Where staff couldn't meet these targets they could be – certainly in some cases – invented them. If you did 'succeed' in meeting targets the rewards in monetary terms could frequently be excessive, even obscene: if you failed, just as frequently you could find yourself out in the cold.

Major inflection point

This is certainly, and this point should be emphasised, not to say that all financial institutions, or large multinational corporations, were run along these line. That is not the case. But what *is* true is that a sufficient number exhibited these kind of characteristics to highlight the reality of a 'behavioural mindset' obsessed with maximising short-term shareholder value – and a belief among some very senior executives that this model constituted a template for success. Certainly for a period in the early and mid–1990s this was an important dimension in mainstream corporate strategy and behaviour. It has cast a long shadow. The investigate process focused on addressing the causes, and effects, in Irish banking will shortly be complete. This will constitute a major inflection point. There will be pain – but also the opportunity for a fresh start based on a new ethical platform. Whether, or not, the resolution on the part of the bank to engage in really fundamental reform remains to be seen. There are some positive indications in this regard.

Ireland is, of course, by no means unique in regard to failings in a corporate culture which is marketed as being consumer–centred and which, instead, had demonstrably failed the consumer. In a recent report 'The Economist' observed that 'there is hardly a corner of US Investment banking which is untouched by scandals'. In the UK, the continued existence of corporate greed within a supposedly new regime of corporate governance continues to engage the attention of both policy makers and the public.

Dance of death

Basically, all of this was a distorted form of the principle expounded by the Nobel Prize winning economist Milton Friedman, that 'the business of business is business' and that pretty well anything over and above this represents a form theft of shareholders wealth. Stated this way it's simply wrong. But from this kind of thinking emerged a belief – shared by top management in some companies, some of the large Institutional Investors holding stakes in companies, and certain Investment Analysts (whose job it is to evaluate the financial prospects of individual companies) – that the overriding objective of business strategy was all about maximising returns to shareholders, even over periods over successive quarters.

It led mentally to a 'dance of death' whereby investor expectations were continually ratcheted up. It tempted, and in many cases almost *impelled*, individuals to behave in a manner consistent with this objective, as was the case with respect to incentives and rewards in companies – salary bonuses, stock options and the rest, for those who 'bought into' the model – together with a willingness you look the other way, when it came to the kind of business practices involved.

People – the big corporate lie

One important dimension of generating profits is to cut costs. Since the 'Business Model' crowded out any regard for morality it lacked any basis for respecting individuals. It is, of course, the case that the survival of the business may depend on reducing the number of people employed. What is at issue in the short-term Shareholder Value model are periodic "culls" of thousands of people, sacrificed on the altar of maximizing shareholder value – careers, lives and family relationships. It was based on a big lie. The model was not, of course, sustainable. It collapsed in on itself in a series of corporate debacles.

1. The 'worth of an individual' can be measured in terms of money, in one form or another. Individuals are a business 'cost' to be minimised (which was really stupid). Individuals are therefore disposable.

2. 'Work' has no intrinsic other than as a set of activities which involve 'getting on', preferably ahead of, and where necessary, at the expense of, the next guy.

3. Customers are basically a <u>means</u> to an end – primarily that of enriching some categories of stake holders over the rest.

4. The 'culture' of an organisation is one in which management require individuals to compartmentalise their lives: trying to live out one set of values behind their hall door and a wholly divergent set of values behind their office door.

5. A society in which money can muscle its way in and displace personal responsibility regarding why we are all here in the first place and which is built upon a business model which 'crowds out' the intrinsic value of each one of us and (keep your voice down) – God.

Ethics

In the last two years there has been a plethora of legislation in the US and across Europe. This legislation encompasses areas such as Corporate Governance, the prevention of the conflict of interest between accounting and consulting, new accounting/auditing standards as well as changes *within* companies themselves. These changes reflected the <u>beginning</u> of an understanding of the interests of other stakeholders in an organization, apart from shareholders. It reflected an acknowledgement that the performance of individuals had to be seen in the context of accountability and compliance and encompassing those and much more, ethics – rather than 'doing the deal'. It reflected the beginning of a wider understanding of the importance of companies as *communitie*s – and communities with wider societal responsibilities, than simply generating wealth as the end and objective for one group of stakeholders.

This takes us into the very heart of the matter. The corporate catharsis through which we are passing is something of an ethical epiphany within the wider business environment.

It is a powerful demonstration of the fact that financial rewards to one group of stakeholders – especially large institutional investors – is at the expense of "crowding out" individual persons. The results are as inevitable as they are disastrous. We should not be surprised at his. Work, any work, has a moral value. It has, therefore an ethical dimension. Here ethics, properly understood, are subjugated to the demands of an economic system – in this case the 'Wall Street' syndrome that 'greed is good'.

From the hall door to the office door

The negative effects on companies and on wider communities cannot be in doubt. A tension is created between, on the one hand, the values by which we try to live behind our hall doors and those, on the other hand, by which we are constrained to live behind the office door. Where the beliefs and values of individuals, in their private lives, converge towards, and ideally are aligned with, those of the values of the work place, there is a powerful 'leverage' effect. One reinforces the other. It is, in the jargon of the economist, a 'positive sum game'.

Conversely, where there is a *divergence,* the intrinsic value of work is subverted: enormous pressure is brought to bear on individuals seeking to develop a career which is a means to the end of allowing them to carry out their wider responsibilities, and on the other hand are encouraged to adapt a corporate mindset, a set of values, a mode of behavior, that is wholly alien to the very idea of ethics. Concepts of 'right' and 'wrong' are effectively hi-jacked.

And so there are the T.V. scenes of senior executives, taken in hand-cuffs from their workplace and into courtrooms. It would be unethical – it would be just plain wrong to judge the behavior or culpability of individuals caught up in this catharsis. We are fallible. Evil has a superficial glamour, especially when it comes in the guise of excessive wealth. And so we compromise – before being conscious of the full effects of what is happening. Our ability to distinguish objectively between right and wrong is diminished.

New Paradigm

There is now a new paradigm taking over in the corporate world. At one level, it is about regulation and, in particular compliance. It is about developing a corporate culture that respects individual persons. Corporate culture is enormously important. The tone is set by leadership from the top. Ethical leadership shapes the values by which the company operates. Employees are empowered to contribute to what is increasingly perceived as a *community* of individuals. It determines the legitimacy – the degree of Trust – attributed to the organization by customers, staff and the wider public.

It comes down to which The Harvard Business Review, in a landmark study some years ago, defined leadership as `humility, with fierce resolve.' Humility is an ethical virtue. Ethics revolves around our human nature, right and wrong, and personal responsibility. The 'coping stone' of responsibility is the concept of 'you' (be it boss or office boy) as another 'I'. It's also about failure and starting again. The Chief Executive, who is a combination of Bill Gates and St Francis of Assisi, has yet to put in an appearance.

This new paradigm is already evident, albeit in an embryonic form. Companies are more highly regulated, compliant and dependent on systems than ever before. But it doesn't nearly go far enough because it doesn't address the core issue of ethics: not Codes of Ethics, which are frequently sets of rules, or a 'wish list' of rules, by which management hope or expect staff to abide. Ethics, properly understood (and that's the hard bit) are the heart of Corporate Culture.

In the short-term Shareholder Value-model, individual persons are simply means to an end of companies seeking to meet the literally insatiable demands of the financial markets. The moral value of the individual person is 'crowded-out' – irrelevant to where the model.

By contrast, in an ethically-driven model individual persons are at the very heart of its *modus operandi*. At the economic level, this new ethical model acknowledges that the intellectual capital embedded in the individual within a knowledge-based economy is the real key to the 'value creation'.

This is enormously important for two reasons: firstly, because it represents a major deficiency in the short-term shareholder value–model, within which individuals are basically viewed as a cost – and are disposable. Secondly because, in any event, the economic power that Institutional Investors have, is based on the notion of capital scarcity. This premise has been made totally redundant by the growth and innovation in the financial markets. Intellectual capital – 'knowledge equity' – is now the scare factor of production and the key to value-creation.

There is also the reality that companies who operate outside of an ethical template inevitably create conflicts and distortions which erode the value of this knowledge equity. More importantly it is devoid of any understanding of the intrinsic value of the individual and the importance for that individual of the moral choices which they make as part of their Daily work.

Ethical deficit

This 'ethical deficit' which became manifested in the Enron debacle has its roots, not alone in a distorted view of the Friedman's model of what business is about – but also in the secularization of society and the deification of money and power. This is not rhetoric – it simply distils the outcomes of case studies of companies that have fallen victim to a flawed paradigm, long past its sell-by date.

Recent Encyclicals of Pope John Paul II, particularly those addressing the value of the individual person, and of relationships, (which are rooted in the Judeo-Christian teaching) – provide a framework from which to develop this ethically-driven model of corporate behavior.

It is possible to discern a new ethically driven paradigm behind all of this. The fact that it is in its embryonic stage does not take from its significance what is evident is a process that is of, quite simply, enormous significance, both to the Regulators and to the Banks themselves. It can be stylized as a progression, in recent decades, from Regulation, through Corporate

Governance and, finally, to Ethics. Not 'business–ethics' or even 'Corporate Social Responsibility' or, least of all, 'Mission Statements' or talk of 'Core–Values'. But Ethics – the real thing.

Take the Regulatory perspective. Regulation is a necessary, <u>but not sufficient</u>, condition to protect the interests of the consumer. It doesn't matter how much regulation you have – at some stage, the only effect is to add to compliance costs, which are then passed on to the consumer.

Corporate Governance seemed to offer a framework within which to ensure that the rights of consumers were properly managed and – at the least – were not compromised through corporate excess. The board of Enron, quite simply, suspended its bright and shiny Corporate Governance structures. And in the wasteland of the post–Enron shakeout, some major banks were found to be complicit in the sacrifice of consumers', and investors', welfare to the great idol of 'shareholder value'.

Which takes us to Ethics. If we define Ethics as, quite simply, 'obedience to the unenforceable', then it is quite clear that it is not something that can be legislated for, or regulated, imposed upon from outside. It is something which is embedded in the values of Corporate leadership – and which is diffused through the whole organisation, impacting at every level, first with staff and, through them, to customers. It is at the core of, but transcends, all governance and compliance.

And what of the actual source of such Ethical Principles? Well, the Judeao-Christian tradition for a start. If there are no values within the organisation, other than perverse financial incentives and short-term shareholder value maximisation, then any serious university student – future management – had better bring in with them their own ethical principles to compliment statutory and compliance requirements.

Consumers – and increasingly staff – see a 'Business Model' in financial services that works against, rather than for, their interests. And they are right. An obsession with maximising shareholder value has chewed up and then discarded employees. In the interest of maximising short-term Shareholder Value, middle management have been put under enormous strain to attain what are, in many cases, unattainable short-term targets. Word is transmitted through the organisation to generate fee and commission-based income, any old how – because in an era of low interest rates and pressurised margins, this is the easy option. No wonder consumers (and employees) saw through it.

There are periodic culls of staff, all of which lead to a perception that staff are not respected and are highly expendable. The interaction between, on the one hand, highly qualified, but over-pressurised and de-moralised staff on the other hand, is state driven by the imperative of pushing products; 'maximising share of wallet' and other business – speak clichés. The reality that staff observe is that, between their hall door, and their office door, they have to get their head around a wholly divergent set of Ethical standards.

Dead man walking

Few believe in this model anymore. It is a dead man walking. Consumers expect to be treated – not just in conformity with Codes of Practice – but in an ethical manner. Ethics was originally, and must be restored to, its primary function of guaranteeing that staff and customers will be treated fairly, with integrity and in a manner that commands Trust.

The Regulation, Corporate Governance and Ethics paradigm helps explain both the failures in Regulation and Governance to date to stamp out corporate greed. More challengingly, it highlights the importance for both Regulators and Banks, of instilling Ethics as the ultimate guarantor of Consumer Protection and, also, of any serious 'value proposition', that engages with the consumer, and leads to sustainable growth and earnings.

This paper was presented at the IBOA Annual Conference, 2005.

Changing Mindsets, Behaviour and a Whole Way of Thinking at AIB

Yesterday's IFSRA Final Report into the AIB overcharging has a consumer focus that will be widely welcomed, writes Ray Kinsella.

In its Final Report on AIB Investigations, published yesterday, the Irish Financial Services Regulatory Authority (IFSRA) returned to deal with unfinished business arising from its Interim Report, issued in July.

The Interim Report identified the key parameters of the overcharging debacle involving some €34 million: the amounts due to be repaid to customers, the numbers and categories of transactions involved, as well as the process for ensuring that restitution was carried out effectively and speedily.

The report also set-out the issues to be addressed in relation to the Faldor offshore scheme, which existed from 1989 to 1996.

Prioritising the restitution was in line with the principles underlying IFSRA 's strategic plan for "putting the consumer at the heart of the regulatory system". It promised in its Final Report to turn to the issues of who knew, when they knew, and why the matter remained unreported for so long. And, of course, to set out what needed to be done to put matters right.

The conclusions reached were tersely summarised by IFSRA's chief executive, Dr Liam O'Reilly: "The failures within AIB uncovered by the investigations are completely unacceptable. We will not tolerate such practices within the financial services industry".

AIB's chief executive, Mr Michael Buckley, accepted the report's findings in full. He acknowledged that procedures for dealing with compliance failures were inadequate and that, at critical times, they simply didn't work.

The bank will, in addition to the measures it has already taken, implement a series of actions required of it by IFSRA. These include, crucially, disciplinary action in regard both to the overcharging issue and, also, to inappropriate share dealings by AIB's subsidiary, AIBIM, in relation to Faldor and other transactions.

Who then knew what was going on?

The form of words used – more than once – in the IFSRA report is striking. "Certain staff and management within certain areas of AIB appear to have been aware..."

IFSRA's investigation will have addressed the issue of accountability thoroughly. Equally, the independent report by DeLoitte, commissioned by AIB following consultation with IFSRA, and overseen by the former CandAG, Mr Lauri McDonnell, delivered to AIB some weeks ago and forwarded to IFSRA, will have dealt with this question. It has been reported by RTE's Charlie Bird that a sub-committee of AIB's board has already initiated a disciplinary process by writing to some 10 individuals.

Both IFSRA and AIB have insisted that "due process" would be subverted by naming individuals. They are right. It is a basic principle of justice that individuals are entitled to be considered innocent until proven guilty.

Even then, there may be mitigating circumstances. Moreover, the public interest, which is central, would almost certainly be undermined by premature disclosure. That doesn't mean that it won't happen, just that it shouldn't.

The form of words used in the report also points to another conclusion. Namely, that what was happening was not known throughout the bank. This is important for a number of reasons.

The words "certain staff and management within certain areas of AIB..." suggest that there were serious deficiencies in communications and in procedures that prevented these breaches of compliance requirements being "fast-tracked" right to the top.

Mr Buckley stated yesterday that he himself was unaware of the overcharging. There is every reason to believe that this is the case. Firstly, this would have been the crucial question addressed by the two reports.

Secondly, because of the statement by IFSRA to a Dáil committee that "AIB, it must be said, has been very active and co-operative right up to board level in addressing this issue since it came to light. Their response includes a commitment to a full and speedy review of systems surrounding all of their charging issues."

The issue of whether the board should have known is a separate matter. What is clear, however, is that there was a major failure in internal controls as well as in the culture of "certain areas within the bank".

So when did they know?

Perhaps the most devastating finding of the report is that the non-compliance in respect of charges existed for almost eight years. An internal memo in 2002 identified the cost of dealing with the issue and the need to inform the regulator. Nothing happened.

All in all, there were at least seven opportunities for "certain staff and management in certain areas of AIB" to identify and/or disclose the breaches of compliance to the relevant regulators. It didn't happen.

Controls and procedures are a proxy – and not the greatest one – for a culture that both demands, and incentivises, compliance and the promotion of good practice. It requires a corporate ethos in which all staff are empowered to bring the values by which they strive to live their lives to the workplace – the office, the branch.

This takes us to the heart of the issue. Ireland has a principles-based regulatory system. IFSRA sets down high-level controls and codes of conduct – it is for the individual institution to comply not just with the letter of the law but also its spirit.

Indeed, what is at issue here is not simply compliance per se but, rather, "obedience to the unenforceable". The short-term shareholder value business model, which was pre-eminent up until recently, crowded out any such considerations. In the case of AIB, it is clear that ethical leadership from the top takes a considerable time to change mindsets, behaviour, and a whole way of thinking.

There is still a long way to go

The focus will now turn to disciplinary procedures which have to be informed, rigorous and impartial. The issue of whether or not IFSRA has sufficient sanctions at its disposal to prevent this deviant behaviour morphing into some other form is another key question.

Ultimately, Dr Liam O'Reilly was surely right in asserting that, notwithstanding its new powers, the real sanctions involve the costs of rectifying breaches of compliance and the reputational costs.

Customers will feel vindicated by the consumer-focused approach by IFSRA, including the remedial action that it has taken. Institutional investors will, no doubt, be relieved that Michael Buckley decided to stay on to put this episode to bed and allow his successor to start with a clean sheet.

Bank staff, whose integrity was highlighted by IFSRA in the Interim Report, will almost certainly feel that the rebuilding of trust is once again down to them. This powerfully reinforces the case for co-opting the IBOA on to the consultative panels. It is helping to rebuild trust, not alone within a single institution, but in an industry of crucial importance to the economy and to society. It deserves its place at the table.

This Article appeared in The Irish Times, December 2004.

Irish Banks Need to Win Back the Trust of Their Staff if They are to Succeed

The Irish banking sector is being undermined by the erosion of trust and a lack of respect for staff, according to Professor Ray Kinsella, who looks at what needs to be done to restore the balance between ethics and success.

The domestic based Irish banks and the wider financial services sector – of which they are core – have an importance to the economy that is not adequately captured by statistical data. Their contribution to employment is highly significant, not least because it is, at least in part, dispersed across the country as well as internationally. The Exchequer is also a major beneficiary more strategically – the IFSC alone generates €1 out of every €10 spent on our health system. Their delivery systems and electronic payments arrangements are the central nervous system of Ireland's highly open 'new economy', which underpins growth and also living standards.

In the early 1990s at least some of the banks lost the plot. They bought into a flawed and subversive business model based on maximizing short-term shareholder value. At the same time, in 1992 the banks and the Irish Bank Officials' Association (IBOA) engaged in a highly divisive strike. There were no winners. Banks felt empowered to initiate work, organisation and remuneration practices that have demonstrably led to a loss of value. Working relationships – and even hitherto close friendship – amongst staff were impacted.

Separately, and in combination, these developments established a highly negative dynamic within the organisations affected. Different 'initiatives' and change – programmes over the years were working against the grain of this dynamic. These inextricably bound-up events – a doomed business model and the bank strike – are the genesis of the 'legacy' issues, and other deficiencies, which culminated in the regulatory investigations in the first half of this year.

This investigative process, undertaken by the Irish Financial Services Regulatory Authority (IFSRA), as well as other departments and agencies in Ireland's new multi tiered regulatory process, will be concluded next month. The outcomes may be painful.

More positively, however, the conclusion of these regulatory investigations provides a wholly unique 'window of opportunity' to develop a new ethically-based business model – and a competitive advantage based on the reality, rather than the rhetoric, of trust and partnership.

The core intermediation function of banking rests on trust and integrity. They were the hallmark of the banking profession. Behind the big issue of the restoration of trust between banks and their customers, not alone in personal financial services but also (as the US' experience in recent years highlight) in investment banking, lies a still deeper issue.

This deeper issue has to do with the re-engineering of banks 'corporate culture' so that, for example, work/life balance, work organisation and systems of remuneration and promotion are determined, first and foremost, by the dignity of the individual person and the intrinsic value of work. People are not a 'resource', alongside capital or technology. The view that they are a 'cost' and, accordingly, disposable, is an expression of the corporate nihilism that is at the heart of this flawed business model. In purely commercial terms, no sustainable value proposition could possibly be based on this view of the individual. It would– and has been – found out by smart consumers, operating in a competitive and efficient set of markets, who have options.

If banks expect customers to trust them, this carries with it an acknowledgment of their duties and responsibilities to staff – which have to convey this trust to customers. Staff cannot communicate an ethic of trust in their relationship with consumers if this very ethic is missing in particular facets of their own work environment.

These are not just concepts trust is an integral part of a healthy societal culture and business models that do not comprehend, and act on, this are semi detached from their customer base. It is not realistic to seek to differentiate between values lived out behind your hall door, and those you are expected to work to behind your office door.

It is not possible to legislate for ethics, for behaviour, yes, not for ethics – which, by definition, involves 'obedience to the unenforceable'. The role of leadership is to demonstrate ethical standards that are then diffused throughout the organisation. The responsibility of leaders to get ethical standards involves a terrifying responsibility. People screw up. They make mistakes. It is the quest for ethics – and the processes by which this is pursued within organisations – that is important. Ethical standards are the 'building blocks' of any sustainable value proposition, and of a credible post-reform business model. It is these standards that will determine whether, or not, the corporate culture is aligned to engage with the consumer, on the basis of verifiable trust.

There is a very real understanding of ethics – and the overriding importance of lived truth in corporate strategy – within the leadership of Irish banking. But it would be naïve to underestimate the difficulties of changing 'legacy' attitudes and 'mindsets' embedded within– that is, in the guts of the organisation – or, indeed, of rooting out inequitable and, therefore, unethical practises that remain very much on the strategic agenda. It can be done. There are examples of institutions where trust is the oxygen that they breathe. They are successful. Quite simply, they bond with the customer – or, more specifically, staffs are *empowered* to bond with the customer. People like working in these institutions.

Reflecting new insights, as well as the impact of the successive disclosures, there has been a substantial effort by banks – in anticipation of prospective penalties and enforcement action – to come to grips with these issues. There has been a rebuilding of trust between banks and the industry body – the Irish Banking Federation (IBF) – and the IBOA.

It is precisely within this framework that what Professor Bill Roche has called 'second–generation' partnership models have an indispensable role to play. Different institutions will have different structures. And both the banks and the IBOA have their own mandate. But there is still a real identity of interest. There is now a unique 'window of opportunity' to push this model forward.

The publications of reports by IFSRA, and the conclusions of other investigations, which will be made public next month, will require, as never before, a partnership approach.

In the post-reform banking system customers will be back at the centre of a principles-based consumer protection supervisory regime. The challenge facing some financial institutions is that the kind of commitment on the part of staff which is imperative to give substance to the vision at the heart of reforms – including the primacy of the interests of the consumer – has been ground down.

These are not malcontents. These are professionals. And even with the genuine changes and the good intentions of bank management, many staff do not like what they see as part of their everyday working environment. It makes no sense whatever not to listen to them. And there is not enough listening going on.

They look at some aspects of micromanagement strategy – and they see a culture of target driven selling as a basis for performance assessment. But cross-selling, for example, retail banking with insurance type products should be about service enhancement – not incentivised pressure-selling. Just because it's legal, it doesn't mean it's ethical or aligned with a principles based consumer protection regime.

Staff listen to platitudes when a colleague takes early retirement – and they know it really counts for nothing. They know how justifiable promotions can get sunk without trace because the individuals are more valuable where they are. They know what every good branch manager knows – that performance metrics don't always measure the worth of a job well done. Expertise is, frequently, walking out the door – leaving a void in customer relations that is not easily filled and leads to loss of value. They know why it's getting harder to retain young staff, who never knew the concept of loyalty – which is hardly surprising, since loyalty is begat by trust.

They look at contract-based remuneration which is being extensively implemented – all very well in its own way – and they know that it can mean hours and weekends away from family with nothing to show for it. They see the dichotomy at the heart of the 80:20 mantra – how do you know who, of the 80, is going to make it into the 20? Sean Quinn once sold gravel from his back garden. You don't know – that's why ethics and good business practise both dictate that all customers be treated with equal respect.

That's why co-opting the IBOA to the distinguished IFSRA Consultative Panels would be more than a wise political decision. It's a strategic imperative, if we are to protect, and build on the domestic banks' contribution to the economy and to national competitiveness. It would show we had learned something over the last decade – and that the importance of trust had been recognised not alone in the political sphere but also in a core sector of the economy.

This Article appeared in Finance, November 2004.

Banks Face a Long Haul to Regain the Public's Confidence

It made no sense to enact legislation of such importance before the results of these reports became available...the IFSRA report is the start of a process that will affect the whole culture of banking in the State, writes Ray Kinsella.

The publication yesterday by the Irish Financial Services Regulatory Authority (IFSRA) of its first report on AIB's failure to report the rate used on certain foreign exchange transactions with customers, and the associated overcharging by the bank of these customers, represents the start of a process that will reshape the landscape of Irish banking.

The IFSRA report will be followed by the publication of additional reports, notably relating to the Faldor offshore scheme, operated to benefit a group of senior bank management during the first half of the 1990s. The bank has already commissioned an independent report, overseen by the former comptroller and auditor general, on these issues.

Then there is the NIB report of the High Court inspectors (the Blaney-Grace report), appointed by the Department of Trade, Enterprise and Employment under the Companies Acts, to inquire into certain commercial practices involving mischarges and the sale of offshore insurance-based products that subverted tax requirements.

This has now been completed and will be published on Friday. This series of reports will result in far-reaching changes in management practice, operational systems and in corporate culture. The issue of whether, and if so what, sanctions are applied is likely to attract attention. But more important over the longer term will be the specific criticisms that the individual reports make and their recommendations for changes. These will affect the whole culture of banking in the State.

The IFSRA report, published yesterday, details the nature and extent of overcharging, beginning with the foreign exchange charges debacle. Once an in-depth forensic investigation had begun, it was inevitable that additional examples of mischarging, albeit reflecting deficiencies in systems, would be identified.

The public, conscious of the successive examples of deficiencies, will understandably be cynical. At the same time, it would be wrong not to acknowledge the quality and depth of the response by AIB's board.

The scale, and voluntary nature of restitution to customers, the toughness and integrity of Dermot Gleeson and the obvious commitment by Michael Buckley to turn things around before his retirement next year were impressive.

A period of reflection is urgently needed when the reporting phase is completed – probably by early September, when the Dáil resumes sitting.

The Republic now has a wholly new model of regulation and enforcement within the banking and financial services sector encompassing not only IFSRA as the "lead regulator", but also the Department of Trade, Enterprise and Employment, Revenue, the Director of Corporate Enforcement as well as the Criminal Assets Bureau. This represents a wholly new dimension in terms of the environment within which banks operate and are regulated.

Against this background, the decision by the Oireachtas immediately before the recess to enact part two of the IFSRA legislation – which encompassed inter alia sanctions – was wrong. It made no sense whatsoever to enact legislation of such importance before the results of these authoritative reports became available.

The fact that the new legislation is not informed by the criticisms responses and proposals contained in the reports, is simply indefensible. It represents a lost opportunity for incorporating the lessons of what has been a major inflection point in the development of banking legislation, regulation and what constitutes "good practice".

There are now three "change forces" in play that will transform the culture and commercial practice of Irish banking. The first is the internal changes that have already taken place in all institutions, especially those under scrutiny. The second relates to the new statutory provisions and supervisory practices: more generally, to the principles-based mode of supervision at the heart of IFSRA. The third "change force" encompasses a much more informed set of customers, hardened by the impact of deficiencies within some banks, who can now avail of the benefits of a much more competitive environment.

The Irish banking system is of enormous economic importance, both to those who use it and to the wider economy. The single greatest challenge facing all of the key stakeholders is the need for the banks to win back legitimacy and trust in the eyes of consumers and of the wider public.

This will not be easy and it will be at the heart of what IFSRA almost certainly sees as a post-September "rehabilitative" phase. This restoration of legitimacy will hinge on whether or not banks have moved away from an obsession with maximising shareholder value to an ethics driven model encompassing a very different view of staff and, by extension, customers.

The short-term shareholder maximisation model has, in the Republic as in other countries, driven a stake through the heart of the legitimacy that the banks once enjoyed.

The core arguments of this model can be simplified to two propositions. The first relates to the internal cost of capital and the need to (re)allocate it accordingly. The second is the premise that costs (including, in particular, staff costs) have to be ruthlessly eliminated. The end-purpose is to continually maximise the value of the bank.

This is a superficial attraction. But it gets things the wrong way round. The whole process is directed to meeting the, literally, insatiable demands of shareholder institutions. It's not about engaging with the customer, except purely as a means to an end.

This business model generated perverse incentives and subverted the lives of staff. It created a culture in which the "legacy issues", that have now come back to haunt NIB and AIB, could flourish. It was never going to be sustainable.

A new business model has not been fully developed. But what is clear is that, while it may be initially at least top-heavy with compliance, its distinguishing characteristic is that it will be ethically driven. It will take as its starting point the fact that people – customers and staff – are at the heart of the model. In staff will be embedded the "knowledge equity" necessary to create sustainable value propositions and to engage with customers in an environment of trust. A process of culture change, across a number of dimensions, is now under way in AIB.

A divergence between the values that people live by behind their hall door and those that are inculcated behind office doors creates an ethical black hole at the very heart of the business model. Regulation and corporate governance is of little avail. There will be subversion of individuals and of good banking practice.

There is not much that the regulator can do about such a situation. It cannot enforce ethics. An ethical corporate culture, properly understood, involves, by its very nature, "obedience to the unenforceable".

There are now a number of key things that need to be done as we move towards a rehabilitative phase. These include:

1   Robust and transparent responses by the institutions to the criticisms raised in the reports, and which are additional to those that they have already undertaken. The response taken by the AIB board to the IFSRA report represents an encouraging start.

2   An ethically-based business model, which would provide a bridge to IFSRA's principals-based regulatory regime. This will take longer and will require the active participation of pension funds and large institutional investors. But it is essential to regaining legitimacy in the eyes of consumers.

3   A more proactive role by the industry as a whole – that is by the Irish Bankers Federation. Such a role needs to focus on unambiguously promoting "best practice" right across the spectrum of member institutions while recognising that at least some of these institutions have long had ethically-based principals as a cornerstone of their corporate philosophy.

4   The Irish Bank Officials Association has a key role to play in a business model that is focused on maximising the contribution of staff to value creation and which can help restore staff morale and public trust.

5   The role of IFSRA is to continue to provide the even–handed leadership which can steer the Irish banking sector through this critical period and, equally important, into a rehabilitative phase, where the public, through IFSRA, can be sure that adequate controls and systems are in place and that there is a high–calibre board to oversee compliance with the spirit, as well as the letter, of the law.

6   Communication with customers and the public is central to getting the message across that all "legacy issues" have been dealt with; that internal controls are rigorous and preclude the possibility of mischarging and that a culture of compliance underpins an ethically driven Irish banking system.

This will be the topic of a landmark conference in UCD involving major banks and regulators, domestic as well as international, that will be held at the end of September in order to facilitate this process of communication in an open and independent forum.

This Article appeared in The Irish Times, July 2004.

Banks Must Recover Confidence and Market Credibility in Order to Survive

Professor Ray Kinsella examines the development and strategy of Ireland's two largest banks in what he calls a 'watershed' year for Irish banking – 2002.

The year 2002 will, in retrospect, be seen as a watershed in the development of the Irish banking and financial sector. At the heart of a change process, that is still ongoing, was, firstly, the decision by AIB to sell Allfirst in exchange for a 22 per cent share in MNT bank and, following hard on the heels of this, the failure by Bank of Ireland to acquire Abbey National in the UK.

It is important to emphasise that developments at the two major retail banks were part of a more substantial transformation, in terms of both strategy and, also, organisational structures. The strong showing of First Active and more particularly the evident success of Irish Life and Permanent – through its acquisition of TSB – in creating a major bank assurance force (that may yet prove a springboard to overseas markets) – has substantially reconfigured the domestic banking franchise. Ulster Bank too has restructured itself. The entry of Bank of Scotland some two years ago had a catalytic effect on the market, showing that the Irish banking sector is, in fact, highly contestable and that this new reality must be built into margins and earnings projections.

Another development of landmark proportions was the establishment of the new Single Regulator. This will result in a greatly enhanced burden of compliance on all financial institutions.

But the real story of 2002 revolves around the developments at AIB Group and the Bank of Ireland. If you look at the banks' performance over the last number of years, some key points are evident:

• There has been, over the longer-term, a progressive rise in the P/E Ratio of the Irish banks.

• This is reflected in the respective share price of the banks. Taking, first, the period since 1986, both of the main groups have progressively strengthened compared to the wider markets.

• Taking a shorter-term perspective (based to 2000 A.D), the Irish banks have continued to outperform the wider markets. Bank of Ireland peaked in mid-2002 and declined subsequently, only to recover lost ground following the termination of its bid for Abbey National.

• AIB's structural problems to do with 'Allfirst' meant that they traded lower than Bank of Ireland, while still outperforming the financial sector as a whole.

Detail, of course, matters. But it's the big picture that is important here. Essentially, over the last decade or so the two main Irish banks have performed strongly relative to the markets.

More important, however, is that compared with what would, at the start of the 1990s, have been seen as a reasonable benchmark – Royal Bank of Scotland (RBS) – they have been left far behind. It is this strategy-driven 'performance gap' compared with RBS, that leaves them both vulnerable to predators. It also provides the focus for an evaluation of where they are at now and what is the key to their future performance.

The starting point for any evaluation is the reality that the 1990s was a period of wholly different – but equally successful – strategic development for both banks. Bank of Ireland, scarred from its experience in the United States in the 1980s – essentially withdrew back to its core domestic franchise. Pat Molloy was enormously successful at retrenching and reducing costs, and establishing a platform on which to build a new strategy. Equally, he steered the ship through what were very choppy waters – it would be easy to forget the courage that was required to commit capital to a subsidiary that continued to haemorrhage over an extended period and then to exit that market on reasonable terms.

This provided the basis for a strategic transformation of the Bank of Ireland into strong local/regional player with a wholly new strategy emerging from Lower Baggot Street with the decision to acquire Cheltenham & Gloucester. This provided a degree of both geographical and earnings diversification and signalled a return of confidence and sense of direction. Given the rapidly evolving nature of the mortgage market, it was hardly the most innovative use of capital. But it did provide a strong pointer to where the bank intended to position itself. And it provided the basis for the abortive bid for Abbey National: the latter was based on the logic of the board strategy, rather than being an individual initiative of its chief executive. In truth, it never looked like succeeding.

The decision by AIB Group to sell Allfirst for a 22 per cent stake in M&T Bank can be seen at a number of levels. To begin with, Berkshire Hathaway has a 5 per cent stake in M&T: market prescience provides a degree of comfort if you are going to do a deal such as this. At a more serious level, while continuing to provide albeit indirect exposure to the US market (and therefore a degree of income diversification), the sale of Allfirst marks the end of what will be seen by monetary historians as a highly successful strategically driven process of geographical expansion.

One example is the 'Case Study' quality of AIB's market entry strategy into Poland. Whatever the future earnings capability post-EU enlargement, the execution of the entry into the Polish market was masterful. The building up and consolidation of AIB's US holdings, which were rebranded in 1998 under the Allfirst banner, was driven by a commitment to compete head on with the emergence of the 'super-regionals' by acquiring scale, notably through the acquisition of Dauphin in 1997.

The decision in 2002 to effectively exit the US market turns that strategy on its head. In terms of strategy, has the Allfirst debacle, and its subsequent sale, brought the global expansion strategy of AIB to a juddering halt?

Keynes famously remarked when asked why he changed his opinions relatively frequently, 'When circumstances change, I alter my conclusions. What do you do, Sir?' Circumstances have changed in terms of the fundamentals of both credit and capital markets and, also, in terms of the type of business model that is appropriate in these changed circumstances. We have seen, for example, the Citigroup beginning, perhaps, to unwind. Equally, there is a silent, largely unnoticed, but enormously significant shift happening – particularly at the corporate level which must have a bearing on the future strategies of both banks. The growth of the capital markets, in all of its dimensions, is leading to a process of 'adverse selection' with regard to the credit markets and to even medium–sized banking institutions. This is a logical starting point for any bank seeking long-term sustainable competitive advantage. It is where we are at in terms of the continually evolving market paradigm. The proposed Abbey National deal lacked conviction. Equally, the decision by AIB Group to reverse what was clearly a long-term strategy would certainly appear to reflect a view that a relatively painless exit from a prospectively difficult situation was preferable to a strategy requiring both commitment and not a little courage.

In both instances, the fear must be of a possible lack of confidence and how best to define and bring forward a new strategy adapted to the changed circumstances. The domestic franchise of both banks is now more important than ever. The market is more competitive and aggressive: margins notably in the mortgage market which is the main driver of domestic credit expansion are much narrower. Against this background, the recent experience of both AIB Group and Bank of Ireland highlight a number of key features in terms of developing a new strategy adapted to greatly changed circumstances both domestically, across the EU and within global markets.

• Neither bank has yet begun to effectively leverage their internal intellectual capital– their 'knowledge equity'.

•Two practical examples may help in making this point. Successive cost–cutting retirement packages are in danger of creating an 'experiential anorexia' within middle management ranks and, more important, in the crucial personal interface with the customer. It is simply not enough to cut out large tranches of over-50s in the drive to reduce costs. Nor has this process been as effectively handled – in terms of organisational learning– as it might. For example, why are certain people taking the 'package' on offer and going? How far does this leave a gap in the banks overall capability – particularly within its crucial domestic franchise? To what extent, for example, have there been 'exit polls' carried out in order to generate some insights into how the culture of the banks could be enhanced. It is possible to say, on good authority, that there is an uninformed 'revolving door' policy of experience out and lower cost workers in that will run counter to the importance of sustainability.

•A second example of the failure to exploit internal 'knowledge equity' can be illustrated from some personal experience. What some initial research strongly points to is that the 'average' branch falls far short, in terms of its earnings generating capability, of what can be called a 'composite' branch: that is, a 'best case' branch within the individual group (which makes it very attainable) – a branch which combines responsiveness, sensitivity to, an empowerment of, staff as well as productive use of management resources. This gap may be of the order of 30–40 per cent. This represents an enormous loss of earnings opportunities. Addressing this gap beats the hell out of short-term cost cutting.

A final point which must be factored into a new strategic direction for the banks relates to the whole issue of the compliance/ethical challenges. There is, as already noted, a whole new regulatory structure – and also a market discipline – that will impel banks to address the issue of ethics – not just in terms of Codes of Practice, important as these are, but of an objective ethical code and understanding of what this implies in terms of management practice. Banks with strong corporate cultures have always had, not just a culture of 'compliance' or even of good 'citizenship' but an ethos that resonates with the Central Bank's 'fit and proper' test.

In retrospect, the 1990s will be seen as a golden period, not alone for the Irish economy but for the Irish financial sector which was, in many ways, at the cutting-edge. This has now changed. The indications are that if either or both of the banks are to survive this will require a recovery in terms of confidence and composure as well as market credibility. The banks will have to address existing internal weaknesses – as well as their undoubted strengths, which were highlighted during the 1990s – as a necessary basis for developing forward-looking strategies.

This Article appeared in Finance, October 2002.

US Fraud a Product of Sickness at Heart of Corporatism

The reported $4 billion accounting fraud at WorldCom will be seen as a major changing point in global corporate management and regulation. The obsession of maximising, at all cost, shareholder value – within a culture that esteems the next quarter's earnings as more important than long-run sustainability of the business, is both flawed and untenable. There are no obvious answers. But the G8, which is meeting in Canada, had better start thinking long and hard about the issue.

The WorldCom debacle is considerably larger than that which brought down Enron. WorldCom has shed 17,000 people. Now the future of the company is in the balance. Investors – including those managing major pension funds – have seen that value of their shares fall from over $60 in 1999 to some 30 cents. What we are talking about here is not economics. Nor are we talking about the volatility of financial markets. This would be off the wall if it weren't so catastrophically damaging to the world economy.

There are important differences between the manipulation of off-balance sheet vehicles that was at the heart of the Enron crisis and the massive mis-statement of WorldCom's profits that is the immediate cause of the WorldCom crisis. But they have much in common, most obviously the deficiencies in auditing practice – and in the corporate culture that facilitated and indeed incentivised these deficiencies.

The reaction of global stock-markets to WorldCom nails down the markets' belief that Enron and WorldCom are not isolated events. They are the product of a sickness at the heart of global corporatism. It is spreading – and the collateral damage cannot yet be estimated. There are, of course, many multi-national companies that are managed with great integrity. But the wider culture in which they operate militates against these virtues. And a process of contagion, which has been triggered by Enron and now reinforced by WorldCom, does not discriminate very well – at least in the short term– between the good, the bad, and the very, very ugly. The first casualty is a lack of confidence in the system.

There are a number of reasons why the WorldCom crisis has – finally – brought us to this point in global corporatism. The WorldCom crisis is a massive shock to the new economy and to the global business environment. Ireland and other small open economies are right in the firing line.

It simply should not be possible for multinational companies to play fast and loose with accounting standards. In reality, the standard-setters are continually playing catch-up – or being ignored. Most important is the fact the auditing profession, which in a number of countries, including Ireland, is an integral part of the formal regulatory process has been found wanting – not all of them of course. But the action of the few has corroded confidence, with all of the knock-on damage that is now evident in company valuations and, by extension, investment capability.

All of the recent evidence resonates with the dance of death by some investment analysts, stressed-out management and institutional investors around the culture of maximising shareholder value: of optimising, manipulating quarterly earnings and short-term market value.

In the wake of the Enron debacle, the Bush administration set-out a series of proposed reforms, aimed at strengthening corporate governance as well as accounting and auditing practices. But with this latest debacle, we are well past the stage where any 10-point plan would be regarded as remotely credible. This is a problem embedded in the bowels of the present corporate culture and it is not going away without radical surgery. It is a global problem and neither regulatory practice nor corporate governance have yet adapted to the global business environment and to the enormous collateral damage that is transmitted through failures such as those of WorldCom.

The large institutional investors must have a much more active role to play – within a more formal system that is closely monitored. Better regulation is imperative. But delivering that better regulation within a fragmented EU regulatory system is a major challenge. More regulation is not the answer. Quite the contrary, it simply highlights the new rules of the game that are there to be shot at by would-be "successful" corporates.

The real issues to be addressed have to do with the shareholder-driven corporate culture, which is rooted in greed. At the risk of overstating, the shareholder value paradigm is redundant. Think about it. Over the last century, we have moved through a series of economic models. We have never seriously questioned the system of ethics that should be the custodian of these models – including the present global market-based economy, within which is embedded a new set of responsibilities that are quite alien to the mid-20th Century model.

The former managing director of Lazard Freres and former US ambassador to France, Mr Felix Rohatyn, was right when he recently pointed out that "ultimately rules are no substitute for ethics...will turn out to be more than a moral imperative: it will turn out to be good business". If we are to seriously address the issues raised by Enron and WorldCom this is a first, and necessary, starting point.

This Appeared article in The Irish Times, June 2002.

Section Two:

The Limits of Corporate Governance

Time for Imagination in Framing Corporate Governance Legislation

In dealing with corporate malaise, we need to go beyond concepts of proper behaviour and think of 'The Common Good', writes Ray Kinsella

The Irish Association of Investment Managers is a highly credible representative body which carries out an important function. It monitors the behaviour of quoted companies on whose value, jobs and living standards are, to a considerable degree, dependent.

Its recent criticism of the board of one of Ireland's largest companies – DCC – has to be taken seriously. At the heart of the criticism is the decision by the board to continue to support its chairman notwithstanding the adverse outcome of a highly complex and protracted civil case. The action of the IAIM is much more than a case of "shareholder activism", it is considered and without precedent.

Corporate governance is a relatively new form of self-regulation of the corporate sector. It deals with high–level controls and with the integrity of procedures, information and values by which a company is managed. The combined code of best practice is the gold standard with which large listed companies are expected to comply.

It is not a prescriptive set of rules. It is much more to do with the ethos of the company the values by which it operates. These are underpinned by the key concept of "stewardship", namely, that the assets of the company managed by individual directors at the board table should be passed on in as good a shape – hopefully better – as when they themselves were entrusted with the responsibility of managing them.

It is an onerous responsibility: jobs, the economy, the interests of employers, pensioners and other stakeholders and the wider common good all hinge on the quality of this stewardship.

The rush to judgment should be resisted. It is wrong in itself, and particularly where not all of the facts are known. Nor is it conducive to fair outcomes.

In the present instance involving DCC and its now-resigned executive chairman Jim Flavin, there are a number of factors which would appear to be incontrovertible.

The first is the outcome of the civil case, which has been extensively deconstructed.

The second is the fact that the Irish Association of Investment Managers has deemed it necessary to intervene publicly in the matter

The third is the fact that DCC's directors are experienced and, it must be assumed, ethical individuals. There is no indication whatsoever that they had an interest in supporting the position they had taken unless they were convinced of its rightness.

Finally, the regulatory framework, and particularly the office of the Director of Corporate Enforcement, appears constrained in taking the lead in resolving the matter.

The dispute is damaging to the company and to trust in the corporate sector. It needs to be resolved and lessons need to be learned. It will not be resolved by more legislation, much less by regulation.

It may be the that the Consolidated Companies Act which is scheduled to find its way before the Dáil in 2009 will set out a way of dealing with issues such as this. But I doubt it. On the other hand, the very fact that the issue is being discussed is indicative of a shaking off of the corporate malaise which mirrors the heart of darkness at the centre of the credit crises.

But there is a possible way forward – not necessarily in this case, though it may provide some pointers. In brief, in redrafting Irish company law, as well as in the teaching of corporate governance, we need to consider reaching out beyond the narrow concepts of behaviour and motivation within which our existing mindset is fixed. Three examples will make this clear.

There is a very rich body of literature centred on 'The Common Good', which reflects the Christian approach to business, and a very practical one it is. Had the "masters of the universe" who precipitated such carnage on the financial markets even a passing acquaintance with the teachings of the Koran, then the world economy would be in a much more stable position than is currently the case.

For Orthodox Jews, the first question they will be asked when they confront their Creator is: "How did you conduct your business affairs?" The Torah and also the Talmud provides an astonishingly prescriptive and detailed guide to conducting business affairs not alone in terms of the law, but more importantly the principle of the law. Tsedek (fairness and justness) and Chessed (goodness) provide the foundation for all business activities within Judaism. They require that one follow not alone the letter of the law, but also its spirit of the law (*Lifnim Mishurat Hadin*).

In the UK, the former archbishop of Canterbury was roundly criticised for suggesting that British Law should take account of the moral principles of other cultures. Such criticisms were wholly wide of the mark. We need to give consideration to what can be learned from other faith traditions which seek to grapple with issues such as preserving the good name of the individual, while at the same time preserving the integrity of the corporate world.

In framing the consolidated company law, the parliamentary draftsmen might find it useful to read widely and think bravely.

This Article appeared in The Irish Times, May 2008

Fragmentation of International Regulatory Governance and the Case for a Single Global Financial Regulator

The Presentation set-out below was developed for an International Conference in November 2000. It highlighted the extent of the fragmentation in global regulation that existed at the time. It also highlighted the fact that this fragmentation left the global system open to the impact of a series of Risks– and the possibility that these risks might combine in what would later be called a Black Swan event. It urged the case for a global financial regulator. The 'Black Swan' event duly appeared in Autumn 2007, which is widely regarded as the beginning of the global financial crisis – though of course the roots were already firmly in place by then. It is included in this set of readings in its original form because the case that it makes: that global regulatory governance is highly fragmented, and that this leaves the system as a whole vulnerable to shocks, has been vindicated and remains one of the most important challenges for global regulatory authorised and governments.

Fragmentation of International Regulatory Governance and the Case for a Single Global Financial Regulator

Professor Ray Kinsella,
Director ,
Centre for Insurance Studies
U.C.D Graduate School of
Business.

Paper presented to **Geneva Association Conference,** organised by JBA/Centre for Insurance Studies, Graduate School of Business, University College Dublin (UCD), Nov 2000

The Rationale for International Financial Regulation

- To offset, or mitigate, 'Market failure' in national/global financial systems and the resultant negative impacts on international trade and investment
- The still 'special' role of banks within the global financial sector and the need to protect depositors funds.
- Increased institutional linkages (Banc Assurance/Conglomerates) between Banks and other financial institutions.
- Risks of cross-border 'contagion'.
- Negative impact of a financial crises on national/international macro-economic conditions
- Need to protect integrated international system against fraud and the consequent increased likelihood of failure.
- Regressive nature of welfare costs associated with a systemic crises in the international financial sector, particularly developing and transitional economies
- Informational asymmetry as between financial institutions, and consumers, in an increasingly distance-independent (electronic) environment and the resultant need to protect consumers.

Context of Global Regulatory Developments

- Increased trade globally in financial services, reflected in capital market activity.

- Increased M & A - driven concentration in Insurance and Banking, with bigger potential impact of failure.

- Increased competition in Insurance and Banking and emergence of new paradigm.

- Increased contestability of market and entry of new non-traditional providers.

- Technology- driven innovation of markets and exchanges.

- Growth in offshore financial services trade.

- Secular decline in the influence and regulatory capability of Central Banks, including their capacity to prevent, or mitigate, 'market failure'.

- Fragmentation of global regulatory and supervisory responsibilities and a correspondingly increased reliance on ad hoc responses to 'market failure' and 'contagion'.

Objectives of Regulators

- Protect depositors funds.

- Prevent, or help contain, 'contagion' spreading across national boundaries.

- Mitigate welfare costs associated with financial crises.

- Enhance market discipline, including improved risk management, promote competition and the strengthening of the global financial system.

- Strengthen consumer protection, including adaptation to new net-based delivery systems.

- Protect the integrity and efficiency of the global financial sector against existing and emerging threats, in particular against criminal and technological subversion.

Regulatory Instruments

Rules-Based	Market-Based
• Capital requirements, including the 2001 BIS proposals.	•Increased transparency of institutions and exchanges.
• EU Insurance solvency requirements.	•Better access by investors to data, including institutions projections.
• Lender of last resort arrangements.	
• ALM based requirements.	•Widening of mandatory disclosure requirements.
• Deposit Insurance.	
• Corporate Governance.	•Incorporation of authoritative rating agencies into surveillance.
• Internal Controls.	
• "Stress Testing" of Balance Sheets.	•Voluntary Codes of Practice.
• Technical Standards in, inter alia, taxation .and accounting.	•Incentivization for the development of a 'culture of compliance' within institutions.
	•Greater accountability to all stakeholders.
These rules incorporate EU Directives well as technical requirements developed within the BIS and in consultation with other regulatory bodies. They also incorporate Codes of Practice and Key Principles, developed as a result of international co-operation among supervisory bodies. In addition, in Islamic banking, there are specific rules requirements, based on the Holy Quoran,with which banks must comply.	Market- based developments include 'Best of World' credit evaluation (including credit scoring), Corporate Governance which go with the grain of, or reinforce, good regulatory and supervisory practice, Risk Metrics including Value at Risk, and *objectively*-based (business) ethics programmes.

Fragmentation of International Regulatory Governance
Key Issues:

- Regulators playing 'catch up' in a rapid transition to a complex, 'New Globalized Economy, characterised by innovation, market volatility and uncertainty.

- Regulatory 'Gaps' in global financial system.

- Demonstrable evidence of 'contagion' (e.g. Russian default and Asian crises of the late 1990's).

- **Lack of robust and properly mandated global system of regulatory governance, adapted to new financial services environment.**

- Secular increase in the role of Capital Markets.

- Disintermediation is impacting on the quality of banks (corporate) loan book and quality of earnings.

- Difficulty of maintaining a balance between, on the one hand, the 'Public Good' arguments for regulation and, on the other hand, acknowledging the limits to intervention and the superiority of market discipline to encourage "Best of World" practise.

- Priority for the IMF to reform its role (post-Meltzer commission) as the primary global financial markets regulatory authority, with the necessary degree of political autonomy (as per the U.S. Fed and the E.C.B) and the capacities and policy instruments to carry out this role.

Challenges

- Alternative Risk Transfer (ART) represents a new paradigm, which is breaking down barriers between banking and (re) Insurance. Catastrophe Insurance, while offering attractive uncorrelated risk diversification opportunities for banks, may also generate highly 'binary' risk.

- This paradigm includes new methodologies for Risk pricing (risk diversification Vs actuarial)

- Disintermediation is leading to 'adverse selection' against banks potentially weakening their risk profile and the prospective robustness of their balance sheet.

- Increased levels of concentration in insurance and banking points to a higher impact/consequences of failure.

- Threat of technological subversion as delivery shifts to a net-based systems.

- Primacy of 'Share holder value' model skews the system towards short-termism and is not sustainable.

Structural Threats to Insurance Markets

•Capacity pressure on traditional insurers, with the emergence of a new market paradigm (including ART).

• Traditional insurers have not yet made the transition to the new, ART driven market paradigm.

• Breaking down the boundaries between banking, (RE) insurance and capital markets, with traditional banking in secular decline, under the pressure of disintermediation and 'adverse selection'.

• Increased market concentration in insurance/banking and associated 'conglomerates' risks.

•Pivotal role of capital markets, whose scale, biological complexity and sensitivity is increasingly beyond the control of authorities.

• Developments in global insurance.

• Switch out of traditional products to equity markets. Resultant 'weight of money'in search of higher returns, is reinforcing the linkage between investor expectations, actual (and latent) financial crises and macroeconomic 'shocks'.

• New risks, which are inherently difficult to predict and price these include:

- Bio-ethical (including genome-related which pose major ethical threats, for which financial institutions are almost wholly unprepared)

- Environmental

- Organisational (technological subversion)

On the Positive Side...

1. Structural reforms, including closures, recapitalisations, and "debt workouts" in countries with weakened financial sectors, have helped strengthen the systems.

2. 2001 Basle capital adequacy proposals are a comprehensive and robust response to latent banking risk.

3. Increased supervisory, co-operation (including agreement on 'Core Principles') and co-ordination between banking   insurance and securities.

4. Lessons drawn by international organisations - including IMF, BIS and OECD - from recent systemic crises.

5. Europe (EU) now constitutes a major capital/banking market 'bloc', with increased access to liquidity and new market opportunities.

On the Positive Side Continued

6.   Growth and integration of global economy, driven by investment in new technologies and increased trade.

7.   Improved risk metrics, to measure and manage VAR, within banks.

8.   Increased emphasis by markets (including Fund Managers) on Corporate Governance, including transparency to market, accountability and internal controls.

9.   Consolidation within banking and insurance may lead to greater cost efficiencies, investment in new delivery systems (thereby increasing competition/contestability, and a more stable transition to disintermediation).

Institutional Threats

- Failure to develop robust international supervisory arrangements whilst operating in an environment of increasing uncertainty.

- Increasingly apparent deficiencies - regulatory 'gaps' in the global governance of converging financial markets, exchanges which are demutualizing and global short-term focussed financial institutions; all of which are on an experiential growth trajectory.

- The absence of an internationally - mandated international organisation, (i.e a reformed I.M.F) capable of dealing in a 'holistic' manner with financial crises: compare this with the current ad hoc, often fortuitous, interventions to stem 'contagion'/market-failure (e.g. in the case of LTCM)

- **Progressive erosion, and secular decline, in the monetary and supervisory influence of national central banks. Hence, the pivotal importance of <u>global</u> regulatory arrangements.**

- The 'Yeats syndrome': "things fall apart, the centre cannot hold".

- Increased delegation of authority by formerly centralised supervisory institutions e.g. increased reliance on lawyers, accountants and actuaries, who now play a quasi-official role in supervisory process.

- Diffusion of prudential regulation by incorporating responsibility for consumer protection within the mandate of 'single financial regulators'.

- Diffusion blurs the focus of prudential regulators (in particular, those with monetary policy responsibilities), who are already over - stretched by credit/capital market innovation affecting Banking and Insurance and security trading as well as organisational threats to prudential stability.

- Absence of a simple, and technically efficient (including liquidity support), regulatory (prudential) mandate within the European Central Bank (ECB) and incorporated within the European Treaties.

- Increased co-operation of international supervisory authorities - banking, securities and insurance - as a 'second -best' response to the latent instability of the emerging global financial markets process.

- The prospective 'death of money' and the inherent difficulties of applying 'public good' arguments to dematerialised commercially-driven e-money.

Behavioural Threats

- Negative sum-game of short-termism amongst global fund managers.

- Primacy of pure Shareholder Value (S.V) among an increasingly concentrated   set of global institutions is deeply flawed at both a conceptual and behavioural level.

- The "Vision Gap": a rigorous and <u>credible</u> development of shareholder value, which would generate <u>sustainable</u> ethical (human capital is now the key 'national resource') corporate and global development.

- Ad hoc migration of supervisory focus from numerical/accountancy-based systems to a process characterised by an increasing reliance upon corporate governance and, also, ethics: the objective (moral) basis of which have not been defined, much less agreed.

Threats to Global Financial Stability:

The 'Leverage Effects':

1. Threats

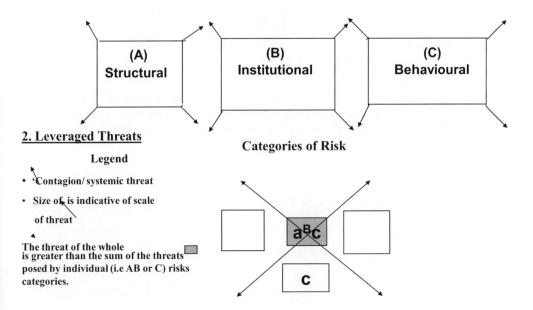

2. Leveraged Threats

Categories of Risk

Legend

- 'Contagion/ systemic threat
- Size of is indicative of scale
  of threat

The threat of the whole
is greater than the sum of the threats
posed by individual (i.e AB or C) risks
categories.

Behavioural Threats

- Negative sum-game of short-termism amongst global fund managers.

- Primacy of pure Shareholder Value (S.V) among an increasingly concentrated set of global institutions is deeply flawed at both a conceptual and behavioural level.

- The "Vision Gap": a rigorous and credible development of shareholder value, which would generate sustainable ethical (human capital is now the key 'national resource') corporate and global development.

- Ad hoc migration of supervisory focus from numerical/accountancy-based systems to a process characterised by an increasing reliance upon corporate governance and, also, ethics: the objective (moral) basis of which have not been defined, much less agreed.

Mandate of a Single Global Financial Regulator

- To prevent, or mitigate, 'market failure' in the efficient operation of global financial services institutions, markets and exchanges.

- To work, on the basis of subsidiary, with national and multilateral regulatory bodies.

- To encourage and facilitate *the highest standards of supervisory practice*, based on *technical excellence* and *competitiveness,* in providing supervisory services to financial service providers.

- To assist in the development of minimum required supervisory standards across all national markets taking account of cultural requirements (e.g. Islamic Banking)

- To provide an international ' lender of last resort' facility- providing short-term liquidity as a response to possible 'contagion', backed up by conditional financing linked to   the reform of the financial systems and the wider economy.

- To develop 'early warning' systems which might indicate incipient financial crises, including possible Cross-border effects,by means of market surveillance and independent evaluation of national financial markets.

- To monitor the compliance of 'designated'[1] institutions with capital adequacy and solvency requirements and, in this regard, to facilitate and, where appropriate, complement the work of national authorities (including the ECB)

[1] 'That is, 'designated' by the single Global Regulator IFRA (in consultation with the relevant 'Home Country') as meeting specific criteria - including size, global reach and complexity of products traded an in which material failures could be expected to have systemic effects.

• To facilitate and incentive the maximum participation of private financial markets and institutions in the reduction of actual or incipient/latent Crises, including, in particular, debt scheduling.

• To undertake and facilitate research into the causes, and appropriate responses to , 'market failure' in the international financial system.

• To monitor the development, and regulatory implications, of electronic (non-central bank) money and to make recommendations to the membership and to other regulatory force.

• To provide a comprehensive regulatory oversight- including intervention where appropriate - of securities exchanges and payments/clearing systems, taking account of the need for competition between exchanges/systems and innovation and, also, the 'public interest' in preventing or mitigating the negative impact of deficiencies in the operation of such systems.

• To work with national authorities and international regulatory bodies to develop an appropriate regulatory and supervisory arrangements for global financial conglomerates.

Multiplicity of Regulators: Overlap and Fragmentation

1. Some Existing Fora

INTERNATIONAL ORGANISATION OF SECURITIES COMMISSIONS

| EU HIGH LEVEL SECURITIES | EU BANKING ADVISORY COMMITTEE | EU INSURANCE COMMITTEE | ESBB BANKING SUPERVISION (MT) |

UCITS CONTACT GROUP

BASLE COMMITTEE ON BANKING SUPERIVISON

FINANCIAL STABILITY FORUM

COMMITTEE ON GLOBAL FINANCIAL SYSTEMS

INTERNATIONAL ASSOCIATION OF INSURANCE SUPERVISORY

FORUM OF EUROPEAN SECURITIES COMMISSIONS

3. Single Global Regulator:

INTERNATIONAL FINANCIAL REGUALTORY AUTHORITY

Ireland Inc's Policeman Needs Practical Support

Republic, as a highly trade–dependent economy, must guard its strong reputation Office of the Director of Corporate Enforcement requires more staff to fulfil its dual role of enforcing rules and raising standards, writes Ray Kinsella.

The Office of the Director of Corporate Enforcement (ODCE) plays a key role in overseeing, and enforcing, compliance with Company law in Ireland. It is, in effect, both the policeman of Ireland Inc, while also playing a central role in educating Company Directors, accountants and auditors in the increasingly complex field of corporate compliance.

For the past two years, the ODCE, which presently has a staff of some 40 officials, has been making the point that its existing staffing levels are 'wholly inadequate' in the light of current activities and prospective challenges. Information obtained by RTE's Business Correspondent Christopher McKevitt, under the FOI, show that it has, so far, met with very limited success from its parent Department (the DETE) and, ultimately, of course, Merrion Street. The numbers are not large. Mr Paul Appleby – the Director of the ODCE – has sought an additional 20 staff, over 2 years. He has been offered eight.

The correspondence released under the FOI is, it should be said, courteous, professional, and clearly driven by the current embargo on Public Sector employment. However, what appears at first sight to be merely a fairly routine negotiation on staffing levels is, in reality, of very great significance to Ireland's International reputation as a location for inward investment, and to the competitiveness of our indigenous companies.

The real significance of the material obtained by Mr. McKevitt is that it demonstrates a lack of insight into just how much the corporate world has changed post–Enron, and the priority which reputable– and therefore robust– businesses attach to compliance. It also demonstrates how the Public Interest in compliance, corporate regulation and standard–setting, can be held hostage to an implacable blunt policy instrument– in this case, an embargo.

It is true that the future fiscal burden associated with an increase of over 100,000 in the Public Sector between 2000 and 2005, is an important factor in achieving *sustainable* high levels of employment and growth. But Leadership is not always best demonstrated in 'holding the line'. Occasionally, flexibility, in response to compelling evidence-based arguments, is the better option. This is just such a case.

The ODCE was established in 2001 against the backdrop of a perceived culture of 'non– compliance' within parts of Ireland Inc. Together with the Auditing and Accounting Standards Boards, and underpinned by the Company Law Reform Group; it was a commendable response by the DETE to the fall-out from the Enron, World Com and other corporate scandals of the late 1990s.

Its mandate is to ensure compliance with the provisions of Company Law and, where necessary, to enforce these standards through prosecution and other sanctions. It monitors the role of auditors, liquidators and receivers in company insolvencies. More generally, it ensures both timely information, through disclosures and, in doing so, enhances the efficiency of our market-based economic model.

Arguably, one of its most important functions, in terms of changing the change in Ireland's corporate mind-set, is its educational role. In a letter to the former Minister for the DETE, back in May 2005, Mr Appleby makes the compelling point that 'we want to help the vast majority of company Directors, and others, comply voluntarily with their legal obligations. But we also need to insure that the minority that seek to evade their responsibilities are brought to account so that the market is aware that non-compliance carries significant risks.' Its most recent Annual Report demonstrates both its success in prosecuting its case as well as in raising the awareness of all of its key stakeholders in the importance of compliance.

There is another vitally important point which has been overlooked and merits highlighting. The ODCE is a crucial component in an entirely transformed regulatory landscape in Ireland.

The Financial Regulator, whose Principles-based model is in sharp contrast to the over-prescriptive and fragmented US system, and its top-heavy UK counterpart, played an indispensable role in even-handedly steering the Irish Banking System through the catharsis of 2004.

Equally, the Criminal Assets Bureau broke new ground internationally in terms of its focus, its extraordinary flexibility, and its effectiveness in combating criminal activity.

The Competition Authority has been vigorous in addressing anti–Trust activities that subvert the efficient and transparent operation of open and competitive markets.

The important point is that, compared with, say, 5 years ago, Ireland now has a 'joined–up and innovative regulatory system'.

It needs to be acknowledged that compliance does not come cheap. It represents a burden on business and one which, ultimately, impacts on the consumer. It would be facile to argue that we have achieved the right balance between, on the one hand, the highest levels of compliance, and, on the other hand, the imperative of minimising the already very considerable burden that this represents.

What we do have, however, is an integrated system that has changed our corporate culture, and has proved highly cost effective. This demonstrably applies to the ODCE, which currently manages on a budget of €5 million, and whose effectiveness of the wider system of which it a part. This system makes a statement about our corporate values. It constitutes the platform upon which Ireland, as a highly trade-dependent economy, can engage internationally on the basis of a strong reputation. Its effective operation is central to national competitiveness.

For all of these reasons, and because it would be entirely consistent with the spirit which is evident in the FOI correspondence that Mr Appleby will, and very soon, obtain the additional staff resources he requires.

However, all the regulation in the world will never guarantee the kind of ethical behaviour, be it in the personal, the public or the corporate sector, to which we aspire. Progress towards this objective requires that we dig deeper still. The roots of the implosion of corporate standards in the United States – and elsewhere – in the 1990s and early 2000s are to be found in a wholly flawed short-term Shareholder Value driven business-model. For all its ostentatious greed, it was always a dead man walking, and so it proved to be.

In the 'new Ireland', where money is increasingly the measure of 'success', and of the value of the human Person, all of the regulation and compliance in the world will not safe-guard us from the collateral impact of this mind–set on business. There is little point to looking to Mr. Appleby and his counterparts to solve this problem.

But we could do a lot worse than reflect on the fact that Ethical business values are at the heart of not alone the Qur'an – and the new wave of Islamic Finance that is now a major force in global capital markets – but also the fact that the first question that is asked of every Jewish business person when they die is 'did you conduct your business affairs honestly?' That's tougher than – but actually at the basis of – all systems of regulation and compliance.

This Article appeared in the Irish Times, March 2007.

Banks Must Rely on Ethical and Innovative Policies to Retain Their Independence

If the takeover of AIB by M&T Bank had gone ahead, it would have had far–reaching and certain consequences, writes Prof Ray Kinsella.

The ownership of major domestically-based institutions matters. Even in a world of integrated globalised financial markets, including increasingly concentrated cross-border institutions, there is an intuitive acknowledgement that the takeover of a major domestic retail bank has far-reaching implications, not alone for customers, but also for public policy.

The disclosure that the board of AIB gave serious consideration to a takeover of the bank by the US based M&T Bank has serious implications.

AIB have been swift to point out that the proposal, which came before the board last autumn, was simply part of a wider strategic review. In a world of intensive pressure on banks to deliver ever-increasing shareholder value, and which is merciless in its retribution on those who fail to do so, keeping all options open is imperative.

It doesn't mean it is sensible – it's just the way things are.

Nonetheless, the fact that the proposal was brought before the board, and at a time when the bank was immersed in the travails of investigations related to over-charging and of the illegal Faldor scheme which existed up to 1996, does concentrate the mind on a number of key issues.

Mainstream thinking highlights the benefits to consumers and to the wider economy of competition, not alone within the domestic environment, but across Europe. The Irish financial sector is highly open in terms of overseas participation. Recent entrants into the retail banking market have been welcomed.

In Ireland, what were the "associated banks" – the core retail clearing banks – grew up with the Irish economy. There was, until relatively recently, an implicate contract of benign oversight as a quid pro quo for a willingness on the part of the banks to lend a sympathetic ear to government initiatives. This contract was enforced by the enormous significance of the banking sector as a whole to the economy, which is still the case. The retail banks themselves employ some 30,000 people, and are a significant contributor to the Exchequer.

All of this bears on the issue of the likely impact of the proposal, had it been endorsed, for takeover of the AIB by M&T Bank.

Some consequences would have been certain. Firstly, there would have been a rationalisation and some downsizing – simply because this would have been built into the funding of the acquisition.

Secondly, the migration of strategy, and possibly key functions, from Ireland would have eroded the contribution by the bank to the domestic economy, and its potential leverage in regard to public policy.

Thirdly, the experience of New Zealand strongly suggests that foreign ownership of the core banking franchise reduces government scope for policy intervention.

Compared with the pre-internal market era, there is a wholly new set of parameters within which governments can operate in respect of safeguarding national banking systems from competition, including takeover.

Protectionism, under the guise of maintaining national champions in the public interest, is explicitly prohibited and rightly seen as subversive of the interests of consumers and of the wider economy.

It is, quite simply, a fact that overseas predators have "run the rule" over both AIB and Bank of Ireland. The possibility of a takeover of either or both is very real. Both banks now operate in a highly-contestable domestic market, with a number of rapidly-growing, domestically-based challengers, such as Irish Life Permanent TSB, as well as recent, and potential, entrants using a variety of traditional and e-based platforms for servicing both customers and new – value propositions.

It is in the interests of the Irish economy and the Irish consumer that at least part of the core domestic banking franchise remains in Irish hands. The example of both RBS and Bank of Scotland highlights the fact that a strong domestic platform can serve a base for significant overseas expansion, with real economic and reputational benefits. Such reputational benefits have a particular resonance for Ireland Inc, not least given the importance of the IFSC and the significance of Ireland as a high-quality location for foreign investment. For this to happen, both of the domestic banks need to take on board not just the rhetoric, but the reality, of a new ethically-based business model.

At the heart of the business model is the restoration of public trust based on a contract with the consumer, not just as an economic entity, but also as an individual.

There remain, for example, wholly anachronistic pockets of discrimination with regard to women customers. Equally important, both banks need to engage with all of their staff not simply on a contractual basis, but rather on the basis of a relationship with those individuals who, ultimately, are responsible for generating shareholder value. The Irish Bank Officials' Association has engaged in a constructive and robust relationship with bank management, and is deserving, not just of trust, but also of a place on the panels that are part of IFSRA's supervisory system.

146

The extent, manner and rationale of significant job-cuts in the case of Bank of Ireland, for instance, require justification that has not been forthcoming

This represents a weakness, not just in the bank's strategic objectives, but also in its capacity to secure itself from a prospective takeover bid from abroad.

It is important, and not just for shareholders, that AIB and Bank of Ireland regain a sense of confidence and direction. An ethically-based and forward-looking business model, operating within the context of significant opportunities generated by economic expansion, is the best guarantor of high performance and continued independence of AIB.

This Article appeared in The Irish Times, May 2005.

Section Three:

Regulation: National and International Perspectives

Changed landscape for financial service providers, consumers and Ombudsmen

Introduction

This crisis is wholly different, in nature and scale, to the cyclical fluctuations which tend to be characteristic of western capitalism. Economic projections by both national and international agencies, including the IMF, have consistently failed to keep pace with the precipitous decline in global growth and trade as a result of the crisis. The erosion of the balance sheets of financial institutions, in the face of a meltdown in market valuations, as well as unprecedented levels of volatility and grave political uncertainties, is without precedent. What makes it even more difficult is the 'feedback' loops between, on the one hand, the effects of 'skewed' macro-economic policies and, on the other hand, the effects of such policies on present and prospective financial stability.

In Ireland – to take just one example – the negative impact of the financial crisis on economic growth and, by extension, employment, living standards and the public finances, has been shockingly abrupt and brutal. Governments fiscal position, and in particular the decline in tax revenues relative to government expenditures, have translated directly into cuts in Public Services on a scale that is hardly conceivable. Ireland is not alone.

This crisis is therefore an inflection in modern history: its nature was such that it could neither be modelled nor firewalled. The true measure of the scale of the crisis is reflected not only in the devastation of lives, as economies continue to stall: notwithstanding the sheer scale of financial interventions by national authorities. These interventions include coordinated international action, including agreements at the recent G20 meeting in London – which have had little discernable effect so far in arresting the crisis.

Looking at the markets, there is, perhaps, a sense of quititude - but that is because they have fallen so far. In the US, unemployment will exceed 10% next year. Its deficit will be of the order of $1 ½ trillion.

In the new landscape, trust has evaporated, confidence is brittle and it not yet clear whether, or not, the nature and scale of Government intervention-which has turned ideologies inside-out and macro-economic policy upside – down – may not yet prove counterproductive. Institution-building – to seek to 'clean up' the mess and to develop regulatory responses – have not been thought through. We remain, for the most part, all at sea.

Root Causes

There is a reason for all of this. The root causes of this crisis are not primarily financial, or economic. Certainly it is possible to identify predisposing factors in these fields – as well as negative feedback effects, such as the impact of the 'Credit Crisis' reducing access by many smaller businesses to even normal financial resources. But these are in general symptomatic of a deeper reality.

The crisis is primarily ethical in nature, with inevitable financial, economic and political consequences. In an absence of a rigorous understanding of the ethical nature of this crisis, it is simply not possible to begin the process of transformation –globally or in Ireland-that is necessary to restore stability and sustainability to the markets. Perhaps I might develop this proposition- because if it is even approximately correct then it certainly impacts on your mandate and your responses to the causalities of the crisis.

Communism, as an ideology with a distinctive 'economic model', was based on Production and historical determinism. The human Person, shorn of the transcendence of being made in the image of-and being redeemed by – the 'Living God', was reduced to a unit of the proletariat. Communism imploded. At the same time, a form of Capitalism-based essentially on the 'Person as Consumer' and driven by what Galbraith, in his prophetic 'The Affluent Society', argued was a 'Wants', as opposed to a 'Needs'- based economy and one which was facilitated by semi-enforced financial indebtedness – gained ascendency in western developed democracies. The legacy endures-in the addiction to indebtedness, with all of the attendant consequences.

It was this form of 'Corporate Capitalism' that was encompassed in-and the key driver of- the 'short-term Shareholder Value' business model. It is this model – riddled with moral and economic contradictions – which has collapsed. This collapse has been catastrophic in its consequences. You see these consequences in your work. There is a news report, brought to my attention by my students: a middle-aged lady has been wiped out by guys 'just following the script' they were given – she is weeping softly to camera, almost in surprise 'they lied to me'

Both ideologies, with their specific 'Business Models', have much in common, which made their collapse both *inevitable* and *foreseeable*. They denied the existence of an objective moral order. They demeaned-and in a very real sense enslaved – the human Person. They had no reference point outside of their own Paradigm.

This, in fact, provides a necessary starting point for both diagnosing the reason for the present catharsis and the template within which recovery and the development of a sustainable economic order, shaped by the characteristics of national economies as well as by innovation and globalisation, can be begun.

The outcome of the global crisis is indeterminate. We don't know 'what's next'. The most recent data and assessments hold out little hope of a 'recovery' (whatever that might mean-it's now a very different world) in the immediate future. Moreover, there are compelling reasons for arguing that the scale of government interventions are creating contingent liabilities that represent a future inflationary threat, which could well lead to a definitive meltdown of Trust. This possibility should not be discounted. Such a collapse of confidence almost happened in October 2008.

We are now entering a new phase of this crisis. Proposals have been put forward in many of the countries represented here – including Ireland – for far-reaching regulatory and supervisory reforms, directed towards strengthening the consumer and addressing weaknesses in both financial institutions and markets, as well as in the regulatory architecture. Every dimension of the 'life cycle' is impacted: from savings to mortgages- from the viability of businesses built up with such effort to the funding of pension schemes.

Significantly, in the light of your deliberations, the basic model of the Ombudsman as a part of the Regulatory regime seems to have been largely left untouched. In part, of course, this is because the work of the Ombudsman does not impact directly on Financial Stability. On the other hand, failures in Financial Stability arising in large part from attempting to constrain a malign and inherently unstable 'Business Model' most certainly impact on your work.

But, I would suggest, it is also something to do with the fact that while there have been extensive changes in Consumer Protection as well as in Conduct of Business arrangements, the basic function of the Ombudsman has been neither 'captured' or 'diluted'. It remains. There are good reasons for this- reasons you will certainly address during your deliberations here in Dublin.

They have something to do with the fact that the Ombudsman is a unique component in the wider structure of Consumer Protection, with a distinctive role to play. This unique contribution to the overall system is because the role of the Ombudsman:

- Is centred on the Individual Person and the individual small business.
- Is independent and therefore credible.
- Is easily accessible.
- Provides a means of seeking, not just redress -but an acknowledgement that ,for whatever reason, they have not been treated with respect.
- Is cost-effective - it substitutes the 'dead hand' of legal intervention for a non-adversarial form of resolution.
- Perhaps most important, it is **trusted** - at a time when there has been an erosion of trust in both institutions and in regulators, this is a singular achievement.
- The Office of the Ombudsman is the catalyst in a *'virtuous learning cycle'*. The investigations, analysis and rulings of the Ombudsman, collectively, contribute to strengthening of standards of consumer protection and oversight in financial institutions. It thereby also contributes to the progressive development of 'Best Practice' within individual countries and across countries covered by the Association.

At a macro level, in the US, Secretary of the Treasury, Tim Geitner has set-out a basic template which, when more fully developed, will be sent to Congress. These reforms will address a number of core issues:

- The need for a less fragmented *regulatory structure*, including the need for a lead regulator, which will almost certainly be the Fed.

- New arrangements for *securitisation* – which certainly helped transmit the financial contagion- and which involve ensuring that originators of Risk retain at least a proportion of risk on their won balance sheet. An important initiative relates to the proposals to regulate OTC *Derivatives*, particularly in relation to clearing and settlement arrangements.
- Then there are proposals for exercising control over levels of *remuneration,* particularly in those institutions which remain in receipt of public funds.

There are parallel movements to tighten up regulation and supervision across the EU, which, of course, has a somewhat different regulatory philosophy to that of the US. In Ireland, recent proposed changes envisage responsibilities for Consumer Protection which had been incorporated into the mandate of the Financial Regulator being taken out of this domain.

These and similar regulatory initiatives amongst OECD countries and in the EU are important: it was the lack of an alignment of the mandate, focus and propensity to intervene - sometimes with very different instruments – among global regulators which has contributed to the extent and the depth of the global financial crisis. But there are major problems.

Globalised financial markets – operating in real time and driven by extraordinary volatility - still do not have a global regulator. There is still a fragmentation of regulatory governance. This makes no sense. In part, this is because some countries wish to retain what they perceive as their national autonomy- though this is a perception rather than a reality because, if the crisis to date proves anything, *it proves that there is no hiding place from financial contagion.*

But there is a yet more fundamental flaw. This is, quite simply, that the basic orthodoxy- the primacy of the short-term Shareholder Value driven model of banking -remains. No lessons have been learnt from the fact that this model was the very epicentre of the crisis. No account has been taken of the fact that there are alternative models: models that take account of a need for more balanced financial systems aligned towards 'The Common Good' (which subsumes objective universal values), rather than simply profitability.

If I might use an analogy, the mainstream model is coming out of Intensive Care, having devastated the hospital, and pretty well all of the patients and medical staff.

It is also true to say that there is little evidence of an understanding of the true nature of the crisis or of what is required. Political institutions are in denial of the kind of the transformational changes that are required. For the most part, while there are many distinguished and committed politicians of great integrity in all of our countries, the reality is that the primary external reference point of each of our *systems* is power. It is certainly not a 'Leadership of service to the Person', which I would contend is what one might expect of a political system aligned – in its mindset and in its institutions, including regulatory institutions to – 'The Common Good'.

With this in mind, our political systems have to address some pretty fundamental questions.

- What is the *Political Counterpart* to the Global Financial Crisis?

- Why did contemporary political ideologies, systems and institutions failed to anticipate, or prevent to even mitigate, the crisis?

- Do the present political systems have immunity from the meltdown that has happened in finance and economics?

- How do our political institutions deal with the social consequences of the crisis and how can we prevent a 'Political Contagion' that could subvert stable democratic institutions in the absence of a 'New Politics'?

- What are the necessary conditions for a 'New Politics' which could underpin a return to global financial and economic stability?

It may be worth adding here that there are objective ethical values that are being violated in political discourse, as well as in our institutional behaviours, and which undermine of the status of the Family. Think of the repossession of what were Homes. The ultimate 'Misery Index' behind many complaints to the Office of the Ombudsman are families – not big institutions but families, worried about loans and insurance, savings and pensions.

These are the problems that cross your desk -and to return to my main theme, they form the narrative of the consequences of the fall of **both** communism and corporate capitalism. The lesson is this: a 'new capitalism' cannot be built on an 'old politics' or on a new paradigm, heavy on regulation but emasculated of Christian values.

So, ladies and gentlemen, thank you for your attention. I know that Joe and his dedicated team have arranged an extraordinarily rewarding Conference for you here in Dublin – and I'm quite sure that that extends to outside of the conference hall, as well as within it.

This Paper was presented at the International Ombudsman Conference: Rethinking the Role of Ombudsman in a post-financial crisis environment and draws, in part, on previous analysis, presented at the recent OSCE Inter-parliamentary Conference and, also, in a Paper for 'Intercom'.

Putting the Pieces Together: Rebuilding the Banks and the Irish Economy

It is clear from the (edited) PWC Report, and from the first published report of the now nationalised Anglo Irish Bank, that the rebuilding of Irish Banking will require radial initiatives in order to regain its hard–won reputation for Principles-based regulatory stability.

Financial Stability is important. It underpins the capacity of our society to mitigate the present 'dark night of the economy' which is being experienced across all sectors and across the entire country. The recent Central Bank forecasts highlight the first decline in real GDP for a quarter of a century, a further 'sharp rise' in unemployment, as well as the 'acute deficit' in the Government's fiscal position, which is set to worsen.

Stabilization can be achieved. It will take reforms in financial regulation, in governance, as well a new corporate ethos based on 'The Common Good' – the primacy of the Human Person over self-interest and the idolatry of markets. Ireland's demographics and intellectual capital constitute advantages. It will require investment in innovative national projects to counterbalance an unhealthy fear and a lack of confidence in our capacity to reconnect with what was a values-based society. It will also require political Trust-building on a scale that is unprecedented. This may require a National Government to utilise the very best talents that are available, and to copper-fasten the political stability necessary to steer the economy through adjustment and rebuilding.

A necessary condition for financial stability is action at a European and at a Global level. This is of central importance to a small open economy like Ireland. The outlook is far from promising. A recent European Central Bank analysis notes that 'despite various and repeated efforts to restore confidence and credibility in financial markets, the situation in the banking system remains fragile'. Just how fragile is reflected in the continual negative sentiment in US Banking, *notwithstanding* Treasury Secretary Guitner's 'package', carrying as it does the full authority of the new President.

To understand how far we have to go, it is important to understand the 'business model', and the mind-set, of the banking sector within which the present problems were spawned. In the UK, the House of Commons Treasury Select Committee recently completed the most incisive dissection of a failed and hollow banking orthodoxy, which has brought the global economy – including Ireland's major trading partners – to the edge of a cliff.

Ireland's banks and credit institutions are caught up in all of this. But we, more than most, had good reason to understand this very basic idea: 'The Common Good' is an infinitely more robust platform on which to build an inclusive and sustainable banking system – and by extension society – than was an intellectually bankrupt short-term Share Holder Value driven model that has taken us to where we are.

Some of the problems which have mired banks in other countries have been avoided by Irish Banks. But the orthodoxy is still the same. The impact of this malign orthodoxy has been compounded by self–inflicted wounds. The Government's recent Recapitalisation Program was almost shot down in flames by 'friendly fire', by an unprecedented debacle of governance and communications.

The core problem at the heart of the global banking collapse was that it had no point of reference outside of itself. Equally, politics is also driven in most developed countries by short-termism and by the acquisition and retention of Power. We have seen – once again – how vulnerable this leaves the Human Person and society. The point of reference which we need to get our head around is 'The Common Good'.

'The Common Good' now requires a calm, measured and innovative approach that is based on the conviction that we can grow through this traumatic experience unfolding before us in each new press release detailing yet more closures and 'lay-offs'. We cannot determine world events, but that which lies within our control can be transformed. We have very little time to make the right choices. There is a tidal flow of disillusionment, anger, and frustration that threatens to swamp not alone our economy, but to overwhelm our political institutions.

Financial stability: the options

This is the background against which the restoration of stability to the banking sector needs to be seen. There are four options. It is painful to spell them out – but this must be done in order to make the case that we can, and must, take charge of our home-grown problems, and in doing so signal to global financial markets and multi-national companies that we are a values-based society with resilience and enormous potential. We need their Trust to make our way in the world.

'All fall down'

The first – the nuclear option – goes something like this. 'Let the banks fail; they have brought this on themselves, on their customers, and on their own employees whom they would not listen to. They have decimated the security of a generation that built this country up. The National Pension Reserve has been raided to bail them out. The way things are going, the next generation may not get an opportunity to work. It has taken a catastrophe to bring home to the banks just how wrong were their models and their mind–sets, their short-termism and their fixation on profits to the exclusion of their customers and their employees. Okay – so it happened in other countries – it didn't have to happen here. Let them go. They are Plcs – how much regard or compassion do they have on other companies up and down the country? Let them sort-out the damage. Most of it has already been incurred: our pensions, our retirement funds, even savings set-aside for nursing homes – all gone.

'Set up a new bank where the rules are written with individuals and families and small businesses in mind. Build up the Credit Unions: they know all about respecting the Person and the local communities, which the banks seem to have forgotten; at least all the profits go back to helping all the ordinary people and business. Let the banks collect their ten cents in the Euro. Take out the Payment System, and establish it as a stand-alone public utility.

'It's the economy which needs to be fixed – not the banks. The €7 billion will not be near enough to recapitalise the banks – the dogs in the street know this. They will be back for more. Forget it – put this money to work in real businesses and transfer it to middle to low income families, where it will be spent to create jobs and not hoarded away to shore-up balance sheets.

Starting again with a clean sheet and an uncomplicated not-for-profit bank that didn't get mixed up in all this toxic 'stuff' would be the best thing that ever happened. What most people need is a bank where the manager has real decision-making power, and is not leaned-on from Head Office with all kinds of targets. Ireland's reputation? The Banks have already done a job on that – when the economy gets going again, they'll catch up with us again and be glad to do business.'

This perception is widely held, in one form or another. It needs to be spoken. There is, for example, a strong case for some form of 'narrow' or risk-free bank. There are also compelling counter-arguments to the perspective set out above. What matters is the *perception* that many people have, and the reality that a once highly trusted set of institutions have lost the Trust not alone but of the public but also many of their staff. That alone points to the need for far-reaching changes in governance, including a much more inclusive, less hierarchical and 'political' corporate culture.

Nationalisation

Nationalisation of AIB and Bank of Ireland cannot easily be dismissed. It is widely accepted that both banks are of genuine 'systemic' importance to the economy. They perform a vital role across a whole range of financial services, both for the Household sector and also for Irish companies both here and in overseas markets. The survival and viability of AIB and Bank of Ireland is inextricably bound-up with being sufficiently responsive to the economy and to proving leadership in achieving an egalitarian and much fairer society.

The nationalisation not alone of Anglo Irish Bank but the *de facto* powers of the Minister of Finance over the commercial conduct of both major institutions as a result both of the Deposit Protection Scheme and the terms of the Recapitalisation mean that *de jure* nationalisation is a real strategic option for Government. Other countries which have nationalised their banks have subsequently returned them to the private sector – and at a profit to the Exchequer. Nationalisation would allow the Deposit Protection scheme to lapse in 2010.

The down-side is that all of the evidence suggests that Government's core competency is not in running business and, with some notable exceptions, in delivering innovative services. Government, like banks, are driven by short-termism. Even the approach which the government has taken to date, namely to appoint more Directors to observe at close quarters a

Business Model which is manifestly flawed, makes little sense. There is also the important issue of ensuring a level playing field between state-controlled, as compared with market-based, institutions.

Recapitalisation

The necessity for Recapitalisation arises from two factors. The first is that while every bank maintains capital to meet <u>unexpected</u> losses, the extents of such losses in Ireland, as well as in other countries, is far beyond anything that was envisaged or predicted. This is clear from the PWC Report. The value of bank's loans and Investments has been impaired to an extent where the financial markets are demanding that banks hold levels of capital far higher than those imposed by the Regulatory Authorities worldwide. Secondly, in the face of prospective losses, banks cannot, and the financial markets will not, provide the quantum of capital needed to allow the banks to resume lending on anything like the scale that the Government is pushing for. In these circumstances, the ultimate nightmare is erosion in the value of assets which would take them below the level of Tier 1 – or core – capital. That is where the lending would have to stop. In practise, the IMF does not envisage this nor would the ECB permit it to happen. But it is important to bear it in mind. The stakes are very high and the 'authorities', under enormous pressures, can sometimes make the wrong call – the failure of Lehman's Brothers in the US is an example.

In addition, banks, having lent excessively in the past, are now not only highly risk-averse, but are operating in an economic environment characterised by unprecedented levels of risk and uncertainty. There may be a role for a Loan Guarantee Scheme, which would mean that the Government effectively co-funded the 'risk premium' in lending to businesses in a high-risk environment.

Deflation is eating into the value of the bank's assets which are declining in value while, at the same time, they are committed to refunding depositors, both retail and wholesale, at par. This is the knife-edge of Trust on which the whole improbable nature of mainstream western banking is balanced.

In these circumstances, the State is the provider of capital of last resort. It's the same story all over the world – governments that are running up enormous contingent liabilities are running out of balance sheet capacity to fund 'stimulus packages' that are simply not working – at least to date. The Irish Government can only fund the €7 billion Recapitalisation programme, to which it is committed, by adding to its own borrowing. The amount which it has provided to the banks – €3.5 billion each – is inadequate, by several orders of magnitude.

This is why what we are confronting is the financial equivalent of 'the Perfect Storm'. This is why the choices which Government make matter. This is why, almost certainly, we need a new politics – and a new 'social contract of Trust', not just to mitigate the decline in, but to serve as a foundation on which to begin rebuilding, the Irish economy.

Recapitalisation, reform and transformation

Recapitalisation can only be effective if it is supported by a set of measures aimed not only at financial reform, but also at economic and social renewal. Budgetary cuts are part of the process, if they are fair and equitable. But, even then, at some stage, a fixation on budgetary policy will create a form of fiscal anorexia that is damaging and counter-productive.

The key point is this: we can only transform that part of a much wider global regulatory catharsis for which we are responsible. But that in itself is important. And, if we get it right, we can help restore Ireland's reputation for resilience, innovation and a values-based society. For global markets weighing up the price of funding Ireland's deficit, and for multi-national companies weighing-up their strategic options in terms of location, what is important is not just fiscal rectitude. It is a conviction on the part of Ireland that it can reconnect with the values that until recently underpinned its international standing as a location for inward investment, and which also challenges the capabilities, and harnesses the gifts, of our young and now pluralist population.

Neither the people of Ireland, nor International Investors, will be convinced by yet another 'plan' or 'strategy', what needs to be done is easily summarised.

- *A New Regulatory Regime.* The existing financial regulatory system was the outcome of an inter-departmental 'turf-war'. It left the Central Bank, which is responsible monetary policy, semi-detached from responsibility for the stability of the banks and the markets through which monetary policy is transmitted. This never made sense. Consumer Protection has been transformed out of recognition. But the synergies between Financial Stability, whose domain is global and which operates in real time, and Consumer Protection, which is essentially domestic and is not time-sensitive. Responsibility for Financial Stability needs to reintegrated into the Central Bank.

- Equally important, the new Governor (the present Governor's extended term of office expires shortly) will need to have very special qualities: a familiarity with the culture of regulation, as well as senior high-level experience in Global Financial markets. They will need to have a familiarity with the whole picture. They will also need to have the clout and moral authority – and the willingness to use both – to restore Trust and confidence and a sense of direction to the Irish Financial Markets. They will need the credibility necessary to rebuild our international reputation. They would also need to have the capacity to contribute, indeed to *lead*, the debate for parallel reforms through the regulatory architecture both within the EU, and globally. By tradition, the post went to the senior official in the Department of Finance. This served us well in the past. In present circumstances, we simply cannot afford to allow tradition to 'crowd-out' selecting the best equipped person for an extraordinarily daunting post.

- What is also clear is that the quality of the regulatory dialogue between, on the one hand, the banks and financial markets, and, on the other hand, the 'Authorities', will have to be greatly strengthened. This whole 'dialogue' is skewed in favour of the banks, which have the resources that the Regulator simply doesn't have. One way to deal with this is to have regular high level exchanges between staff   in the banks and in the Regulator/Central Bank. This would provide the new Central Bank with access to not alone highly specialised mathematical models driving the banks 'Business Models', but it would also ensure that the Central Bank knew precisely what was happening 'on the streets': at present, market participants are simply way ahead in their knowledge of what's happening. The 'authorities' are in catch-up mode– always a little breathless and a little late.

- Mergers of some credit institutions are structurally and strategically essential.

- None of this will work unless there is a radical change in the corporate culture of our financial institutions. Both banks and also financial markets have become separated from their constitutive purposes. The markets were manipulated – and turned rogue. Banks were seduced by greed into a model which recognised no external point of reference other than short-term profits for one category of stakeholders.

- The reality is that banks only create value by serving the needs of depositors, as well as borrowers: by utilising and respecting the talents of their employees and by them recognising that there is a broader purpose which they serve. Dr. Liam O'Reilly, the first Financial Regulator, highlighted the point that there are many thousands of decent, ethical and highly professional individuals working in banks up and down the country. They, like the public, have been held hostage to a malign culture that simply has to change. There are models there which could help inform such change. These include Islamic Banking, as well as institutions based on the pioneering work of Ciara Lubik. What is needed is not so much more Non-Executive Directors looking over the shoulders of those that are there. We need more expert Directors, trained to know what to look out for and strong enough to be the 'dissonant voice'. We need the Consumer Panels, including Trade Union representatives, not telling the CEO how to lead the bank but looking out for the welfare not just of its members but, even more importantly, 'The Common Good', which is a wider matter.

- What is lacking is the willingness to climb over the wall of conventional thinking, inertia, and self-interest. The public – this generation whose pension reserves have been raided – and the next generation who have been deprived of jobs and decent public services – deserve no less than a wholly new culture within our banks. The Government now have the power to do this, and it will be a measure of their conviction whether, or not, they have the courage to take on this challenge.

- Auditors are a part of the Regulatory process; their role in central to ensuring financial stability. It hasn't, for whatever reason, worked. There is now a case for stripping out a pure 'audit function', distinct from the provision of one which encompasses non-audit service, and whose sole-focus is ensuring the integrity and transparency and accessibility in plain English of all of the information necessary for Regulators, Boards, and the markets, to make informed decisions.

- The problem of bad loans and impaired assets that now weigh down banks balance sheets has to be tackled Those assets – in particular, houses, apartments and land banks which have an intrinsic value – can be separated out from unrecoverable losses and write-offs This is where the Government needs to think big and to think laterally. There are, as was pointed out recently by Vincent Brown in The Last Word, many homeless people and families coexisting alongside boarded-up houses and empty apartments. This does not make economic sense, and reflects an impoverished thinking and an inability to see what is staring us in the face. It is clear what needs to be done. In addition, a 'value' will have to be struck for land banks that constitute the collateral for loans that are 'warehoused' on bank's balance sheets. This land provides an extraordinary opportunity for the State to invest in whole range of amenities which are desperately needed. This is not about the National Development Plan – this is about common sense. We do need more sporting facilities – we do need facilities that can bring communities together. We do need land both on which our young companies develop and which, when we get on top of this problem, can provide the foundation for projects attracting multi-national investment. If we allow ourselves to be hypnotised by present difficulties, we will simply never be able to reshape our future. The reality is that land is available at a price which could not have been conceived of by Government two or three years ago. The difference is this; the driving force behind developing this land must be 'The Common Good' of the people of Ireland. We need to think big as well as responsibly if we are to grow our way out of deflation.

- The biggest single opportunity that now exists is the prospect for the development of the International Medical Services Centre (IMSC). The case for a project on this scale was put forward in Croke Park a number of years ago and has been further refined since then. Firstly, Ireland already has major multinational companies – leaders in pharmaceutical and medical devices – and we need to anchor these here. It has outstanding researchers in its under-funded universities. We are at the threshold of a whole new knowledge revolution in medical services. The scope for developing technologies – from ethically-based genetic technologies, to nano-technology – is virtually limitless. Innovation continues even during the most protracted cycle. An IMSC, based in the West of Ireland – and Westport is an obvious 'hub' which has already signalled its willingness to promote such a project – would not only be a viable project in its own right. It would serve as a clear signal that Ireland Inc. was in the business of transformation. The IFSC was launched in 1987 – at the nadir of that depressing decade – and succeeded beyond all expectations because of the leadership and vision and quality of the value proposition that Ireland put together. The template is there.

- Transformation of Anglo-Irish Bank. The possibility of using Anglo-Irish Bank as a 'bad bank' has been mooted. This would be misconceived for two reasons. Firstly, because it would serve as an enduring metaphor for loss and pain. Such negativity is the last thing we need. At quite another level, there is a major challenge which successive Governments have failed to address. The counterpart to the Government's budgetary cuts is its Plan for

'The Smart Economy' – that is, a Knowledge-Driven Economy based on new and emergent technologies. We need to get real. The number of top scientists and technologists on the Boards of banks and financial institutions is negligible. The number of scientists and technologists which are recruited by the banks in decision making roles is negligible. This makes no sense. There is a compelling case, therefore, for running off Anglo's existing business and, as a nationalised bank, focusing on building up a critical mass of skills and capabilities in understanding technology, on pricing technology risk, and in providing the necessary credit and capital market services to support our own science and technology-based entrepreneurs. This would also incentivize champions of change in the major institutions. There is simply no 'joined-up' thinking in this area. Science Ireland plays a key role, but it needs the support of the financial infrastructure of the country, which could bring enormous leverage to its efforts. The transformation of Anglo into a nationalised financial institution that understands science and technology, and whose governance and services are properly aligned to national development objectives provides an extraordinary opportunity to take a medium-term approach to a vital development objective. Such a transformation would demonstrate to the international markets Ireland's capacity to think innovatively.

Societal transformation

The kind of transformation which Ireland needs to come through this evolving crisis is not restricted to the financial sector and the economy. Even more important is the kind of social revolution that is needed to reconnect ourselves to the value-system from which modern Ireland emerged. The single most important institution in stabilising society and in avoiding the enormously disruptive impact of a break-down in political institutions is the Family. We should not be embarrassed to make this case, not alone because the role of the Family is enshrined in our Constitution, but also because all of the evidence points to the fact that a strong family-based society is more resilient in the face a 'shocks'. For the newly unemployed and for young people suddenly confronted by the reality of negative equity the Family is where they go for support and to regroup. The Family provides the values-based learning environment for children which can help mitigate both the shock of a suddenly unemployed parent as well as the enormously self-destructive trends in our society; trends which have contributed both to the financial catastrophe, and which constitute an enormous fiscal burden across every Government department.

Successive Governments have shirked from this and effectively emasculated the family unit – in much the same way that, as Financial Times columnist Martin Wolf has pointed-out, has occurred in Britain. A range of initiatives, from reversing existing discrimination in tax treatments of families including those on lower incomes, to new incentives for individuals wishing to be stay-at-home parents – including those who would like to work from home – would do more for the medium-term recovery of Ireland, than any bail-out from the banks, necessary though this may be. It should not be forgotten that the work of Simon Kutznets, who essentially developed the US National Accounting System for their economy, highlighted the fact that some of the most important services were excluded from national accounts and GNP – and these included family-related services. This 'social capital' is the essential foundation for financial, economic and social transformation.

This global crisis has confounded all predictions, defied every effort by national government and international agencies to stall its momentum and to stop it continuing to metastasise into still more malignant strains. Its outcome is indeterminate: what matters is the quality of policy and personal responses to what is essentially a moral crisis, with catastrophic financial, economic and political consequences. It is worth recalling what the great scholastic philosopher, Dom Ansvar Vonier once pointed out: 'It is a law of the universe that certain things happen only in response to prayer'. We should know.

This is a significantly longer version of the article 'Putting the Pieces Back Together Again' which appeared in the Irish Examiner, February 2009.

Is Nationalisation of the Banking System now Inevitable?

There is now a compelling argument for the Government to consider nationalisation of the major Irish Headquartered Credit Institutions: AIB and Bank of Ireland. A probable consequence would be the need to also nationalise Irish Life Permanent TSB. This will not be well received – the Government in its interventions has done at least as well, and in some respects better, than the authorities in other developed countries. But it may be the least-worst option now confronting an economy entering the portholes of a recession that is unprecedented in terms of its suddenness, severity, and its impact on living standards and public services.

AIB and Bank of Ireland are, by some distance, the largest Credit Institutions in the State. They dominate the payments system – which allows businesses and individuals to make payments. In this sense, they are of 'systemic importance' in a way that is not true of Anglo Irish Bank. Irish Life & Permanent, while not of the same importance in terms of making payments and providing credit, is nevertheless, a large sophisticated conglomerate, and is certainly of strategic importance.

Both of the major banks have, in the last two years since the Global Credit Crises began to manifest its malign effects, emphasised their relative strength in relation to regulatory capital requirements, and the quality of their assets. The Government have made the same case; their argument is that both banks have the capacity to come through the present crises. There is some merit in this argument. Conversely, there has been a radical shift in market sentiment, both globally and in Ireland. At a global level, we are now looking at a second, and even third round of right-offs and losses by major institutions that would be inconceivable some five years ago. In the face of this tsunami, Governments have struggled reactively to keep their banking systems on the life support of liquidity provision, recapitalisation, and other interventions. In both the US and in Britain, institutions have been taken into public ownership. The Rubicon has been crossed.

These developments have obviously impacted on the Irish banking system. They have been exacerbated by self-inflicted damage. The problem is this. The impact of two distinct credit crises building-up within the domestic economy, together with the continued sharp deterioration in the international economy, which is absolutely central for Ireland as a Small Open Economy – is now feeding back into the bank's balance sheets. Forecasts that were reasonably robust even six months ago are no longer valid. The international markets have turned up-side-down prevailing regulatory standards of capital adequacy. The markets are demanding more capital of all banks. The combination of deterioration in the Irish Economy together with new strict requirements for providing capital against accounts that have fallen into arrears, is putting the banks under enormous pressure. Moreover, the scope for raising capital from highly cynical and risk-averse investors is, at present, minimal.

There are, as noted, two credit crises now operating within the Irish Financial System. The first – and most obvious one – is the increased cost and stricter conditionality attaching to bank lending. The Government, in successive statements, have insisted that banks make credit available. The problem is that the banks are now facing into an economic environment which carries a much higher probability of default. There is a paradox in criticising the banks on the one hand, for excessive and imprudent lending in the past, while on the other hand, insisting that they make more credit available in what is manifestly a much more difficult economic environment. There is, in other words, a high 'risk premium' attached to lending.

One possible way around this would be for the Government to introduce a Loan Guarantee Scheme, which I suggested some weeks ago, and which would help to reduce the disincentive to lend. It may now be too late for this. Share-prices have reached levels that bear no relationship whatsoever to the real value of credit institutions, but which are, in effect, a judgement, not alone on us as a society, but also a view that our Credit Institutions have virtually (and that word is important) run out of strategic options. All of this has been compounded by excessive lending to the property sector. The point here is that while the bank's exposure to retail property remained within the sectoral limits imposed by the Regulator, banks were lending into what they must have known – and experienced professional middle to senior bankers did know – was an over-heated property market that flew in the face of the laws of supply and demand and was incapable of defying, at some stage, the law of gravity. Still, the sales culture prevailed – the product of a malign short-term Share Holder value maximisation model that was unethical, and had wholly lost any connection to the concept of 'The Common Good'.

'The Common Good' is not some ethereal platitudinous concept. It is a first cousin to the 'Public Interest' which runs right through the Deposit Protection (Credit Institutions) Act 2008. It means that banks take into account in their governance, strategy, and in their management the reality that whatever value they create should be attributed not alone to shareholders, but also to depositors, to customers, to employees – and most of all society. The present banking model does not reflect this reality and yet it is 'society' that has underwritten its stability and it is the next generation that will be left picking up the costs of the mistakes and failure to factor in The Common Good.

In an ideal world, it would be in the national interest for AIB and Bank of Ireland, as well as Irish life and Permanent – (with their competitors) to survive and prosper. There would have to be changes in regulation – in particular, legislation that rejoined 'the Central Bank' with the prudential (financial stability) part of the 'Financial Regulator', changes in governance that go beyond simple regulation, and a new breed of management that are incentivised primarily by doing a good and important job well, and less by the number of stock options; and changes that ensure that the operation of banks, in terms of lending practice, is aligned to the pulse beat of the Irish economy, and not to movements in global stock markets. Equally, it would be in the national interest to transform Anglo-Irish Bank into a research and development/technology bank, that had a real depth of expertise from board level down in technology and development and which could invest in the kind of knowledge economy which is at the heart of the government's medium term strategy.

Ireland's attraction as a centre for Multi-National investment is best served by an open, market-based financial system. But 'the Markets' are delivering a verdict on Ireland and on its financial institutions. This requires us to think about what is necessary in the national interest, rather than what is desirable. This raises the question of public ownership for a limited period. In terms of our international reputation, the Rubicon has already been crossed. Large tracts of the Western Financial System now operate within the penumbra of public ownership. It is simply not the case that there is not talented highly ethical professional operating within Irish Financial Institutions. There are, but they have not been able to work their way through to the top due to a flawed business model that gives far too low a priority to the interest of all stake-holder, and in particular The Common Good. Not just of this generation, but of the next. Equally, it is absurd to believe that the core competency of Government is running any kind of business.

We need to rebuild both our banking system, and our economy – and also our societal values – from the ground upwards. In these circumstances what is important is 'The Common Good'. What is important is a functioning national payments system. What is important is that Credit is available to viable businesses and households and is not constrained by an erosion of capital and the volatility of global financial markets that are now fuelled by fear because what is of growing concern is evidence of an 'informal' credit crises – an erosion of Trust among businesses that is reinforcing the effects of the formal credit crunch. This represents a dangerous escalation, and one which the Government must move swiftly to address.

Nationalisation provides a means of achieving these objectives. It puts it up to the Government to align what it sees as the requirements for mitigating this crises and promoting economic recovery, with the operation of banks which would be under its control. It also puts the burden of providing Leadership – 'humility with fierce resolve' – at the top of not alone of the financial sector, but also, the wider economy and our country.

Recapitalisation Will Not Lead to Business as Usual for Banks

The Statement by the Minister for Finance on Re-Capitalisation has brought some recovery in the share–price of Irish Banks, *albeit* from exceptionally low levels. The Ministers' initiative is welcome, if overdue, and provides a window of opportunity to bring some measure of stability to the Irish Financial System, it is important to grasp this opportunity – there may not be another one. It is unlikely to wait upon lengthy discussion such as, it would appear, are envisaged.

Capital plays a key role in ensuring the stability of Credit Institutions. Its function is to help absorb unexpected shocks. Standards of capital adequacy are set by the EU in line with the Bank for International Settlements (BIS) – the *de facto* Central Bank of developed economies. By these standards, Irish Institutions are adequately capitalised. It is, however, the markets who have reasserted themselves as the ultimate arbiter of capital adequacy. These same markets have unambiguously signalled their demand for Irish Banks to strengthen their capital base. This reflects a number of factors, including the large existing and even larger prospective write-downs and the implications for banks' loan-books of the vicious collapse in economic growth, employment, and in the public finances. In addition, banks in other countries have recapitalised.

The Government have no other possible option than to recapitalise Irish Credit Institutions. In reality, it is the responsibility of banks themselves to take action to strengthen their capital-base.

This normally involves a Rights issue, these are not normal times. Other options can include retained earnings. While there are differences across the banks, the scale of recent and likely future bad loans – as we enter the portal of recession – means that this is simply not an option. AIB and Bank of Ireland could raise additional capital from the sell-off of overseas subsidiaries. But not enough.

Had the banks' move to recapitalise in the immediate aftermath of the Deposit Protection Scheme, it is possible that they would have met with a sympathetic response from the capital markets and large institutional investors. That moment has passed. Failure to act early and decisively has meant that the proper responsibility of banks has devolved onto Government. That means onto the productive sector of an economy in crises, and whom the banks are, by their nature, meant to support. It also means those in need in our society – right across the spectrum – because the cost of this recapitalisation will further exacerbate recent cuts in public services. It is a high price for a small and vulnerable open economy to pay for the collateral damage caused by a foreseeable and inevitable, financial crises; crises, moreover, which has metastasised into an unprecedented economic recession, the full magnitude of which we can only guess.

The recapitalisation initiative is not a detailed plan which the Government intends to press ahead with decisively. It is, instead, 'an approach to recapitalisation', setting-out broad parameters, within an extensive time-frame, and the exact form of which still remains to be announced.

The key elements are three-fold. Firstly, there is the willingness of the state to 'supplement and encourage private investment in the recapitalisation if credit institutions...with State participation'. Secondly, there is an indicative amount for a Private/State recapitalisation fund – €10 billion. Thirdly, there is a decision that the mechanism for the State's participation would be either through the National Pension Reserve Fund, 'or otherwise'.

It is imperative that the initiative succeed – yet, there is no guarantee that it will. The amount of the fund, as well as the time-scale, and even more so, the nature of the co-funding, is highly problematic. Even if it does, it will make a necessary, but limited contribution, to financial stabilisation, and to mitigating the effects of the malign financial pathology on growth, jobs and public services.

There are four issues that need to be addressed:

Firstly, there is the case made previously in these pages, and whose importance could hardly be overestimated, that the business-model is inherently unstable, unbalanced, and without any economic or ethical foundation. This has to change. Management give, and are incentivised, to give overriding priority to the interests of shareholders, at the expense of depositors (who provide core stable resources), borrowers (who provide the demand for funds which drives profitability), employees (who create the embedded value of the business) – and the 'public interest'.

'The Public Interest' is at the heart of the deposit protection scheme. It is invoked by the minister throughout the act. Distinguished and highly credible non-executive directors have been appointed to each of the covered institutions to monitor 'the Public Interest'. They are, however, observing more closely and diligently, a model which has brought about the present state of affairs and which remains fundamentally unchanged.

Secondly, the issues of co-funding by the Government with external Private Equity. In general, such institutions are focused on securing high returns, and over a short time period. It is this mind-set that spawned the present crisis. Institutions would also be coming in on the back of the Deposit Protection Scheme, underwritten by the Irish people, and buttressed by co-investment by the state. Hardly a 'Public Interest' perspective. Thirdly, the re-capitalization intuitive ignores the whole issue of consolidation. This is, quite simply, flying in the face of what is necessary – and what is known to be necessary and which is, moreover, provided for in the Act.

Fourthly, there is the prospect of using the National Pension Reserve Fund (NPRF) to help re-capitalize the banks. This may be necessary – but it makes it no less reprehensible. The NPRF is an important and far seeing initiative intended to help fund future pension provision in this country in the light of a projected growth in total population as well as in the proportion of older people. Irish credit institutions did not cause the global financial crisis. They remained within the parameters set-down by the Regulator. Nonetheless, the culture of pushing product, the flaws of the business model and the sheer scale of the losses and write-offs provide the back drop against which this raid on the NPRF needs to 'evaluated'. The Minister has left himself a let-out clause; re-capitalization is to be supported by the State via NPF 'or otherwise'. Flexibility is a good thing – but the intent is pretty clear. This subversion of a sensible and far seeing initiative is a metaphor for the lasting damage caused by adventurism.

Re-capitalization will not lead 'business as usual', banks are now highly risk averse – there is more risk in this system. Excessive lending in these circumstances could trigger more bad loans, further cut backs and a vicious cycle. In these circumstances there may be a case for some form of Loan Guarantee Fund so as to mitigate for the banks the risk premium, which is constraining the availability of credit to business and households.

The process of re-building our financial system and economy within a value-based society will take a generation to achieve. Still, it is the least we owe to those who will inherit the problems which we helped to create.

This Article appeared in The Irish Times, December 2008.

Northern Bank: from Liquidity Crisis to Solvency Crisis, a Case Study

A 'Run' on Northern Rock, which is a major credit institution based in the most sophisticated financial markets in the world, is a shocking event. It is a Central Banker's worst nightmare. It is shocking, first to the legions of savers who have entrusted their money to the institution. It is this *Trust* that underpins the whole banking system, in all countries. It is shocking to Investors who have seen the market valuation of banking institutions plummet overnight, albeit with some recovery since. These Investors include Pension Funds, who manage the future living standards of millions. Certainly, management at Northern Rock will be in a state of shock. After all, it is an institution which is fully compliant with national and EU regulatory requirements and is overseen by the UK Financial Services Authority (FSA). Its funding model is skewed towards a greater dependence on more volatile wholesale money markets to fund mortgages. Yet it is not in any way unique in this – pretty well all banks rely, to a greater or lesser degree, on the wholesale markets for funding.

But arguably the greatest shock will have been felt by the FSA (which regulates banks in the UK) and especially by the Bank of England (which is responsible for Financial Stability). The Bank has seen a lot over the centuries. But even they cannot have anticipated being called upon the meet their most traditional roles – lender of last resort – to a regulated institution, in so dramatic a crisis

But, and here is the point, for savers simply to have discarded (to date) the reassurances, not alone of the Bank of England but of the Chancellor for the Exchequer, is telling us something pretty important about the deep-seated crisis in, and across, global credit and capital markets. Despite the most emphatic reassurances from 'the great and the good', the queues are still outside the branches. This, alone, sets the present crisis apart from other 'market events' of recent times – such as the 1987 US equity markets collapse, as well as the Asian banking crisis and the Long-Term Capital Management Hedge (LTCM) – Fund meltdown on the late 1990s. Somehow, these were seen by the public as exotic events, semi-detached from the real economy and real life. 'Bank Runs' were supposed to be confined to banking textbooks. The Northern Rock has brought it back on to the streets of the UK and Dublin.

There is another feature of the Northern Bank 'Run' that sends shivers down the spines of the financial authorities and investors alike: it's called 'contagion'. It is a virus-like collapse of confidence, leading to massive re-pricing of risk across markets and involves the transmission of a shockwave over a whole set of inter-related global markets. In this case, the 'epicentre' of the shock was the US 'sub-prime' mortgage market.

Sub-prime is a euphemism for high-risk, *prospectively* high return, on investment. In this case 'dodgy loans' would be a better description. It is easy lending when official rates are at an historic low of 2 per cent, but when, as was inevitable, rates began to rise so too did the rate of defaults in the sub-prime market – and, here is the twist, the demand for 'securitised investments', (parcels of these mortgages, sliced into different tranches) which were sold to investors in order to fund yet more such lending, also dried-up. More generally, liquidity simply melted, with a 'flight to quality' to government bonds.

This has lead markets to much more costly access to funds among banks themselves. Banks are being left with massive paper-based investments, intended to fund large, over-priced, corporate activity, on their books.

This contagion has now spread across global markets. Its impact has been felt in Germany. But it is Northern Rock, because of the size of its mortgage book and its dependence on wholesale markets which has caught pneumonia. It may recover – it is a compliant and regulated institution. Guarantees of unlimited funds by the Bank of England and a Chancellor desperate to stop the contagion is a pretty powerful anti-biotic. It may be taken over by a larger institution. What all of this means is that the crises is less about Northern Rock than about the unease and uncertainty in the financial markets generally and by fears of what may yet be waiting in the long grass.

Where will it end? The timing is not great. Global growth, while robust, is slowing. Oil prices are high and rising. There is a great deal of political risk out there. A contagion and a 'Run' on a major financial institution are the last things that the international economy needs – but they are a pointer to deep-seated structural problems that exist and need to be dealt with.

The real genesis of this crisis is greed, pure and simple. Remember the gospel of Gordan Gecko in the film 'Wall Street' – 'greed is good'. This greed was encapsulated in a flawed business model, aimed at maximising short-term shareholder value. We saw some of the results of this greed in the post Enron banking debacles in the early 2000s. It's still there, except it's morphed into a slightly different form.

It is not the decent, competent and professional bankers, who work within the system with whom the responsibility lies; it is the model itself, with all of its pressures and targets which remain, for the most part, an integral element of the culture in large parts of the global banking arena.

In the present instance, the greed was clearly evident in mid 2006, in the incessant 'search for [higher] yield', within a low – interest rate environment awash with capital. It was rooted in so called 'innovative' funding vehicles, which all too easily made the resources available to invest increasingly risky and opaque investments. By autumn 2006, the ECB was writing that the volatility within the capital markets exceeded that in the run-up to LTCM. The price of gold, always a sure indicator, has steadily moved northward. All the ingredients were there to see but there was nobody around to say 'stop'.

The hard question that cannot be dodged is this: could it happen in Ireland? The fact that it happened in the UK, means it could happen in any well-regulated and well-capitalised EU banking system. It's unlikely to happen here directly – but the indirect effects, in terms of access to, and the cost of credit, as well as the transmission of financial instability into a slow-down in an economy which is so heavily dependent on the global trade and capital flows – are inevitable. We are talking lower growth, employment and the certainty of 'cuts'. One thing for sure is that the Treasury Departments in all banks will be 'stress-testing' their Asset and Liability Management Models, lines of credit and contingency plans. But, really it is not an Irish problem, but a global one. Our own culture of materialism has just left us even more vulnerable.

No one is in charge. The transition from national to international and now to global financial markets has not been matched by a strengthening in what Gordon Brown in the early 1990s famously called the 'global financial architecture'. The markets are too complex, too smart and too 'real-time' to be properly overseen by a competing patchwork of multinational institutions, professional bodies involved in standard-setting and informal cooperation among central banks. Bear this in mind: the LTCM crisis, as well as the Asian banking debacle, was stopped in its tracks by the President of the New York Fed President Bill McDonagh – that wasn't his job. The fact is that he just happened to be around and had the courage and the credibility to step in. They were small-scale compared with what's happening today. So, who's in charge and what instruments are available to them to do their job?

It is only fair to say that much has improved in recent years. This includes, in particular, the Basle II agreement, which has strengthened the capital base of banks and made them more calibrated to risks, including off-balance sheet risks. There is more stress testing in scenario planning. There are more transparent accounting systems, alongside better modelling. But, the present crisis has happened, notwithstanding all of this.

The last thing we need is a highly prescriptive SOX type regime, which was introduced by the US in the wake of the Enron crisis and was basically a form of regulatory imperialism. But what we do need is a global authority to replace the present fragmented system – one that spans all of the different sectors operating within and across the capital, credit and (re) insurance markets. It is crucial that the governance of any such institution is truly global. But try selling that to the larger national central banks.

We need to deal directly with existing anomalies that, while they have a useful role, are also unregulated landmines. Hedge funds should be much more closely regulated. It's not a popular message, but the case, which I have argued elsewhere, is unassailable.

Even more fundamentally, we need to take account of the fact that 'Markets' are there to serve the real economy – from which they have become semi-detached. Markets, as the Compendium of the Social teaching of the Catholic Church, so presciently point out, are an extraordinarily useful mechanism that has enhanced economic welfare and the development of civilisation. But the constitutive purpose of markets has been lost sight of. They have been subverted and undermined – what we have now is a form of idolatry of the markets. It is this that has allowed the financial markets to be used as a conduit for greed, instead of a mechanism for enhancing stable global savings and investment.

Pessimism, for which economists are notorious, can be an indulgence. But it is difficult to believe that this present crisis has run its course, much less that the authorities have either the answers or the capacity to face up the scale of what needs to be done. Northern Rock is a symptom of a wider malign disease that threatens the global financial system. Real people and families in the prosperous (which may yet prove an illusion) and especially in the poorer debt-ridden countries, are at the sharp end of this crisis.

This Article Appeared in the Irish Examiner, December 2008.

EU-wide Approach Needed

What the Government has done is brave and necessary, and Europe should follow suit, writes Ray Kinsella.

The Dáil, in scrutinising and enacting the Credit Institutions (Financial Support) Bill 2008, has performed a signal service in copper-fastening the stability of the Irish financial system and, by extension, the wider economy. Their deliberations may, in retrospect, prove to be the catalyst that the EU has needed to develop a financial markets intervention model that actually works and which can help stabilise global markets.

The scope for scrutinising the legislation was, of course, highly constrained.

Firstly, there were market-driven time pressures. The stability that flowed back into Irish markets following the Government's action is a precious commodity. The legislation needed to be put in place.

Secondly, the spectre of the recent rejection by the US House of Representatives of the Paulson package hung over Leinster House. At the same time, questions had to be asked, clarifications sought, and assurances given. The Act is the better for this scrutiny.

A number of issues have arisen in the immediate aftermath. The first relates to the coverage of the arrangements and, in particular, to the case for broadening its scope.

It was right that the Irish authorities, in the first instance, crafted the arrangements around Irish-headquartered banks and credit institutions. These institutions – unlike those headquartered in other EU countries – are the direct responsibility of the Financial Regulator and of the Government. These institutions had been targeted by speculators. Their importance to the stability of the wider economy can hardly be overstated.

Having said that, there are a number of institutions – Ulster Bank and HBOS, (which are subsidiaries of British parent groups), and also National Irish Bank, (which is a branch operation of a major European group) – which have a significant presence in Irish retail markets. They provide competition and choice, and bring different service propositions to Irish customers. Having begun with the core task of stabilising Irish-headquartered institutions, the Government would surely be right in including these institutions within the scope of the arrangement.

The UK authorities have raised the question of the compatibility of the new arrangements with EU competition policy. Their criticism is just a little wide of the mark. The responsibility for the financial stability of an institution lies, first and foremost, with its board, and ultimately with the regulatory authorities of the home country.

The UK authorities have developed their own strategy for stabilising UK markets. That is properly a matter for them. It is entirely legitimate for the UK to lobby the Irish Government on behalf of its institutions.

But any suggestion that what Ireland has done is contrary to EU competition law is simply misconceived. There is little point in talking about competition or distortions in competition in an environment in which the very survival of institutions can be undermined.

The EU Commission has sent out a very strong signal to this effect in its references to its need to respond reflexively. The UK authorities know this. In calmer times, they will affirm publicly the reality that the overriding priority now is for all European countries to work together, firstly to stabilise the markets and then, to ensure that whatever forms of intervention are made, are consistent with open and competitive markets. The Irish financial markets intervention model initiative meets this test – but it goes further. It is the only such initiative – right across the globe – that has demonstrably worked. It has assuaged the concerns, and the opportunism, of the most merciless and dispassionate critics – the markets themselves.

In contrast to interventions based on nationalising troubled institutions or which socialise toxic products, the Irish model is focused on protecting depositors as well as on reassuring institutions in the wholesale markets which are funding Irish institutions. It provides guidance as to the actions that are now needed at a European level.

It is no longer tenable to have piecemeal and inconsistent approaches to interventions aimed at stabilising EU financial markets. What is needed is a unified EU-wide approach. Europe needs the kind of radical thinking that underpins the Irish initiative.

The point is this: the EU regulatory system, set-out in a whole raft of directives, is based on the authorisation of institutions on the basis that they conform to specific requirements. These are extensive and very detailed. They are there to protect depositors and to underpin, so far as possible, the stability of Europe's markets.

The EU finance council now has an opportunity to do precisely what the Irish authorities have done. A two-year guarantee that all deposits in EU-authorised institutions would be insured would go very far indeed towards stabilising the markets. The markets themselves are beginning to pressurise governments to move in this direction.

Europe needs to be brave. Sensitised by the implications of the most serious crises in financial markets, European governments need to show conviction in their regulatory framework and engage in fundamental reforms at a global level, including the establishment of a global central bank.

More than a decade ago, British Prime Minister Gordon Brown was pushing the idea of changes in global financial architecture, and significantly, British EU Commissioner Peter Mandelson is now promoting this idea.

In Ireland, we now have two years within which to make this initiative work. It is not the shareholders with banks who have restored calm to Irish institutions and markets. There has been a massive transfer of goodwill to the banks, from the people of Ireland. It is they who have underwritten the future of the banks and brought them back from the brink.

Goodwill is a two-way thing. The banks need to respond constructively, imaginatively and immediately to this goodwill.

This will require a change in the mind-set of the boards. Their responsibility is not just to shareholders. They have an equal responsibility to their customers, to depositors, to their employees and to the wider community. This balance has not been there in the past. But it is a model which recent events demonstrate is demonstrably more robust than one based on maximising short-term shareholder value. The latter is not just conceptually redundant in an environment where there is no shortage of capital; it has created a target-driven environment, incentivised by obscene levels of remuneration, and which is wholly destructive of the person within the institutions themselves and in the wider community.

Change should not be primarily a matter of regulation from on high, or even the exercise of very extensive powers granted to the Minister under the legislation. The banks have grown up with the Irish economy. They have the knowledge and the clout to respond to the needs of the economy, which, with all the goodwill in the world, banks headquartered outside the State simply do not have. The boards need – to use that tired old cliché – to think outside the box.

The Government, having stabilised financial markets, now has a more solid foundation on which to craft not alone the budget, but also a pathway which will bring the country through recession. If it listens to what is being said deep in the long grass, there is much more that can be done – and at no cost. We have to anchor foreign direct investment within the country. But there is a great deal more that can be done to develop Irish industry and services. Regulation, in different forms, is important. In Ireland, we have turned it into an industry, which is semi-detached from the realities of managing a business and which is simply suffocating enterprise. Addressing this problem would rejuvenate entrepreneurship, but it will take radical surgery.

The banks need to provide explicit indication that they will support all businesses, and in particular small businesses, through the hard times ahead. The Government needs to make it worthwhile for Irish businesses to employ additional workers and to expand their facilities.

Our destiny is in our hands to a greater extent than we might perhaps believe.

This Article appeared in The Irish Times, October 2008.

AIB's place in Ireland Matters

If the takeover of AIB by MandT Bank had gone ahead, it would have had far–reaching and certain consequences, writes Prof Ray Kinsella.

The ownership of major domestically-based institutions matters. Even in a world of integrated globalised financial markets, including increasingly concentrated cross-border institutions, there is an intuitive acknowledgement that the takeover of a major domestic retail bank has far–reaching implications, not alone for customers but also for public policy.

The disclosure that the board of AIB gave serious consideration to a takeover of the bank by the US based MandT Bank has serious implications.

AIB have been swift to point out that the proposal, which came before the board last autumn, was simply part of a wider strategic review. In a world of intensive pressure on banks to deliver ever-increasing shareholder value, and which is merciless in its retribution on those who fail to do so, keeping all options open is imperative.

It doesn't mean it is sensible – it's just the way things are.

Nonetheless, the fact that the proposal was brought before the board, and at a time when the bank was immersed in the travails of investigations related to over-charging and of the illegal Faldor scheme which existed up to 1996, does concentrate the mind on a number of key issues.

Mainstream thinking highlights the benefits to consumers and to the wider economy of competition, not alone within the domestic environment, but across Europe. The Irish financial sector is highly open in terms of overseas participation. Recent entrants into the retail banking market have been welcomed.

In Ireland, what were the "associated banks" – the core retail clearing banks – grew up with the Irish economy. There was, until relatively recently, an implicate contract of benign oversight as a quid pro quo for a willingness on the part of the banks to lend a sympathetic ear to government initiatives. This contract was enforced by the enormous significance of the banking sector as a whole to the economy, which is still the case. The retail banks themselves employ some 30,000 people, and are a significant contributor to the Exchequer.

All of this bears on the issue of the likely impact of the proposal, had it been endorsed for takeover of the AIB by MandT Bank.

Some consequences would have been certain. Firstly, there would have been a rationalisation and some downsizing – simply because this would have been built into the funding of the acquisition. Secondly, the migration of strategy, and possibly key functions, from Ireland would have eroded the contribution by the bank to the domestic economy, and its potential leverage in regard to public policy.

Thirdly, the experience of New Zealand strongly suggests that foreign ownership of the core banking franchise reduces government scope for policy intervention.

Compared with the pre-internal market era, there is a wholly new set of parameters within which governments can operate in respect of safeguarding national banking systems from competition, including takeover.

Protectionism, under the guise of maintaining national champions in the public interest, is explicitly prohibited and rightly seen as subversive of the interests of consumers and of the wider economy.

It is, quite simply, a fact that overseas predators have "run the rule" over both AIB and Bank of Ireland. The possibility of a takeover of either or both is very real. Both banks now operate in a highly-contestable domestic market, with a number of rapidly-growing, domestically - based challengers, such as Irish Life Permanent TSB, as well as recent, and potential, entrants using a variety of traditional and e-based platforms for servicing both customers and new-value propositions.

It is in the interests of the Irish economy and the Irish consumer that at least part of the core domestic banking franchise remains in Irish hands. The example of both RBS and Bank of Scotland highlights the fact that a strong domestic platform can serve a base for significant overseas expansion, with real economic and reputational benefits. Such reputational benefits have a particular resonance for Ireland Inc, not least given the importance of the IFSC and the significance of Ireland as a high-location for foreign investment. For this to happen, both of the domestic banks need to take on board not just the rhetoric, but the reality, of a new ethically-based business model.

At the heart of the business model is the restoration of public trust based on a contract with the consumer, not just as an economic entity, but also as an individual.

There remain, for example, wholly anachronistic pockets of discrimination with regard to women customers. Equally important, both banks need to engage with all of their staff not simply on a contractual basis, but rather on the basis of a relationship with those individuals who, ultimately, are responsible for generating shareholder value. The Irish Bank Officials' Association has engaged in a constructive and robust relationship with bank management, and is deserving, not just of trust, but also of a place on the panels that are part of IFSRA's supervisory system.

The extent, manner and rationale of significant job-cuts in the case of Bank of Ireland, for instance, require justification that has not been forthcoming. This represents a weakness, not just in the bank's strategic objectives, but also in its capacity to secure itself from a prospective takeover bid from abroad. It is important, and not just for shareholders, that AIB and Bank of Ireland regain a sense of confidence and direction. An ethically-based and forward-looking business model, operating within the context of significant opportunities generated by economic expansion, is the best guarantor of high performance and continued independence of AIB.

This Article Appeared in The Irish Times, May 2005.

Changing Mindsets, Behaviour and a Whole Way of Thinking at AIB

Yesterday's IFSRA Final Report into the AIB overcharging has a consumer focus that will be widely welcomed, writes Ray Kinsella.

In its Final Report on AIB Investigations, published yesterday, the Irish Financial Services Regulatory Authority (IFSRA) returned to deal with unfinished business arising from its Interim Report, issued in July.

The Interim Report identified the key parameters of the overcharging debacle involving some €34 million: the amounts due to be repaid to customers, the numbers and categories of transactions involved, as well as the process for ensuring that restitution was carried out effectively and speedily.

The report also set out the issues to be addressed in relation to the Faldor offshore scheme, which existed from 1989 to 1996.

Prioritising the restitution was in line with the principles underlying IFSRA's strategic plan for "putting the consumer at the heart of the regulatory system". It promised in its Final Report to turn to the issues of who knew, when they knew, and why the matter remained unreported for so long. And, of course, to set out what needed to be done to put matters right.

The conclusions reached were tersely summarised by IFSRA's chief executive, Dr Liam O'Reilly: "The failures within AIB uncovered by the investigations are completely unacceptable. We will not tolerate such practices within the financial services industry."

AIB's chief executive, Mr Michael Buckley, accepted the report's findings in full. He acknowledged that procedures for dealing with compliance failures were inadequate and that, at critical times, they simply didn't work.

The bank will, in addition to the measures it has already taken, implement a series of actions required of it by IFSRA. These include, crucially, disciplinary action in regard both to the overcharging issue and, also, to inappropriate share dealings by AIB's subsidiary, AIBIM, in relation to Faldor and other transactions.

Who then knew what was going on?

The form of words used – more than once – in the IFSRA report is striking. "Certain staff and management within certain areas of AIB appear to have been aware..."

IFSRA's investigation will have addressed the issue of accountability thoroughly. Equally, the independent report by DeLoitte, commissioned by AIB following consultation with IFSRA, and overseen by the former CandAG, Mr Lauri McDonnell, delivered to AIB some weeks ago and forwarded to IFSRA, will have dealt with this question. It has been reported by RTE's Charlie Bird that a sub–committee of AIB's board has already initiated a disciplinary process by writing to some 10 individuals.

Both IFSRA and AIB have insisted that "due process" would be subverted by naming individuals. They are right. It is a basic principle of justice that individuals are entitled to be considered innocent until proven guilty.

Even then, there may be mitigating circumstances. Moreover, the public interest, which is central, would almost certainly be undermined by premature disclosure. That doesn't mean that it won't happen, just that it shouldn't.

The form of words used in the report also points to another conclusion. Namely, that what was happening was not known throughout the bank. This is important for a number of reasons.

The words "certain staff and management within certain areas of AIB..." suggest that there were serious deficiencies in communications and in procedures that prevented these breaches of compliance requirements being "fast-tracked" right to the top.

Mr Buckley stated yesterday that he himself was unaware of the overcharging. There is every reason to believe that this is the case. Firstly, this would have been the crucial question addressed by the two reports.

Secondly, because of the statement by IFSRA to a Dáil committee that "AIB, it must be said, has been very active and co-operative right up to board level in addressing this issue since it came to light. Their response includes a commitment to a full and speedy review of systems surrounding all of their charging issues".

The issue of whether the board should have known is a separate matter. What is clear, however, is that there was a major failure in internal controls as well as in the culture of "certain areas within the bank".

So when did they know?

Perhaps the most devastating finding of the report is that the non-compliance in respect of charges existed for almost eight years. An internal memo in 2002 identified the cost of dealing with the issue and the need to inform the regulator. Nothing happened.

All in all, there were at least seven opportunities for "certain staff and management in certain areas of AIB" to identify and/or disclose the breaches of compliance to the relevant regulators. It didn't happen.

Controls and procedures are a proxy – and not the greatest one – for a culture that both demands, and incentivises, compliance and the promotion of good practice. It requires a corporate ethos in which all staff are empowered to bring the values by which they strive to live their lives to the workplace – the office, the branch.

This takes us to the heart of the issue. Ireland has a principles-based regulatory system. IFSRA sets down high-level controls and codes of conduct – it is for the individual institution to comply not just with the letter of the law but also its spirit.

Indeed, what is at issue here is not simply compliance per se but, rather, "obedience to the unenforceable". The short-term shareholder value business model, which was pre-eminent up until recently, crowded out any such considerations. In the case of AIB, it is clear that ethical leadership from the top takes a considerable time to change mindsets, behaviour, and a whole way of thinking.

There is still a long way to go

The focus will now turn to disciplinary procedures which have to be informed, rigorous and impartial. The issue of whether or not IFSRA has sufficient sanctions at its disposal to prevent this deviant behaviour morphing into some other form is another key question.

Ultimately, Dr Liam O'Reilly was surely right in asserting that, notwithstanding its new powers, the real sanctions involve the costs of rectifying breaches of compliance and the reputational costs.

Customers will feel vindicated by the consumer-focused approach by IFSRA, including the remedial action that it has taken. Institutional investors will, no doubt, be relieved that Michael Buckley decided to stay on to put this episode to bed and allow his successor to start with a clean sheet.

Bank staff, whose integrity was highlighted by IFSRA in the Interim Report, will almost certainly feel that the rebuilding of trust is once again down to them. This powerfully reinforces the case for co-opting the IBOA on to the consultative panels. It is helping to rebuild trust, not alone within a single institution, but in an industry of crucial importance to the economy and to society. It deserves its place at the table.

This Article Appeared in The Irish Times, December 2004.

Prevention of System Errors is the Key Issue

A policy of systematic overcharging would be not merely delinquent but tantamount to commercial suicide, writes Ray Kinsella

It's called "operational risk". It means any failure in systems or protocol subverts the effectiveness of a bank's operations, including those that underpin customer relationships and the value of the banks brand. More specifically, it involves ending up on the financial or, even worse, the news pages for all the wrong reasons.

It may be small comfort to AIB customers who have been overcharged to know that they have been the victims of a systems failure as opposed to being simply overcharged as a matter of commercial practice. However, the distinction is important in terms of organisational integrity as compared with effectiveness – and in identifying how best to protect customers against any repetition.

Banks, globally, have long operated in an environment which is obsessed with maximising shareholder value.

The short-term focus of this – impelled by the behaviour of institutional investors – has been largely responsible for the seismic cracks which have appeared in major corporate entities, notably in the US.

This has created a culture that generates pressure right throughout the organisation and is fixated on "maximising its share of the wallet". Because more than 40 per cent (and rising) of bank income is generated by fees and commissions (non-interest income), it is little wonder that charges have become a highly sensitive issue.

Maximising fee-based income is pushed at every division, at every level and in pretty well every bank. The problem is that there is a tension between this objective and that of cultivating a "high-trust" customer relationship.

The more competitive the environment, the more difficult it is to get this balance right. AIB, like other banks, has invested hugely in CRM (customer relationship management), and marketing strategies based on customer relationships. A systems error in this area is seriously bad for both the bank and the customer.

If competitive pressures are important then so too is the greatly increased compliance burden – both statutory and non-statutory – on all financial institutions. Consumer protection is at the heart of compliance.

The Irish Financial Services Regulatory Authority (IFSRA), which was established only two years ago, has already developed a highly pro-active expert capability which is now scrutinising this overcharging episode.

A policy of systematic overcharging involving non-compliance with established fee notification protocol would have been not merely delinquent but tantamount to commercial suicide.

It would run wholly counter to an ethos of "good citizenship" and "corporate social responsibility", which is where all banks are seeking to position themselves. The prospective damage, in terms of reputation and brand management, would be simply out of all proportion to any increase in fee income.

This leaves a systems failure as the probable cause of the over-charging. The difficulty that banks have in addressing this is the "Oh yeah?" syndrome, which is a product of an essentially adversarial relationship that has been allowed to develop across the financial services spectrum.

Banks are spending tonnes of money to counteract this and the last thing that they (and, even more importantly, their customers) need is such investment being wasted by systems failures.

Currently all financial institutions are busy implementing Basle II, which, amongst other things, involves allocating capital against prospective market risk, including a failure in operational effectiveness.

It must be a concern for regulatory authorities and bank management that an error can be embedded within a bank's systems for an extended period without being identified.

The error happened to relate to bank charges on a relatively small subset of its transaction with customers. It could, in principle, just as easily have related to the banking and capital markets side of its business. We have, over the past year, seen failings in the control systems of global banks, such as National Australia Bank and even Goldman Sachs.

One problem here is that internal controls tend to lag behind commercial practice, although this should not be the case. Potential problems should be identified by human expertise, and/or diagnostic software.

These kinds of problems can never be wholly eliminated. The issue is reducing the scope for, and probability of, such failures.

In this regard, it is surprising that banks are so narrowly focused in their systems testing, overlooking approaches that have a great deal to offer in terms of reducing the probability of such a failure.

AIB will have learned from the effectiveness of its response to the Allfirst debacle that credibility hinges on a pro-active and transparent response. Restitution, a core concern for the IFSRA, can be taken as read.

And, indeed, the IFSRA's response to this failure in consumer protection systems will have boosted the confidence of consumers that their interests are being safeguarded.

In retrospect, the real lesson of this, and failings in other multi-national banks, may be that the internal controls systems are simply not sufficient.

This Article Appeared in The Irish Times, May 2004.

Regulatory Regime Changed Beyond Recognition

The Faldor debacle could not happen under current regulations, writes Ray Kinsella, who says the only effective regulatory system is based on ethics.

The successive disclosures of failings in controls, procedures and, most important of all, in practices, have made this a bad week not only for AIB but, even more importantly, for the wider Irish financial services sector.

And it's not over yet. Sometime over the next few weeks the report commissioned by the Tánaiste, Ms Harney, into failings at National Irish Bank (NIB) will be published. Once again, the whole issue of the subversion of consumer's trust in financial institutions will be debated.

The "high-trust" relationship between the consumer and the management of the financial service provider is the "contract" on which all of the other elements of the value-proposition to the customer – efficiency, transparency, competition and innovation – must be built. Trust is hard-won and, in the absence of integrity and leadership, easily lost.

There is an important distinction between what might be called the "foreign exchange reporting debacle" – which was a reporting failure compounded by corporate communications breakdown – and the disclosure regarding the AIB Investment Management/Faldor off-shore banking scheme, which spanned from 1989 to 1996.

The first issue deals with operational efficiency and, of course, it's hugely important. But the second one strikes at the very heart of what banking and financial services are all about, namely "fit and proper standards" in management.

A failing to appreciate just how important core banking values and practices are to the trust which customers and other stakeholders invest in management is something approaching a "black-hole" in the vision of an institution's management.

Some hard things have to be said. The first one is this: the short-term shareholder-value maximisation model on which banking, and particularly investment banking, has been based is fatally flawed. The notion that an institution, the life-blood of which is integrity and trust, can operate by looking over its shoulder every quarter at its share-value rating is absurd.

The "dance of death" whereby stock analysts, the large institutional investors and top management each try to second guess one another in predicting and messaging forecasts, has been at the heart of the collapse of the short-term shareholder value model in the US.

It has caused enormous collateral damage and the regulators, notably the Securities and Exchange Commission, have wreaked a savage vengeance on the major banks for buying in to such a model.

The victims have not only been the consumers and small investors but also middle and lower-grade management who have been cajoled and bullied into accepting a code of values that was entirely alien to that which they instinctively felt was right. The responsibility for this rests unequivocally with a wholly flawed view of leadership. Leadership, as the Harvard Business Review has pointed out, is "humility with fierce resolve".

In the Republic, the culture of greed, which characterised the late 1980s and early 1990s, was a societal phenomenon, which inevitably infected the financial services sector. But that has changed. The DIRT and other related scandals sensitised people to the erosion of the "high-trust" relationship that was being subverted by perverse incentives, corrupt sales practices and "mé féin-ism".

The whole regulatory and compliance system has now changed. It's important to point out that the Faldor debacle, disclosed by AIB on Thursday, simply could not have happened after the Investment Intermediaries Act was enacted in 1996. This Act put in place codes of practice that are effectively binding. Equally, within AIB, the enormous investment in risk management and compliance initiated post-Rusnak would wholly preclude the possibility of such practices today.

The regulatory system now in place vindicates the right of consumers to expect a set of ethical principles that permeate the whole organisation.

What has also changed is the scale and scope of financial regulation. We are now looking at an infrastructure that embraces not only the Irish Financial Services Regulatory Authority but also a wider network of agencies – including the Criminal Assets Bureau, the Office of the Director of Corporate Enforcement and the Revenue Commissioners – all of which are now communicating effectively with each other.

It would be wrong not to acknowledge that financial institutions – as well as the regulators – have also "raised their game". To a public that is jaded by a drip-feed of debacles that may seem cold-comfort. But it's the truth.

I have seen it in my classroom, where post-graduate students have talked with the leaders of these agencies and with management responsible for implementing internal controls and the implementation of compliance. It is a different world, compared with even five years ago, into which my students are moving.

The new reality is that the Irish financial sector is now regulated more rigorously and according to higher standards than at any time in the past.

This is not in any way to condone the legacy-old sins that are being revealed. Instead, it is to welcome the fact that the financial services industry, which employ's tens of thousands and serves as the central nervous system of our economy, is now encompassed within a rigorous and transparent compliance system. And that's important, because that is the benchmark against which international investors, fund managers, service providers and rating agencies assess the credibility of our economy and the standards by which Ireland Inc operates.

186

That is why we do not need more regulation. From the perspective of the customer this just adds to costs and undermines competitiveness. And no amount of regulation can wholly guarantee protection against subversion.

That's why, when the governor of the Central Bank meets with the Oireachtas All-Party Committee and the public service, the emphasis should not be on more regulation but on implementation and, more especially, the need to focus on corporate culture and ethics.

The key point is this. In all countries, including Ireland, we are witnessing a profound shift in what can only be termed as the "regulatory paradigm" within which financial institutions operate. We have moved from "box-ticking" regulation, through corporate governance, to a realisation that the only truly effective regulatory system is based on ethics – "obedience to the unenforceable".

This Article Appeared in The Irish Times, May 2004.

EU Initiative Needed to Solve Regulatory Gap in

Indemnity Insurance

There exists a major regulatory anomaly in Ireland in respect of Medical Indemnity/Insurance contracts Professor Ray Kinsella writes. Unless it is addressed, in terms of legislation and regulatory process, it will constitute a threat, not alone to the patient but, also, to the wider public interest.

This anomaly, in one form or another, is not unique to Ireland. It is a 'gap' in the fabric of EU regulatory and supervisory legislation and will, ultimately, have to be addressed in Brussels. When the dust settles – as it will – over the present dispute between the Government, MDU and Hospital Consultants, the full implications of the situation existing prior to the implementation of the Clinical Indemnity Scheme (CIS) for Consultants, on February 1st 2004 will become apparent.

Absence of certainty

Commercial 'Insurance Undertakings' had exited the Medical Indemnity Market – largely because of the knock-on effects of the increased number and costs of claims, on premia being paid by Government and (jointly) by consultants. Medical indemnity was then provided by two provident-type institutions – the Medical Defence Society (MDU) and the Medical Protection Society (MPS). MDU – at the heart of present discussions – provided, inter alia, 'discretionary' cover i.e. there was an absence of certainty, though it should be added that in practice they had not rejected any claim. The companies were fully compliant with UK company law. Also, MDU are reportedly moving away from an essentially pay as you go system to an insurance/reinsurance model, going forward.

But...

But – and it is a very important but – these were not 'Insurance Undertakings', as defined in EU Directives and Irish Insurance Law. They were not, therefore, encompassed within the very strict, pan-EU, regime regarding reserving, solvency and the run-off of claims. Nor are they covered by the consumer protection regime of the Irish Financial Services Authority (IFRSA). They were – and are – quite simply – 'non-regulated entities' in the terminology of the IFRSA.

It really shouldn't have happened – potentially it put patients (and by extension consultants) at risk and was wholly contrary to the whole idea of the Single Regulator (IFRSA). In fairness, no one – regulators, academics, policymakers or analysts – picked up on it.

It is important to point out that this is part of a more general regulatory issue that the Government will have to confront. There are a number of ways of looking at this. The state, in general, insures on a pay-as-you-go basis as do some mutual and provident institutions in some EU countries. Individual and private sector entities still insure e.g. liability cover, for the most part, through 'insurance undertaking', that are fully funded. They are quite different in terms of accounting practice and, also, the cost of funding. It's not a 'level playing field'.

But take a further step. Increasingly, large companies are part self-insuring; this can be very sensible in some instances – the danger is that the company and the 'Insurance Undertaking' who is underwriting part of the risk may use very different accounting and presentational methods. This could lead to what one leading authority has called a form of 'regulatory arbitrage'.

What all of this means is that firstly there is an emerging un–funded liability, within both the public and the private sectors, the size of which we don't know. What the medical indemnity issue proves is that you cannot really afford to take your eye off the ball i.e. consistency and transparency in relation to funding arrangements. Secondly, this is complicated by differences in accounting procedures.

Thirdly, there are latent dangers in terms of competition policy as between e.g. the states pay-as-you-go approach and that of 'insurance undertakings'. A very uneven 'playing field'. The medical indemnity issue illustrates some of these issues – and very real problems – in microcosm.

CIS – putting the package together

The introduction of CIS – based on the legal liability of the enterprise, rather than that of the individual(s) may yet prove a template for other countries. Essentially it provides free indemnity cover for consultants working in public hospitals and – because the public-private mix is the cornerstone of the acute system in Ireland – it also covers private procedures in 'designated' beds in public hospitals. In regard to wok carried out by consultants in private hospitals – such as the Mater Private, St. Vincent's Private, the Blackrock Clinic and later this year, the new Galway Clinic – the Government have, it would appear offered to pay the premia relating to exposures above €1 million. Consultants will be indemnified for work carried out under the National Purchase Treatment Fund.

At one level, all of this replaces a patchwork of arrangements whereby Government bore 90 per cent cost of cover, to the MDU or MPS, with Consultants paying the residual – quite considerable – premia costs.

So, for much of the scheme, the CIS – based with the State Claims Agency in the National Treasury Management Agency (NTMA) – will simply replace what was generating into a rapidly escalating volume of expenditure by Government. But it is tidier, less fragmented and – most important of all – incorporates a National Risk Identification System.

Total potential exposures and consultants

There are two points that are not – yet – clear. The first is the total potential exposures – in terms of future claims – which the CIS are taking over. Medical indemnity is a notoriously 'long-tailed' exposure. The second is the financing deal which will underpin the negotiated package: one which deals, in particular, with the potential exposures of consultants in respect of incidents which happened prior to February 1st 2004, when the Minister introduced the scheme over the head of the consultants

It is regrettable that matters came to such a head – after all, it has, in the event, proved necessary to take another month to try hammer out a fair and equitable arrangement. The Consultants are, by far, the most vulnerable section of those covered by the CIS, since patients were at risk depending on whether their insurer would, or could, cover such exposures.

In practice, the Government would have found it difficult to walk away from successful litigation by a patient in a situation where most consultants believed they were dealing with certainty of funding (in cooperation with Government) from a de facto 'Insurance Undertaking'.

Nonetheless, the transition was always likely to be difficult and should not detract from the Government's success in developing and implementing the new scheme and – almost certainly – in working with the MDU and the Consultants to provide fair and equitable arrangements in regard to retrospective (i.e. prior to February 1st 2004) exposures.

Regulatory 'time–warp'

All of this leaves a number of absolutely fundamental regulatory and supervisory issues to be dealt with, as part of a settlement, or to be resolved in the near-term.

Firstly, the MDU, and also the MPS, arguably exist – in terms of EU supervisory practice – in a historical 'Time Warp'. This is not to say that they do not provide a range of valuable services for their membership. What is at issue is the reality that they are 'unregulated entities', compared with 'Insurance Undertakings' who provide complimentary/substitute products.

In the event of a re-entry of commercial insurers into this market in Ireland, we would have the same 'twin-track' regulatory processes as existed in the 1990s: substitutable products being provided, on the one hand, by (heavily) regulated insurers and, on the other hand, 'unregulated entities'.

In practice, it is difficult to envisage a re-entry of commercial insurers – partly because of the CIS taking out a large chunk of the potential market and partly because of the uncertainty (and therefore difficult to price) nature of clinical risks. But even the possibility of such a 'gap' is contrary to regulatory 'best practise' and against the whole intent of the IFSRA.

Regulatory inconsistency

There is another issue. Even if commercial insurers do not re-enter – at least in the short to medium term – there are still two regulatory arrangements in place in regard to integrated medical indemnity risk. Firstly, there is the CIS, managed by the State Claims Agency (part of the NTMA), which is accountable to the Dáil and ultimately comes within the remit of the Minister for Finance.

Then there are the MDU and the MPS which, as matters stand, are neither 'regulated entities' (as commercial 'insurance entities' would be) nor is it easy to see to who they are accountable, within the jurisdiction.

A Private Consultant, operating in a private hospital, could have (a) private cover by an unregulated entity with the 'excess' of €1 million funded by the State (b) If he/she were engaged in National Treatment Purchase fund work, cover provided by the CIS. These arrangements cannot be satisfactory. They do not e.g. conform to the principles set-out by Government itself in 'Better Regulation' (Department of An Taoiseach 2004).

Internationalisation of exposures: an EU issue

The procedures operated by the State Claims Agency in respect of the CIS are as rigorous as could reasonably be anticipated in 2000.

Still, there are issues that may prove difficult. Medical consultants operate across sectors (Public/Private), as well as a North/South basis. More importantly, they increasingly operate in an international (EU and US, mainly) domain. This requires consistency of indemnity arrangements, to begin with across the EU. It requires rigorous protocols, based initially on [a development of] the NTMA (Amendment) Act, 2000. More generally, this whole anomaly of the CIS being accountable to the Dáil (though not formally regulated/supervised according to EU/IFRSA standards; MDU is not tenable.

There remains an unpredictable element. The state is now back in the insurance business. One of the most far-sighted elements of the CIS is the introduction of the National Incident Report System. This should – given management commitment, investment in I.T. and especially in training – generate a considerable reduction in clinical risk, by identifying 'clusters of incidents'; thereby reducing the number and costs of claims. In this environment, there are three possible trajectories, each with very different regulatory and policy implications.

The first simply assumes that the CIS will produce a cost-effective set of outcomes. Central to this will be the quality of claims settlement, as opposed to claims management. The second assumes that the State Claims Agency will be so successful that, at some future time, the issue of privatisation will arise. It's inevitable. Effectively, the CIS will have resolved with the 'market failure' – stemming from the exit of commercial insurers – which presently exists, opening up new possibilities. The fact that the whole scheme is 'un-funded' may be its 'Achilles heel'. The third scenario is rather different.

It presupposes that, notwithstanding the inherent strengths of the CIS initiative, the State will be left as an 'Insurer of Last Resort', within an environment of escalating medical cost inflation and litigation generated by 'moral hazard' ('the States picking up the tab' mentality, reinforcing Irelands 'compensation culture') and the uncertainty generated by seismic advances in clinical and therapeutic advances – partly driven by the application of the human genome project. From the Exchequer's perspective, it's not a pretty picture.

None of this should detract from the quality of the CIS as a world-class management innovation. But it is only prudent to identify the actual – and potential – regulatory anomalies, as well as the uncertainties with which it will have to cope with over the next decade.

We need legislation now to centralise all regulation in the field of medical indemnity/ insurance within the IFRSA in order to ensure consistency and transparency.

And we need to begin talking with Brussels about how best to develop responses to the wider issues, relating to the protection of patients in the event of an 'adverse incident' within a wholly new, emerging acute care scenario, within and across, the EU.

Article appeared in Finance, March 2004.

IFSRA Bill Should be Withdrawn

Responding to the publication of the IFSRA Bill which allows for a single regulatory structure in Ireland, Ray Kinsella says that the institutional structure and mandate of the regulatory arrangements envisaged in the Bill are fatally flawed and therefore the Bill should be shelved.

The Central Bank and Financial Services Authority Bill 2002 will, effectively, implement a single regulatory structure for Ireland, encompassing prudential supervision, consumer protection, and monetary policy. The structure and remit of the Bill were agreed in substance by the Minister for Finance and the Tánaiste as long ago as February 2001. There is a compelling – indeed an overwhelming – case for the view that the institutional structure and mandate of the regulatory arrangements envisaged in the Bill are fatally flawed and that the Bill should be withdrawn.

Background and proposed structure of Single Regulator

The proposed Single Regulator was born of scandals within the Irish financial services sector during the 1990s. Following the Report of the Implementation Advisory Group on the Establishment of the Single Regulatory Authority (the McDowell report) in 1999, there was an extensive period of trench warfare as key institutional stakeholders fought over location, remit and structure of the proposed Single Regulator. In February 2000, the Tánaiste and the Minister for Finance, Mr McCreevy, reached agreement on a structure and indicated that the Government would be putting forward proposals for legislation.

Essentially what is proposed in the Bill is a regulatory structure – the Central Bank of Ireland and Financial Services Authority (CBIFSA). This will encompass a new authority – the Irish Financial Services Regulatory Authority (IFSRA) – that will be responsible for prudential regulation of banking and insurance and also for consumer protection. The proposals also envisage an interim board, which will appoint a chief executive and a director of consumer protection. On the establishment of the IFSRA, the latter will take over the functions of the director of consumer affairs. The new structure will also include an Irish Monetary Authority (IMA) whose job it will be to 'carry out the administrative functions required by the role of the Governor within the ESCB and to manage the external reserves'. Simple it's not.

It's important to make the point that some rationalisation of financial regulation – to correspond with changes in the marketplace – makes sense. Specifically, it makes sense to bring banking, insurance and securities within the single regulatory regime. Equally – while international practices vary across different countries – there is a strong case for constituting the Central Bank as this single prudential regulator. This is especially the case in Ireland, where the Bank has evolved over the last ten or fifteen years as the de facto single regulator (except for insurance). The crux of the matter relates to bringing responsibility for consumer protection, including conduct of business arrangements, within these arrangements. That is what the Bill proposes. That is where it is flawed.

Systemic dangers

It's important to be clear what we are talking about here; that is, the capacity of the Central Bank to respond quickly and effectively to a systemic shock (whether of domestic or international origin), which threatens to undermine the stability of the financial system and, thereby, undermine the real economy. How likely, in practise, is this to happen? During the 1980s and 1990s there were a series of financial crises right across the developed and transitional economies. Some of the largest global financial institutions – Daiwa, Sumitomo, Morgan Granville, Barings… the list goes on. They did not threaten the wider system.

An authoritative study by the 'Group of 30' into the management and supervision of global financial institutions and the potential for systemic risk, argued that

'The growth in size, velocity and complexity of international transactions, and the higher concentration of trading activity in a relatively small number of institutions that play a leading role in multiple markets, suggest that regulators will find it increasingly difficult to improvise effective crisis-management in the event of a shock occurring.'

The threshold of concern for the study group was a shock that would not only threaten a major financial institution, but could cascade through the international financial system threatening additional major institutions, and, in turn, the financial infrastructure of the entire international system itself. While past shocks and crises have not risen to this level, those in the study group agreed that such a situation could not be ruled out.

The case against the legislation

The case against proceeding with this legislation – and specifically the integration of prudential supervision with consumer protection, including conduct of business rules, rests on the following arguments:

• The complexity of the institutional arrangements, which are proposed in the Bill.

As noted above, what is envisaged is an amalgamation of diverse functions and an alphabet soup of anagrams that is so uniquely opaque as to militate against any prospect of efficient and transparent regulation.

• More specifically, the proposed integration of prudential regulation with consumer protection will involve bringing together, within a single highly complex institutional structure, quite distinct policy objectives. It is worth pointing out that the whole thrust of the Central Bank over the last 20 years or so has been to shed responsibility for consumer protection to a more appropriate institution, so that it can focus on its main monetary policy and the stability of the bank system.

The net effect of the proposals in the Bill will be a weakening of Ireland's albeit already limited capacity to respond to a major systemic shock. At the same time, consumers of financial services and products would be considerably disadvantaged, compared with alternative institutional arrangements: namely an enlarged Director of Consumer Affairs which could ensure timely redress for consumers across an ever-widening spectrum of financial services. This is a huge agenda for consumers and one infinitely better handled in an existing, experienced institution – the Director for Consumer Affairs – than in a set of arguments transposed to a wholly different Institution, the Central Bank.

• Then there is the issue of timing in regard to the bringing forward of this Bill. The timing is inexplicable – other than simply an exercise in 'clearing the decks' prior to the election. Internal controls are at the heart of the supervisory process. There are enormously important lessons to be learned from the failure of Internal Controls and Risk Management procedures in Allfirst / AIB. The Ludwig Report provides substantive insights into areas that may need further strengthening in terms of existing legislation. But there has been no systematic public evaluation of any of the Ludwig findings. Nor has the Central Bank's own report been published. Nor is there any indication of when the Reports of the FBI, the US Federal Reserve, and the Maryland Regulatory Authorities will be available.

• At the level of the EU, the most important point to be made is that the European Central Bank (ECB) lacks a substantive regulatory and supervisory role. This deficiency was built into the Treaty. The idea was, effectively, to leave financial regulation within the control of national (Home Country) authorities. And so the provisions of the Treaty are – in sharp contrast with the Delors model – labyrinthine. They were meant to impede, rather than to facilitate, progress towards a single system of EU financial regulation. This made no sense in the early 1990s: it makes even less sense now when national borders have been wholly redundant by the growth of global financial service providers.

These considerations are not grandiose or removed from the reality of the Irish financial services marketplace. Quite the contrary. It is precisely because we have a highly open financial sector; it is precisely because the IFSC is a microcosm of global financial markets that we had really better take into account developments in the broader international context in which the proposed Bill is being brought forward and expected to work.

The real problem with the Bill is, of course, well known. It embodies a structure, which was prescribed at the outset – i.e. a single regulatory authority for prudential supervision and consumer protection – rather than one that emerged from an open-ended and EU-informed discussion.

In summary, can it seriously be suggested that the proposed regulatory arrangements in the Bill – encompassing an organisational structure that is elephantine to put it kindly – could possibly deal effectively with a sudden systemic crisis either within the Irish financial system or in the wider European and global markets of which Ireland is now a small subset?

The Bill should be withdrawn. The reality is that prudential supervision and consumer protection have a very different focus. They deal with different issues and require very different skills and competencies. It simply makes no sense whatsoever to lump them together within a single organisation. There is a very real possibility of a conflict of interest leading to one gaining ascendancy or 'crowding out' the other. To put this more positively, it makes far more sense to have one institution – the Central Bank – focussing on prudential and solvency issues – which feed directly into its role in implementing monetary policy within the ECB; and a separate institution with a clear and undiluted focus on consumer protection.

Such a structure would allow each agency to get on with its respective responsibilities.

But perhaps, most of all, what is needed is time to reflect; to absorb the lessons of recent domestic and international events; to develop a set of proposals that reflect the challenges of a global financial environment that is characterised by unprecedented complexity and uncertainty; and to consider what should be the European (and, in this regard, the Irish) contribution to a new system of international regulatory governance. All of this is a very long way from the proposed Bill. It should be shelved.

The above is an extract from his paper entitled, 'EU and International Regulatory Arrangements and the case against the Central Bank and Financial Services Authority Bill 2002'.

'Global Institutions, National Supervision and Systemic Risk' by John Heimann, Merrill Lynch and Lord Alexander of Weedon, NatWest Group.

This article appeared in Finance, April 2002.

Ludwig Analysis Provides Opportunity to Scrutinise Plans for Single Regulator

The upcoming Bill's plan to lump prudential supervision and consumer protection together within a single body makes no sense whatsoever, argues Ray Kinsella.

The Ludwig report analysis of the failings in Allfirst Bank and the recommendations made have already resonated through the international banking markets and regulatory agencies.

They are almost certain to prove, in retrospect, the catalyst for a restructuring in risk management and, equally important, in what is perceived to be the trading-based culture and mindset of the major banking institutions. The report's recommendations also provide significant food for thought for the international regulatory authorities – because internal control systems were subverted with a knock-on effect on the bank's capital resources. There is also the fact that these deficiencies remained undetected not alone within the institution, but also from the scrutiny of external auditors and supervisors.

These are centrally important issues and no doubt will receive attention in the outstanding reports on events at Allfirst. But there is another issue which has attracted scant attention but may prove to be the single most important impact of Mr Ludwig's report.

It was not within his remit to evaluate the adequacy of the existing regulatory system in Ireland nor, more importantly, of the prospective regime involving the establishment of a Single Regulatory Authority. Nonetheless, albeit unintentionally, the Ludwig report provides such an opportunity. Due to be introduced before the end of the current Dáil term – is a Bill which proposes extensive changes in regulatory arrangements. There are several important issues.

One is that consolidating such arrangements in respect of prudential and solvency requirements – across credit institutions, insurance companies, and the financial markets and exchanges through which they trade – is sensible. Developments in domestic and international markets, involving a convergence between banking and insurance, points to the need to adapt Ireland's formerly compartmentalised approach to regulation into a single agency. At present it spans several Government Departments and bodies.

The second issue about which the different institutions and Government Departments argued was whether this institution should be a "greenfield" agency or encompassed within the Central Bank which, over the last 10 or 15 years had, de facto, evolved as a quasi-prudential regulator – with the single exception of insurance.

While different views were expressed, there was always a compelling case for devolving responsibility for solvency requirements and supervision of insurance institutions to the Central Bank. The reality is that the Bank, responsible for monetary policy within the

European central banking system, had to have responsibility also for the stability of the institutions. Banking and insurance institutions in global financial markets are inextricably linked and are the markets through which monetary policy is transmitted.

The third point – the crux of the matter – relates to bringing responsibility for prudential and solvency requirements in together with consumer protection, including conduct of business arrangements. That is what the Bill proposes.

The proposed Single Regulator, encompassing both prudential supervision and consumer protection, was born of the scandals within the Irish financial services sector of the 1990s. Following the Report of the Implementation Advisory Group on the Establishment of the Single Regulatory Authority (the McDowell report) in 1999, there was an extensive period of trench warfare as key institutional stakeholders fought over location, remit and structure of the proposed Single Regulator.

In February 2000, the Tánaiste and the Minister for Finance, Mr McCreevy, said that agreement had been reached on a structure and that the Government would be putting forward proposals for implementation.

Essentially what is proposed in the Bill is a regulatory structure – the Central Bank of Ireland and Financial Services Authority (CBIFSA). This will encompass a new authority – the Irish Financial Services Regulatory Authority (IFSRA) – which will be responsible for prudential regulation of banking and insurance and also for consumer protection. The proposals also envisage an interim board which will appoint a chief executive and a director of consumer protection. But on the establishment of the IFSRA, the latter will take over the functions of the Director of Consumer Affairs.

If you are confused at this stage, do not read on. Because the new structure will also include an Irish Monetary Authority (IMA) whose job it will be to "carry out the administrative functions required by the role of the Governor within the ESCB and to manage the external reserves": a task it should be said which has moved along effectively within the existing Central Bank system for quite some time.

The Central Bank Act requires banks to have regard to the quality of their internal control systems, which are monitored by the bank. The experience at Allfirst and in other banks where there was a trading-related collapse in internal controls demonstrates the impact which a subversion of these controls can have on capital adequacy and the bank's overall solvency.

It is never sensible to overstate an argument. And it is certainly the case that the proposals in the Bill and outlined above have received the most detailed consideration from experts, at a policy and a political level. Nevertheless, one is inevitably forced to conclude – especially after the Ludwig report – that this element of the Bill is flawed, overly complex, and compromises seriously the capacity of a Single Regulator to undertake its prudential responsibilities. Equally important, it is also very much a "second-best" instrument for consumer protection, compared with existing arrangements in financial services.

Can anyone seriously imagine that the proposed regulatory arrangements, embedded within an organisational structure that is elephantine to put it kindly, could possibly deal effectively with a sudden systemic crisis either within the Irish financial system or in the wider European and global markets of which Ireland is now a small subset?

The Bill should be withdrawn and these provisions recast. The reality is that prudential supervision and consumer protection have a very different focus. They deal with different issues and require very different skills and competencies. It simply makes no sense whatsoever to lump them together within a single organisation. There is a very real possibility of a conflict of interest leading to one gaining an ascendancy or crowding-out the other.

To put this more positively, it makes far more sense to have one institution – the Central Bank – focusing on prudential and solvency issues which feed directly into its role in implementing monetary policy within the ECB; and a separate institution with a clear and undiluted focus on consumer protection. Such a structure would contribute to simplicity and allow each agency to get on with its respective responsibilities. This would not be possible with the Bill's proposed structure.

This Article appeared in The Irish Times, March 2002.

Fraud Shows Banks' Controls Playing Catch-up and Regulators Arriving Late

The massive fraud at AIB's US subsidiary, Allfirst, shows how internal controls are always playing catch-up, suggests Ray Kinsella. It is a gap that will have to be bridged.

It will take some time before all the investigations now under way are completed. Moreover, a rush to judgment is never a smart idea. Nevertheless, there are already a number of points about the events at AIB's US subsidiary – Allfirst Bank – that are clear.

Some of these have to do with the failure of the internal control systems and the likely effect on AIB Group. Some of them have to do with the increasing difficulty within all banks of managing risk within the context of a globalised financial market of unprecedented complexity. The latter raises issues regarding the vulnerability of the global financial system – of which Ireland is a very small subset – to a global systemic shock.

AIB has acknowledged that there was a failure in the internal control systems within Allfirst Bank. This was the problem which brought about the collapse of Barings Bank some years ago – an event which, despite the relatively small size of Barings, sent a shock wave through the entire global banking system. One rogue trader decimated the entire capital base of one of the oldest British banks.

Comparisons between Allfirst and Barings are totally overstated. To begin with, Barings' Singapore subsidiary, within which Nick Leeson worked, was a small operation which generated for a short period enormous profits.

Secondly, Barings' management was manifestly culpable for not acting on clear and obvious deficiencies in the internal control systems in Singapore.

Thirdly, the management as a whole was clearly out of its depth in terms of understanding the markets in which Nick Leeson was trading: the management chose to ignore the poor quality of the earnings stream, reflected in the fact that one small unit could generate such a high proportion of total profits.

None of these arguments applies to Allfirst Bank. To begin with, AIB Group, in pursuing during the 1990s a strategy of global diversification, has developed in Maryland a robust and profitable organisation. Secondly, while the impact of the alleged fraud is significant, in terms of the impact on AIB's capital base it still leaves the group very well capitalised in terms of international benchmarks.

Thirdly, the alleged fraud was – unlike the Barings case – highly complex. But, crucially, it was picked up by the bank's control systems, albeit not until a significant amount of damage had been done. The situation was significant, but certainly far short of critical.

200

Perhaps the most important difference is the manner in which management has, to date, handled the debacle. The proactive approach by group management, which has been highly transparent to the markets, will have gone some way to reassuring large institutional investors. The decision to take the capital charge in the current year was absolutely correct; having said that, the breakdown in internal controls in Allfirst should not have happened.

There will be collateral damage in terms of market perception. Like most large international banks, AIB Group has a highly sophisticated risk-management system. Some of the questions that need to be asked will focus on the management process and some on how the bank's settlements procedures could have been subverted to such an extent.

The reality is that internal controls in all banks are continually playing catch-up with both financial and technical innovation within the markets.

A shock such as this has become increasingly probable within a market environment in which internal control systems increasingly lag behind the complexity of the markets which they are intended to monitor – and the regulatory authorities generally arrive a little breathless and a little late.

Certainly, supervisory authorities are increasingly monitoring the quality of internal controls, but it is not easy to see how this gap can be bridged. Moreover, the prospective risks embedded in this environment are exacerbated by the increasing scope for externally – generated attacks on a banking system whose central nervous system is technology – dependent and therefore vulnerable to subversion.

There is an additional issue which the Allfirst shock throws into sharp relief. In an environment of increasingly concentrated and integrated financial markets, there is quite simply, nobody in charge. The long-term capital management (LTCM) crisis of the late 1990s and the Asian banking crisis would have been immeasurably worse in their impact on financial markets had the New York Fed not stepped in. That's not its job; it is not responsible for maintaining the stability of the global financial system. Then, again, neither is the IMF.

The Bank for International Settlements plays a pivotal role, but it does not have a global mandate. Nor does it have the policy instruments needed to contain a full-blown systemic crisis. And the European Central Bank is only now beginning to develop a supervisory capability. Responsibility still rests primarily with national authorities whose banks trade on global markets.

This fragmentation of responsibility is, quite simply, scary. It may not be so easy to deal with the next crisis – and there will be one as we head into prospectively a period of low economic growth and heightened political risk. It's poor comfort for AIB shareholders, but at a global level the Allfirst shock may have the effect of concentrating minds.

This Article appeared in The Irish Times, February 2002.

Scrap the Single Regulator and make way for

European Supervision

Ray Kinsella argues that it is still not too late to ditch the whole principle of a single regulatory authority for financial services and to support moves for the European Central Bank to have a real role in financial supervision.

The Report of the Implementation Group on the Single Financial Regulator (The McDowell Group) has been 'on ice' for about a year. The Group of Experts was established by the Dáil, following on an evaluation of failures in governance within the financial sector. The Government's intentions in regard to institutional arrangements for a single regulator remain to be clarified: whether, for example, the Single Regulator is to be located within a revamped Central Bank or within a new 'greenfield' institution. Similarly, the scope and mandate of the proposed new Single Regulator has not been announced; specifically, whether it is to encompass consumer protection, as well as prudential regulation. Policy uncertainty is the last thing one wants in the financial sector, more especially within an environment of change and uncertainty. The issue is hugely important: it needs to be resolved.

Reasons to re-think

My argument is that, in this instance, the delay that has occurred (for whatever reason) has, in fact, been fortuitous. Notwithstanding the rigor of the Group's analysis, the whole project needs to be completely rethought from scratch. There are a number of reasons for this.

The first relates to a 'gap' in the governance and regulation the international financial system. In an environment which is now truly global, and in which market and systems integration will continue to increase, there is, quite simply, no one in charge. The nearest we have to a global regulator is a committee of the Bank for International Settlements (BIS). It has played an absolutely indispensable role in the oversight of international financial stability, but its writ is not universal nor do its recommendations have a binding force except via national authority. The IMF, in the wake of the 'Asian Crisis', acutely conscious of the impact of instability on global macroeconomic conditions, is seemingly aiming to fill this leadership gap, but this would require a change in its statutes. However this issue is resolved, it is clear that a major international regulatory initiative – my guess would be as part of the programme of the incoming post-Clinton US Administration – is on the way. Pre-empting this global uncertainty here in Ireland makes no sense.

Then there is the EU. At the heart of the Maastricht Treaty on EMU, there is a fundamental flaw. This 'Black Hole' has to do with Article 105 (of which more below) and will have to be addressed in order to support the ESCB EU-wide monetary policy mandate with appropriate prudential responsibilities. A 'fudge' is probable but an amendment of the Treaty is what is really required. Whatever option is adopted, there will be important knock-on implications for the regulatory/supervisory capabilities of the European Central Bank (ECB). To proceed with the Single Regulator at this stage – to second-guess what may come out of the Article 105 issue – would be to risk undermining the future relevance and effectiveness of Ireland's Regulatory System.

A third reason has to do with rapidly developing internet-based crime and how regulatory authorities should deal with it. The problem is again a global one: the transition to internet banking represents a paradigm shift for national regulators. Law-enforcement agencies around the world are rapidly accumulating experience of new forms of net-based financial crime. The stakes are incalculable.

In this regard, the words of former Bank of England Regulator Brian Quinn – "Regulators usually arrive a little breathless and a little late" – are more than a little chilling.

Much of the experience that is now available on the regulation of internet-based crime was not factored into the discussions of the structure and the mandate of the Single Regulator. This, in itself, would be a sufficient for saying "Okay – better do this again from scratch and be sure we get it right". But when one also considers the uncertainty and problematic regulatory environment at the global and EU level, as well as the technological changes impacting on the robustness of prudential regulation – the case for starting over becomes nothing less than compelling. It is important to go back to basics to underpin the strength of this argument.

Back to basics

There are two reasons why the regulation and supervision of financial services are justified. It is useful to spell them out because it provides an insight into how the regulatory/supervisory function is best organised in terms of institutional arrangements here in Ireland.

The first reason has to do with consumer protection. The argument here is broadly similar to that which applies to other key services/utilities, e.g. telecoms. That is, individual consumers are disadvantaged because of a lack of information necessary to make an informed decision. This justifies intervention in the form of regulation, to inform and protect the consumer. The extent of regulation may be a matter of degree. Large corporate customers will be in a better position to make informed decisions on using a service, compared with, say, retail customers. This is reinforced by the fact that certain financial services transactions are hugely important for an individual: e.g. taking out a mortgage. The cost to an individual of such a transaction going wrong is pretty important. That is why the Director of Consumer Affairs' mandate needs to be strengthened in any future regulatory/supervisory arrangement.

A second reason has to do with the prudent management of institutions in the interests of the stability of the wider financial system, and it has two separate, but related parts. The first part has to do with the need for a credible – and hence independent – external regulation to ensure that depositors' funds – the very basis of intermediation – are not put at risk because of deficiencies in a firm in e.g. the calibre of management, the quality of internal controls and, more generally, the capacity of the institution to manage (in the broadest sense of the word) risk. Capital adequacy (and, in the case of insurance, solvency margins) play a particularly important role in this regard.

The second part relates to the need to maintain market confidence – in an institution, a market or an exchange – so as to avoid, or mitigate, the social costs (quite apart, that is, from the private losses to share/bond holders) of 'contagion', which may follow a collapse in confidence.

And the importance of this prudential role hinges on the crucial role played by institutions within the wider economy – their role in money transactions and the key role of their liabilities – and, also, on the leverage built into the structure of their balance sheet. These qualities make banks uniquely important – and uniquely vulnerable: the consequence of a failure (or even the threat of a failure) generates consequences ('externalities') that greatly exceed the private costs of failure. So much for the basic rationale for regulation and supervision which should be built into a robust institutional structure for Ireland. Against this background, it may be useful to develop some of the key points summarised earlier.

Maastricht: regulatory 'black hole'

The primary influence on Irish financial regulations has been the EU. The Single Market Programme (SMP), in particular, has largely determined the substantive content and scope of national regulation. Having said that, the SMP did not affect existing institutional arrangements in respect of financial regulation.

In Ireland, the Central Bank has in recent years evolved into the de facto Single Regulator (aside from insurance) alongside its primary monetary policy role. It is scheduled to take responsibility for insurance intermediaries later this year: Given market developments (bank assurance), there is a compelling case for the transfer of responsibility for solvency of insurance companies to the Central Bank, just as it supervises capital adequacy for the banking sector.

The introduction of EMU has effected a separation between, on the one hand, the EU-wide jurisdictions of the Single Monetary policy (the domain of the ECB) and national regulatory and supervisory policy (as provided for in Article 105 of the Maastricht Treaty). This dichotomy has further exacerbated the ECB's lack of capacity in regard to prudential regulation – a 'black hole' in the Maastricht Treaty on EMU.

EU policy gaps

The logic of the Euro and the Single Monetary Policy for the EU requires that the ECB should have a substantial regulatory capacity – enshrined proactively in the Treaty – in order to safeguard stability and, where appropriate, to intervene, in order to mitigate the effects of contagion or arising systemic 'shocks'.

That is not what was provided for in the Treaty. In sharp contrast to the Delors framework for EMU, the provisions of the Maastricht model are tortuous: the basic premise is that responsibility for supervision should remain at the national level, with the ECB playing a minor supporting role. Article 105 (5) assigns to the ECB the task of:

'...contributing to the smooth conduct of national policy pursued by competent authority relating to the prudential supervision of credit institutions and the stability of the system'

This resonates with a recent perspective of the ECB:

'The overall framework for cooperation within the Euro area essentially aims at reinforcing preventive measures against bank fragility'

However, in cases of instability, the same framework can be used to deal with any cross-border implications of such a crisis, and to limit contagion.

Supervisions stand ready to inform the Euro-system as soon as a banking crisis arises, and the BSC is in a position to address the relevant issues.

The need for a timely exchange of information is essential in order to enable competent national authorities to deal with cross-border implications.[45]

It is clear that the development of policy remains at the national level with the ECB having a purely supportive role, 'contributing to the...conduct of national policy'. Even in Stage I, it was clear that this was a misjudgement: a black hole at the centre of the EU financial system. The extent of structural change, including increased linkages across the EU that have occurred since then, has reinforced the gap between the national perspective built into the treaty and where the market is at.

More recently, the ECB has moved to address the latent difficulties inherent in its lack of regulatory/supervisory capability. It has, notably, established a Banking Supervisory Committee (BSC) which directly and through sub-groups has identified key issues and how they might be addressed. By bringing together officials from both the ECB and national authorities, it has also strengthened cooperation in financial supervision.

This reactive national perspective built into the ECB, via Article 105 (5), is wholly at variance with the nature of developments in EU financial markets, and the potential threats they face. These threats include:

• The significant, M&A driven, process of market concentration in banks, insurance and capital markets.

• The development of complex trans–EU (and global) financial conglomerates.

---

[45]ECB Bulletin, April 2000

• The significant increase in cross-border transactions, including money market inter-bank transactions created by the Single monetary policy.

• The near explosive growth of internet-based financial service providers and the threat of technological subversion which cannot be addressed, let alone resolved, at a national level.

Each one of these factors reinforces the case for the EU having a substantial responsibility for, and capacity in, prudential regulation. In aggregate, however, these factors constitute a compelling case for a revision of the Treaty, to ensure that the ECB (and, by extension, the EU itself) has the capacity to protect the stability of the markets through which its money policy is transmitted. And, as financial institutions grow, through mergers, into EU (rather than national) entities, there is surely an unarguable case for adapting prudential structures to this new EU–regime.

The Asian Banking crises of the late 1990s, and the Long Term Capital Management debacle, highlighted how crises are now truly global in nature. The international community – including the EU – was caught flat-footed. The New York Fed (which encompasses prudential authority with its monetary policy role) intervened to resolve both crises.

We may not be so lucky next time. The idea that coordination of EU national supervisory authorities (especially where a Single Regulatory may have a double focus of Consumer Protection as well as prudential responsibility) – which is the current situation – is risible. It indicates an obtuseness of the dynamics of (global) financial crises and the clout, leadership and speed of response required to address them; hence, again, the need for the EU to get its act together and to adapt its capacities (as the IMF is) to the new global paradigm. This requires an amendment of the Treaty rather than waffle about 'closer coordination'.

Optimal regulatory arrangements

The next stage of the argument has a very direct bearing on the mandate and institutional arrangements for the proposed Single Regulator and, also, whether or not we should proceed to its establishment without further detailed consideration.

In addressing this issue there are a number of points to be made. Firstly, there are a wide variety of institutional arrangements in relation to supervision across the Community. In most countries the Central Bank is either the prudential regulator or has a major role. These differences reflect unique national peculiarities of culture and customs. But the more important issue is whether, in principle, one institutional structure is inherently more robust to existing and future challenges and efficient. In addressing this issue, two propositions can be advanced.

The first is, quite simply, that where a Central Bank has responsibility for the implementation and/or the conduct of monetary policy, it should also have responsibility for the stability and integrity of the institutions, exchanges and markets through which monetary policy is transmitted that is my first Proposition.

There are several reasons for this. In the event of a systemic shock, the capacity of the Central Bank to manage the provision of liquidity – to act as lender of last resort – is easier, where it has a close working relationship based on detailed supervisory knowledge with institutions. Equally, in carrying out its monetary policy role, its prudential responsibilities provide important information, which facilitates the conduct of monetary policy.

My second proposition is that consumer protection and prudential regulation are quite distinct disciplines. They may, of course, overlap. Consumer protection is more easily assured when a bank is well capitalised and appropriately regulated.

Transparency and accountability are more easily ensured – and potential conflict of focus avoided – when consumer protection is managed separately from prudential regulation.

Consumer protection is focussed on micro issues, such as conduct of business rules, whereas prudential regulation is concerned with macro, or systemic, effects: the consequence of deficient prudential regulation (as we have seen time and time again in the 1990s), are potentially enormously costly. They are also highly time-sensitive: the impact is now and is transmitted with biological sensitivity throughout highly integrated markets. Finally, the skills and competences required in each discipline are quite distinct.

Global governance

There is a widening gap in global financial governance. This is not to say that there is not intensive cooperation among prudential authorities within, and across, markets. There is. There has been considerable progress in developing sets of principles and Codes of Best Practice. Moreover, there is an intensive dialogue between the leading banks and the regulatory authorities in regard to utilising new risk metrics, which will contribute to prudential stability. These are important developments.

But there is a growing recognition that a legitimate, accountable, global system of prudential regulation simply does not exist at present. The NY Fed held the line when LTCM, and the Asian Bank crises, threatened global financial – and macroeconomic – instability. But they may not next time. Some form of major initiative, possibly involving the IMF in cooperation with the BIS, is inescapable. And soon.

The ECB, for its part, needs to participate in this debate as a principal. There are forceful arguments for the ECB accepting responsibility for EU-wide prudential regulation as a response to market developments that could threaten the stability of the EU-system and, equally, as natural complement to its primary monetary policy mandate.

No short cuts

Against this background, Ireland's Single Regulator initiative should be deferred. There are no short cuts to stability. Instead, the Government should – for all of the reasons set out above – establish a Banking Commission (there are important precedents in Ireland's financial history) to address appropriate forms of regulation within the broader context of structural change in Ireland's financial markets. At the same time, it should publish a consultative paper, which could serve as the basis for much needed rigorous debate and consultation (external as well as domestic) on the issues. The 1990s have seen a veritable deluge of financial/supervisory legislation in Ireland. The work of a Banking Commission would provide time to address the process of consolidating this plethora of legislation and greatly contribute to the operational effectiveness of whatever institutional arrangements for regulation are put forward by the commission.

And finally...

My own evaluation is that what is required is to:

• Retain prudential regulation within the Central Bank for all financial institutes, markets and exchanges. While commissioning a fundamental review of how internal structures of the Bank should be reconfigured (Mission – Principles – Objectives – Instruments – Skills/Competencies – Procedures – Controls – Oversights) to accommodate this new mandate.

• Extend and develop the Office of the Director of Consumer Affairs (it also needs a new name) to encompass Consumer Protection across all (financial) products and services.

• A co-ordinating Financial Compliance Directorate, supported by investment in MIS systems, to facilitate information flows.

• Establish a consultative financial market forum, chaired by the Secretary General of the Department of Finance with a brief to bridge the regulatory market divide and to ensure worldclass standards (informed by market investment in this field) in risk metrics, and also to evaluate the strategic implications for Ireland of ongoing structural change in EU and global financial markets and architecture.

• A programme of consolidating and rationalising financial services regulatory legislation, within an electronic template, as an urgent priority.

This Article appeared in Finance, July 2000.

No Bank Can Afford to be 'Complacent' After

Barings Debacle

The official report of the Bank of England's Board of Banking Supervision on the collapse of Barings Bank largely confirmed what the markets already knew: the £820 million collapse of the bank in February was attributed to the activities of Nick Leeson, its chief trader in Singapore.

More fundamentally, it was due to a catastrophic failure of internal controls within Barings Bank which facilitated the continuation of unauthorised trading activities. The report includes criticisms of supervisory practice by the Bank of England and of Barings auditors.

Barings was an elite bank in the heart of London. A bank which encompasses competent and well-regarded teams servicing an alpha client list. It collapsed against the background of a statutorily-based supervisory system which addressed, in specific terms, those key issues that lay at the root of the failure of Barings.

The report has a chilling relevance to all those who belong to the "it couldn't happen here" school. In a lecture at the University of Ulster, some three years ago, Brian Quinn, Head of Supervision and member of the Board who compiled the report, pointed out that:

"The failure of Johnson Matthey in 1984...brought home the message that even quite large banks could have life-threatening deficiencies of systems and controls. It was clear that... supervision over the control of internal administrative systems was now sufficiently important to be included specifically in the criteria for authorisation. Both these deficiencies were addressed in the 1987 Banking Act and in the Bank's Statement of Principles.

"To be authorised, a bank must satisfy the Bank of England that it maintains adequate accounting and other records; has adequate systems of control of the business and of its records; has non-executive directors where appropriate; and has satisfactory arrangements for internal and external audit.

The bank has supervised compliance with these requirements in two ways. It has sent in its own "review teams" of bankers and accountants, mainly seconded from the major firms. Secondly, using the specification of its power in Section 39 of the 1987 Act, the bank has required all banks to provide it with reports covering the adequacy of systems and controls, and of the accuracy of supervisory statistical returns. Those reports are prepared by reporting accountants engaged by and paid for by the banks."

The Barings debacle, quite simply, should not have happened. But it did. That's why no bank, however large and well managed, can afford to be complacent. There are four key financial themes which all banks and supervisors need to address: internal controls, capital, corporate governance and supervision.

Internal controls are defined by the Cadbury Committee as: "The whole system of controls, financial or otherwise, established to provide reasonable assurance of (a) effective and efficient operations; (b) reliable financial information and reporting; and (c) compliance with laws and regulations."[46]

Their purpose is to safeguard the financial integrity of a bank. In the case of Barings, the key points are that robust internal controls are a condition of authorisation and that they are subject to ongoing scrutiny by various aspects of the supervisory process. The issue, therefore, is one of whether the organisation understands the nature and importance of controls, whether they are bedded down in a "compliance culture" within the organisation and whether they are enforced. Barings failed on all three counts.

Two developments impacting on internal controls have placed pressures on banks: technology which can increase the potential for undermining internal controls, and off-balance sheet instruments which can significantly alter risk profiles.

At the heart of the Barings debacle was a failure to reconcile two quite separate cultures within a single management ethos. Barings prospered on the basis of traditional (on-balance sheet) merchant banking activities.

These it understood. The trading culture of the derivatives (off-balance sheet) market is fundamentally different. Barings management – and the control system – never got to grips with how best to integrate these into an informed, cohesive and robust entity. There are important lessons here for conglomerates.

Perhaps the single most extraordinary aspect of the Barings collapse was the manner in which the supervision of internal controls allowed the bank's capital – at the very heart of prudent bank management – to be mismanaged, eroded, and finally, wiped out.

It is arguable that Barings – as a small to medium sized merchant bank – should not have been in the business of derivatives trading in the first place. Not simply because it was not where the bank's core strengths lay; nor because senior management didn't understand them, but, also, because they lacked the capital to be a serious player on the scale commensurate with the profits that were, supposedly, being generated.

The Bank of England's rules are clear: "Capital...must be of an amount which is commensurate with the nature and scale of the institution's operations..."[47] But when things began to go wrong, the supervisory system should have worked.

The provisions of the Cadbury Code relating to high level and internal controls and, more recently, of the Greenbury Code on executive remuneration, provide a corpus of "best practise" on corporate governance. Deficiencies in this area are central to an understanding of the reasons for the failure of Barings and its relevance to other financial institutions.

---

[46] Cadbury Committee
[47] Bank of England

For banks, the quality of earnings is everything. Profits generated by speculation in what were or should have been essentially non-core activities in a peripheral market manifestly fail the quality test. And when the system of executive remuneration, including bonus payments, feed on such profits, the extent to which good governance can be compromised is clear.

The report identifies what were, in retrospect, important procedural failings in the Bank of England's supervision of Barings. But its recommendation that the bank strengthen its understanding of the derivatives market rather misses the point. The collapse had little to do with the more exotic forms of off-balance sheet instruments. What the report does not state is that the overall supervisory structure in the UK is fundamentally flawed. It is a patchwork of statutory and self-regulating systems, of overlapping, and sometimes competing, regulatory bodies. Problems arising from a lack of co-ordination are inevitable. Basically, the Financial Services Act, 1986 was a disaster. It needs to be fundamentally revamped. But this will not happen. In these circumstances, the idea of taking responsibility for banking supervision away from the Bank of England and giving it to yet another body is daft.

In fact, though its critics would be loath to admit it, there is substantial evidence which indicates that the bank's supervisory record is much more robust than might seem apparent. This is all the more so, given the size of the UK banking sector and the difficulties of maintaining systemic stability which it has at a time of unprecedented strain arising from innovation, competition and globalisation.

What will change is the bank's supervisory style. This has always, even within the present formalistic system, been very civilised and courteous. Also, market intelligence – what the boys talk about at their favourite watering hole – will be strengthened.

Again, this is something which the bank has always seen as important – it is precisely why there are external members on the Board of Banking Supervision. The system did not work this time.

This article appeared in The Irish Times, July 1995.

Section Four:

The Global Financial Crises: The Meltdown of Trust and its Consequences

Alternative Economic Vision of "Spirit of Ireland"

Offers Hope

Ireland is a chastened country. Successive economic forecasts provide confirmation of an implosion that is creating a vortex at the heart of our economy, and the wider society – including public services – which it underpins.

On the external front, the contraction in world trade, together with the pressure on US foreign investment arising from Barack Obama's legislation, give additional impetus to this vortex which is swallowing up jobs, lives and domestic industry. It is not partisan, but only the hard reality, that the politics which have led us into this cul-de-sac are incapable of identifying a way forward.

But, there is a way forward. Unlikely as it seems, we are being offered an opportunity to re-imagine the economy, and in doing so, restore both our confidence and our international standing.

The announcement, by Graham O'Donnell, of a new national energy initiative is transformational. It is based on our capacity to jointly harness Ireland's uniquely favourable wind-flow, and the potential for hydro–electric generation offered by ice-sculpted valleys running into the Atlantic.

Nothing like this has been conceived before. The logo "Spirit of Ireland" does less than justice to what is envisaged – which is reimagining how our economy and society could be. It is eminently clear from the critical mass of research, drawing on both Irish and international expertise, that this can be done, starting, more or less, now. The economics of the initiative are compelling.

Ireland's economic future is inextricably bound up with the cost, and the security, of a stable and sustainable supply of energy in a form compliant with our responsibilities under the Kyoto protocol. The most recent (2008) National Competitiveness Report by Forfás highlights this reality:

"This report highlights that Ireland is highly dependent on imported fossil fuels, which present a range of challenges...With respect to electricity cost competitiveness, Ireland ranks as the second most expensive country in the EU15...Irish businesses and consumers are exposed to volatile and increasing international prices for oil and gas...Our reliance on imported fossil fuels endangers our security of supply and raises the carbon intensity of the Irish economy...Significant change will be required if we are to meet our Kyoto targets. Achieving our security of supply and environmental objectives in a fashion that does not further weaken our energy cost competitiveness is an acute challenge."*

Electricity costs for Irish industry have risen inexorably over the last decade – significantly faster than those of our trading competitors. They are now, according to the most recent data published by the Central Bank, the second highest in the EU15. The cost of electricity to households has followed a similar pattern – they, too, are the second highest in the EU. The cost of imported fuel is some €3 billion a year. The reality is that our capacity is inadequate, our costs excessive, and our whole generating infrastructure deficient and not aligned to our own indigenous energy capabilities.

The Spirit of Ireland Initiative provides a robust platform for:

- Transforming Ireland's medium-term economic performance.

- Reducing uncertainty, which is at present imposing a severe economic penalty on business and Government, not least within a largely self-fixated banking model and foreign exchange markets that are, at best, indifferent.

- Restoring national morale and confidence in our ability, wholly against the odds, to innovate and, once again, provide a template for other countries to seek to emulate.

- Fiscal stabilisation, and greater certainty, will contribute to a restoration of Ireland's international reputation and policy credibility.

- Leveraging Ireland's "Golden Demographics", which is one of its few embedded competitive advantages, compared with other EU and OECD countries. The initiative provides a compelling justification for pro-active investment in higher education, and for expanding, rather than closing down, skill-based third-level courses and research.

It is worth emphasising that Central Statistic Office data suggests that the present demographics provide a unique window of opportunity which will close within 20 years, leading to significant increases in older, as well as the overall, dependency ratios.

Furthermore, the funding would not represent a further burden on an exchequer running out of balance–sheet capacity. Instead it provides the means for progressively returning to fiscal stability and paying off the costs of fiscal and political profligacy.

The initiative is not aspirational. It is rooted in established engineering and project management protocols. The scale of the project is vast. Downstream applications are limited only by the inventiveness of the Irish people. The first wave employment opportunities are in the tens of thousands – the key constraint here being the commitment of the people of Ireland and, secondly, the willingness of the present political order to support it without any regard whatever to patronage, and still less to control.

One of the terrible aspects of the recession has been the unravelling of expertise. Engineers are emigrating, whole classes of postgraduate students are seeking shelter within the third-level sector or setting aside their hard-won knowledge and capabilities. There is still time to reverse this process. We have the people with the necessary skills and with every incentive to engage proactively with this initiative.

What is in prospect is a whole new wave of industries and specialised service providers, following on from the epic energy engineering "core" of the project itself. The scale of Spirit of Ireland is, prophetically, proportionate to that of the country's existing and even more so, prospective, problems. And all of this potential, which is waiting to be harnessed, is configured around natural endowments of air, water and the human creativity of one of the youngest populations within the OECD.

It is, however, the proposed governance of the Spirit of Ireland initiative which truly sets it apart. The hubris that brought Ireland to its knees in the latter stages of the Celtic Tiger was characterised by societal fragmentation, driven by greed. We lost the run of ourselves and lost sight of our neighbour.

Spirit of Ireland is the complete antithesis of this mindset. It proposes that the wealth – in the form of energy, and all of the other activities that will be animated by this energy – be held in trusteeship for the people of Ireland. The proposed legal framework envisages that the gifts of our natural resources are the legacy of this, and future, generations, and must remain so. The fruits of this initiative will not be privatised, or parcelled out for private or institutional interests. This far–sighted vision throws into sharp relief the extent to which our natural resources have, in the past, been sold out or sold cheaply.

This is not a Government – or even a political – initiative. It is, quite simply, driven by the vision, tenacity and generosity of Graham O'Donnell, a successful entrepreneur working in this field, co–operating with a gifted academic team led by Prof Igor Shvets. The integrity and clear-sightedness of the initiative has brought on board a wide range of Irish and international experts. The sole motivation of this team has been the interests of the people of Ireland, and the willingness to engage inclusively with all of the people in order to make it happen.

This is the public good as a vital force in transforming, not just our energy supplies and our economic trajectory, but the whole manner in which Ireland, as a community, can function. That, surely, is transformational.

The response to my recent article ("We've screwed up, that's the truth of it" – April 23rd) – which argued for a whole new political ethos – found an extraordinary resonance across all ages and shades of political opinion. This response is embodied in the Spirit of Ireland initiative which is not just the only option open to us in our current bleak circumstances; it is the very best possible option.

Spirit of Ireland puts our future firmly into the hands of the people of Ireland, and the onus for supporting and empowering this initiative on to the politicians of a political system which is passing.

*Source: National Competitiveness Report 2008 (Vol. I) 1.2.6.

This Article appeared in the Irish Times, May 2009.

The Global Economic Crisis and its Impact on Ireland; Only Transformational Change Can Bring us Back From the Brink

The global financial crisis, which originated in the subprime mortgage market of the United States in the early years of this decade, has metastasized into the single greatest economic 'shock' to western liberal democracies, short of war.

This crisis is wholly different, in nature and scale, to the cyclical fluctuations which tend to be characteristic of western capitalism. Economic projections by both national and international agencies, including the IMF, forecasters have consistently failed to keep pace with the precipitous decline in global growth and trade as a result of the crisis. It has levelled long standing global financial institutions, destroying whole market sectors in the process. The erosion of the balance sheets of financial institutions, in the face of a meltdown in market valuations, as well as grave uncertainties, is without precedent.

In Ireland, the impact on economic growth and, by extension, employment, living standards and the public finances, has been shockingly abrupt and brutal. Governments fiscal position, and in particular the decline in tax revenues relative to government expenditures, have translated directly into cuts in Public Services on a scale that is hardly conceivable.

Ireland has had three 'Budgets' in the space of one year and still the fiscal deficit and borrowing requirement are beyond anything that could have been conceived even a year ago.

This reflects three factors: Firstly, the small and open nature of the Irish economy-we are highly vulnerable to the recession in the international economy as well as to the implosion in market confidence. Secondly, while Irish credit institutions avoided large exposure to so – called 'toxic assets'- the product of the kind of malign 'Business Model' that has impacted on banks and financial institutions in some other countries ,they are impacted by the effects on international credit and capital markets. Thirdly, our economy is suffering from self-inflicted wounds. These have taken the form of excessive lending to the whole spectrum of property and construction related sectors, as well corporate behaviour that has caused reputational damage to Ireland abroad and a loss of morale and Trust at home.

Collectively, these have pushed Ireland's economy into economic dislocation and deflation; they are generating economic and social stresses on individuals, Families and domestic businesses not seen before. There are no precedents – and whether measured by CSO data, or the insights of the St.Vincent de Paul Society, the situation continues to deteriorate. There is growing pressure on our political institutions. Politically, Ireland and indeed other developed economies, are being impelled into a different place-for which the nationalisation of banks stands as an apt metaphor.

The pastoral implications and challenges are enormous.

This crisis is an inflection point: it could neither be modelled nor can it be firewalled. The true measure of the scale of the crisis is reflected not only in the devastation of lives, as economies continue to stall notwithstanding the sheer scale of financial interventions by national authorities – as well as coordinated international action, including agreements at the recent G20 meeting in London – which have had little discernable effect so far in arresting the crisis..

There is a reason for this. The root causes of this crisis are not primarily financial, or economic. Certainly it is possible to identify predisposing factors in these fields – as well as negative feedback effects, such as the impact of the 'Credit Crisis' on the decline in access by business to even normal financial resources. But these are in general symptomatic of a deeper reality.

The crisis is primarily ethical in nature, with inevitable financial, economic and political consequences. In an absence of a rigorous understanding of the ethical nature of this crisis, it is simply not possible to begin the process of transformation – globally or in Ireland - that is necessary to restore stability and sustainability.*

Communism, as an ideology with a distinctive 'economic model' was based on Production and historical determinism. The Human Person, shorn of the transcendence of being made in the image of-and being redeemed by – the 'Living God', was reduced to a unit of the proletariat. Communism imploded. At the same time, a form of Capitalism-based essentially on the 'Person' as consumer and driven by what Galbraith, in his prophetic 'The Affluent Society', argued was a 'Wants', as opposed to a 'Needs'- based economy and one facilitated by semi-enforced financial indebtedness, gained ascendency in western developed democracies. It was this that was encompassed in – and the key driver of – the 'short-term Shareholder Value' business model. It is this model -riddled with moral and economic contradictions-which has collapsed. This collapse is catastrophic in its consequences.

Both ideologies, with their specific 'Business Models', have much in common, which made their collapse both inevitable and foreseeable. They denied the existence of an objective moral order. They demeaned – and in a very real sense *enslaved* – the human Person. They had no reference point outside of their own Paradigm.

This, in fact, provides a necessary starting point for both diagnosing the reason for the present catharsis and the template within which recovery and the development of a sustainable economic order, shaped by the characteristics of national economies as well as by innovation and globalisation, can be begun.

This must be said. The Catholic Church has developed the most rigorous critique of the conditions for a sustainable and just economic order. It is embedded in the Scriptures. It has been developed in successive Encyclicals. It is set out in the monumental 'Compendium of the Social Teaching of the Catholic Church' – a resource of truly global significance. It is predicated on a rigorous understanding of 'The Common Good', at the heart of which is the human Person.

The outcome of the global crisis is indeterminate. The most recent data and assessment from the IMF are bleak. Moreover, there are compelling reasons for arguing that the scale of government interventions are creating contingent liabilities that represent a future inflationary threat , which could well lead to a definitive meltdown of Trust. This possibility should not be discounted. Such a collapse of confidence almost happened in October 2008.

The Irish economy – a small sub set of global markets-faces the most serious challenges. The difficulties and pressures confronting Government are formidable. It is no platitude to say that they need prayers – after all, it was the denial of this reality, and all that it implies, that lead inexorably to the present crisis.

It is also true to say that there is little evidence of an understanding of the true nature of the crisis or of what is required. We are following misconceived economic policies; political institutions are in denial of the kind of the transformational changes that are required. There are objective ethical values that are being violated in political discourse as well as in our institutional behaviours and in the undermining of the status of the Family.

Ireland is a Christian nation in the truest, most inclusive, sense of the word. The great Benedictine scholar Dom Anscar Vonier once wrote: 'Christ could not be the living power He is without deeply modifying the ethical sense of the nations that worship Him....Now, the lessons of history are that wherever the name of Christ is alive ,there we find great ethical assurance and certainty...'('The Personality of Christ').

This generation is – as Pope John Paul II warned, in his address in Limerick, 'crowding-Christ, across pretty well all economic social and political domains. There are consequences – and they form the narrative of the fall of both communism and corporate capitalism. In Ireland, the lesson is this: A 'new capitalism' cannot be built on an 'old politics' or on an 'ethical' sense emasculated of our Christian values.

This Article was published for the Irish Times, April 2009.

We've Screwed Up – That's the Truth of It

The emergency Budget was seriously misconceived and our existing politics are incapable of resolving our problems. We are in dire need of political realignment and valued-based politics that eschews cronyism.

The Global economic crisis, as it is manifest in the wasteland of what was once the Celtic Tiger, is now entering a final and arguably devastating phase. Our political institutions and systems of governance are coming under inexorable pressure in the face of inadequate policy responses to the rise in unemployment, the decimation of the domestic economy, and a palpable feeling of quiet desperation among individuals and families and businesses.

The most recent assessment of the global economy by the International Monetary Fund – and its evaluation of Ireland's financial sector – makes sombre but not unexpected reading. The most recent Central Statistic Office data for the final quarter of 2008 shows a sharp decline in investment. Meanwhile, the live register is now escalating and is set to reach new levels before the end of this year.

This would strain the most robust and inclusive political system. In the case of Ireland, which faces both local elections and a contentious referendum, there is every possibility that what has happened will test the limits of tolerance of a population that is not without experience of the pains of unemployment and emigration.

We are looking at a fracturing and realignment of political institutions which do not speak to the sensibilities of a young generation they have beggared, nor to the needs of those who felt themselves entitled to something better having contributed much of their lives to the development of the Irish economy.

The roots of this latent political crisis are – like those of the global financial crisis – starkly ethical in nature. We have a political system largely rooted in obsolete divisions and, in the view of many, emasculated of the values which once animated them. This is not to say there are not highly committed professional and ethical politicians; there are, and many will be, not without some courage, knocking on doors.

The tragedy is, they are a "dead man walking". The defining characteristics of the system as a whole is a culture of power instead of service to the person. Our essentially adversarial political institutions have demonstrated little relevance to the imperative to restoring hope, and a sense of direction, at a time of unprecedented stress in modern Irish history.

It cannot be right that, for our legislature and political systems, it continues to be "business as usual" while, in virtually every other domain of our national life, the most painful adjustments are being made without consolation or consensus.

We have screwed up – that's the truth of it. We cannot build a new capitalism on old politics. Rebuilding trust in our institutions and in our political system – as much in the financial sector – will requires a values-based leadership. The time for political rhetoric and the old fashioned ardfheis-based nonsense is long past.

Political institutions and the system of governance are semi-detached from the pulse–beat of individuals who have lost their jobs, businesses teetering on the brink of failure, and families that are crushed by the circumstances in which they have suddenly found themselves.

They are still dominated by an apprenticeship system, which favours those who have served their time over those who can contribute most to addressing the problems now confronting the country.

The system of ministerial appointments makes little or no sense. All too frequently, it is geographically-based. Even more fundamentally, they commonly lack the relevant expertise to direct, with a sure and experienced hand, policy in the departments to which they are appointed. There is no formal training required from ministers from their first day in office. This simply makes no sense. It would not happen in any other profession or vocation.

Our political landscape is littered by "silos", each driven by their own agenda and political dynamic. There is the ambiguity of the relationship between, on the one hand, the legislature, and, on the other hand, the executive. This ambiguity leaves itself open to the "capture" of policy; it leaves itself open to the de facto delegation of key areas of responsibility to quangos of different kinds. Conversely, it can, and does, inhibit those within the public sector who have a real capacity to contribute, from putting their head above the parapet. The old political canard of the first priority on getting power being to retain it corrodes and demeans the very nature of what politics should be about.

The contradictions, ambiguities and inefficiencies in all of this, are all too evident in the manner in which we have responded to the economic crisis that continues to gather momentum across the entire economic landscape. The resources generated during the years of the (healthy) Celtic Tiger were, in substantial part, dissipated in a process of political largess. The legacy of the last 10 or 15 years can be stylised as being represented by interminable tribunals, legislation, much of which has served only to increase the burden on basic freedoms as well as on basic businesses, and regulation, which has turned to dust under the stress of recent events. These deficiencies raise the question, for example, of why it is only in an unprecedented deflationary period, we have appointed "An Bord Snip" to seek out inefficiencies in public expenditure. It is difficult to explain this either through a lack of political leadership and foresight. Equally, we have a Commission on Taxation – one that is expert and one that will produce an excellent report – side–by–side with ad hoc responses to a crisis that continues to gather momentum.

The anomalies and contradictions that riddle our taxation system have been evident for well over a decade. Neither markets, nor the lives of people, can await the production of reports. We have had too many reports. Paradoxically, the Government will commission external agencies to prepare detailed reports when all the knowledge necessary is already within their own departments. There is an acute lack of confidence in our own expertise and in our own resources.

The three budgets that have followed in rapid succession as Government failed to keep up with events, are a mess of additional levies and ad hoc taxes which result in a totally fragmented funding system. All

of the time, the landmine of unfunded pension liabilities remains deep in the long grass and a clear and present threat not only to those who are employed, but even to those who have recently, or will in the near future, lose their jobs. It makes no sense to prioritise the allocation of resources, written as IOUs on our future, to financial institutions over businesses whose survival is essential not alone to individual families, but to the wider economy – and by extension to the banking system.

We have our priorities all wrong. We are spending undreamt of sums of money – which we do not have – to support utilities which are skewed in favour of shareholders (and that is the supreme irony, since their interests have been entirely subverted by a malign business model) – while we continue to have a fragmented, unfair and multi–tiered healthcare system. That too does not make sense.

The recent Budget was seriously misconceived. What was needed was a budget written in our factories and on our farms; in our hospitals and in our homes. What we got was a malign orthodoxy that impressed no one but will do great harm.

The test of a good budget is whether or not the economic and fiscal dynamic is likely to sustain jobs, incomes and public services over the medium term; whether it will restore confidence and a sense of trust and, thirdly, whether it promotes those institutions that underpin social solidarity in the face of unprecedented social strain. The Budget fails these tests. The window of opportunity has shut and we face a period of grave economic, social and political strain and instability.

We will not get through this crisis if our political institutions and system of governance do not change radically. We should be clear that, economic stabilisation, much less recovery, will be stymied by alienation from our political system, by fragmentation of political support, and by the very real prospect of a rise in disenchantment and extremism among the tens of thousands who have joined the dole queue.

We need a realignment of politics in Ireland – we need democratic choices that mean something to contemporary society. We need a sense of right and wrong. We need a whole new political ethic premised on values based leadership.

We need to engage individuals who have little interest in power as such, who have a commitment as well as a widely acknowledged expertise that is capable of restoring trust, confidence and a sense of direction.

This article was published in the Irish Times, April 2009.

Irish Banking System and the Global Credit Crisis

More than a year after the onset of the international credit crisis, the IMF, in its most recent *Financial Stability Report*, has warned that 'global financial markets continue to be fragile and indicators of systemic risk remain elevated'. It is not only the IMF. In June, the European Central Bank (ECB) warned that 'the risks to the Euro area financial stability system had, on balance, increased compared with the previous 6 months'. This, it argued, pointed to 'a protracted adjustment period within the financial system as banks seek to increase their liquidity and capital positions'. They are having a difficult time doing both. This unprecedented financial crisis is not going away. Indeed, there is a persuasive argument, based partly on levels of volatility, that behind the façade of 'Business as Usual', the system is increasingly vulnerable to tectonic shocks with unknowable consequences for the real economy of jobs, trade and living standards.

As recently as two weeks ago, the two titans of the mortgage markets in the US – Fanny Mae and Freddie Mac – which between them hold some $6 trillion worth of mortgages, and already enjoyed privileged access to the capital markets, tethered on the brink of failure. Had the US authorities not stepped into provide additional guarantees, they would have effectively failed. They are not out of the water yet. In the UK, the Alliance and Leister Building Society has been acquired by Banco Santander, as the UK mortgage sector goes deeper into crisis.

With each new collapse and/or 'near miss' the credibility of the authorities is being further eroded. The next time round – and there will be a next time – neither investors nor the public may trust in the capacity of the markets or the regulators to contain the implosion. Recent data from the US on the acceleration of foreclosures on mortgages – the epicentre of the initial crisis – together with the fact that an increasing number of people are simply walking away from mortgages that are mired in negative equity – is a pathogen within the system that has the capacity to bring about its collapse. All of this highlights the case for a global Central Bank, as argued some months in these pages (*Irish Times February 2008*).

These developments raise important issues for Irish publicly quoted banks: AIB, Anglo–Irish, Bank of Ireland and Irish Life and Permanent and, by extension, the wider economy. The recent recovery in share prices is well-founded. Such was the extent of the decline in share prices over the last 12 months or so that, prior to the recent recovery, share prices had fallen – on average – by some 70 per cent compared with the previous 12 months.

Such declines are not justified by reference to their balance-sheets or recent performance, as AIB's recent results demonstrate. It is an axiom of financial theory that markets are efficient and rational. But the operation of markets over the last decade has been subverted by a Business Model that is flawed, and rooted in greed and excess. It is not functioning effectively. It is a rogue market, spawned by the malign sub-prime debacle to which it gave birth and the parallel universe of 'structured finance'. It is now beset by uncertainty and fear. The credibility of policy has dissipated.

The US and other world Central Banks have injected hundreds of billions of euro into global credit markets – effectively exchanging publicly funded equity for the toxic debt acquired by banks in their pursuit of short-term shareholder value. Even this hasn't succeeded in regenerating trust on the part of the financial markets. There is also a limit to which Central Banks can – or should – burden their balance sheets with 'investments' that are non-marketable. The potential dangers to policy effectiveness and credibility are obvious.

The Irish economy is structurally stronger than it was in the 1980s. Equally, the banks, while exposed in varying degrees to prospective write-offs, have balance sheets fully compliant with regulatory requirements. The Financial Regulator imposes limits on the extent of exposures by banks to specific sectors. Importantly, unlike their European peers, the liquidity position of Irish banks was presciently 'stress-tested' before the onset of the crisis. They also have access to liquidity from the European Central Bank (ECB).

However, higher write-offs and the decline in the demand for mortgages and loans, as well as a lack of market confidence and difficulties on the funding side experienced by all banks, have inevitably impacted on their share-price performance.

This has been reinforced by the fact that Ireland is no longer 'flavour of the month' with International Institutional Investors. The 'Celtic Tiger' was always a niche play within their portfolio and, in any event, there is no longer any incentive to acquire Irish bank shares in order to gain indirect exposure to the Irish economy. In the present savage 'bear' market in global equities, financial stocks have been hammered and Irish banks' shares have been a casualty. Domestic investors lack the stomach for 'value investing' in institutions that would appear to be undervalued, while international investors have simply lost interest. Against this background, the recent modest strengthening is encouraging.

The four listed banks – each with a very different 'Business Model' – have an importance to the Irish economy that would be difficult to overstate. It's not alone the jobs, and the quality of these jobs. It's the 'knowledge-base' encompassed within the banks' branch network. It's also about the sensitivity of domestically-owned and headquartered banks to the pulse of the Irish economy and their informal role as a conduit for public policy directed towards The Common Good. The IFSC, to take one example, would never have happened in the absence of a commitment by Irish banks.

Compared with twelve months ago, and taking a short to medium-term view, the market value of Irish banks has contracted. Smaller banks generally find it more difficult and/or expensive to raise capital. The issue here is not that the banks need to raise capital from a regulatory perspective; rather, the market reserves to itself the right to decide on what it regards as a sufficiently robust capital base.

There are a number of options open to the banks. They could seek to 'sit out' the recession, on the basis of the latent strength of the economy, the quality of their recent performance and, also, their balance sheets. The markets have, it is reasonable to assume, factored all of this into the existing share-levels.

This option of 'sitting it out', however, may leave individual banks vulnerable to take–over. It is quite certain that more than one potential predator has run the slide–rule over them – and they will almost certainly have redone their homework in recent times. An attempted takeover could, in principle, be friendly or hostile. One point is clear: the implications would be very far-reaching indeed.

Another option would be for one, or more, of the banks to initiate merger talks. This would require the consent of the Financial Regulator and The Competition Authority. The fact that the Irish banking system is now an integral part of the EU Internal Market, together with the ease of entry through new technology-based platforms, means that the implications for competition would be very different compared with the past.

A merger would reduce the absolute number of competitors, particularly in retail, business and mortgage finance. But the Irish banking market would remain contestable – any attempt to exploit market dominance would attract new entrants.

The Irish financial system has been enormously enriched, in terms of consumer choice, alternative 'business models' and competition by the entry of overseas based banks. This is really what the EU Internal Market is all about. Nonetheless, if one or more of the listed banks were to be taken over, particularity through a hostile takeover, there would be a serious and lasting loss of welfare for the Irish economy.

A newly merged bank would be less vulnerable to a take–over. It would almost certainly find it easier and cheaper to raise additional capital, should this be necessary. In the mid and late 1960s Dr Ken Whittaker, the economic architect of modern Ireland impelled the then eight Irish clearing banks to merge in order to form four larger and stronger banks, capable of competing with an influx of overseas banks. The same logic – *albeit* in different circumstances – applies in today's environment.

A merger would inevitably lead to job losses and the closure of some branches. It is the staff that create value in any bank. In order for a merger to succeed, it would be imperative that management, staff and the IBOA engage in dialogue, in an environment of trust and respect. A post–merger rationalisation process has to be set against the possible consequences of an overseas acquisition of one of the core banks, at the heart of the Irish financial system. This would involve not alone job losses, but also the migration of key management, operational and technical functions abroad.

There is another perspective that needs to be factored into any attempt to understand, let alone resolve, this crisis. It began within the banking system. It was transmitted across the banking sector and credit markets. The sheer scale of the fallout from what has been a monumental failure in leadership within the global banking system is simply incalculable. The banks have been – and continue to be – insulated from the consequences of their actions at two different levels. Firstly, by shareholders (including Pension Funds – the irony!), whose investment in the banks has been diluted by capital–raising to mitigate disastrous strategic and operational decisions. Secondly, the banks have been 'bailed out' by governments and global central banks. The Business Model within which banks operate needs to change. So does the mind–set. 'Business as Usual' is no longer an option – not after what has happened and its cost in human terms.

It is important that whatever of the options noted above is pursued that the banks be proactive. Leadership requires that they demonstrate that they are not fixated on maximising short-term shareholder value. They have other stakeholders, whose commitment and loyalty has helped generated shareholder value. Households are now struggling with mortgages, including 100 per cent/40 year term, on properties that have fallen sharply in value – mortgages that banks were marketing aggressively as recently as last year. Business are confronted with an economy at the cusp of recession while, at the same time, being subject to much stricter conditions and requirements in relation to funding.

The Irish listed banks prospered during the years of the Celtic Tiger. It is in their strategic interest, and that of the country, that they demonstrate an understanding of this reality: sustainability and profitability are built on real relationships and public trust, rather than on a fixation with shareholder value through the pursuit of a metric/targets-driven culture imposed on staff. It is in the hard times that the sincerity of such 'relationships' are truly tested.

This Article appeared in Finance, December 2008.

Causes and Effects of Worldwide Financial Turmoil

Ray Kinsella highlights possible reasons for the current turbulence in financial markets – and lessons that can be learned from the situation.

The scale of the crisis – the rapidity with which it morphed from something that seemed essentially semi-detached from the lives of most individuals into one which threatened the entire stability of western financial markets – was astonishing in its rapidity. As recently as last April, the Central Bank's authoritative forecast was for economic growth of about 2 per cent with a recovery in 2009. Even more recently, the European Central Bank was generally benign in its mid–summer forecasts, strongly indicating that a cut in interest rates was not to be expected. Then the full extent of the crisis became evident in markets around the world sending the contagion coursing through the veins of all markets and threatening in a manner which was clear and unambiguous, the entire global economy.

The role of the State is now far more intrusive in financial services than could ever have been conceived possible. Governments, whose political values and ideologies are wholly opposed to such intervention and who are now grappling with what this means have little to be triumphant about.

If some form of nationalisation of a second or even third–best solution, then it is important to be aware of the dangers of statism. Because this much is clear – governments may be nationalising all or parts of individual institutions but did not the crisis occur precisely within a de-facto nationalisation in the form of regulations and in the tacit linkages between big banking and big government? A check list of the dangers would include the fact that public ownership:

- Tends to undermine the operation of markets and of market based economies.

- Assumes that the public sector has the skills necessary to restore trust in these institutions.

- Ignores the incentives for engaging in opportunistic, political or ideologically based interference.

- Represents an enormous set–back for the principles on which the international Trade Organisation (ITO) and, more immediately, the EU internal market is based.

- Suggests that the solution to what is a deep-seated moral contagion can be (re)solved by socialising institutions.

At the same time, it should be said that it does provide an opportunity to reengineer the short-terms value maximisation model because it will explicitly factor in 'The Common Good'. It will insist not alone on the protection of depositors, but on the underlying principal that without depositors, there can be no intermediation, and therefore the rights of the depositor should rate at least equally with those of the investor. It gives pause for thought that the sustainable value created by banks should be shared more equitably across the institution, rather than appropriated in a wholly disproportionate manner by the very, very few.

Possible root causes

Excessive liquidity and excessively low interest rates at the beginning of this decade were not the cause of the crisis. They were permissive factors. Nor was the sale of mortgages to the sub-prime sector of the US housing market on a 'originate and distribute' model wholly responsible, although it was the seedbed.

The securitisation of assets – notably mortgages which were sold with little regard to rigorous risk evaluation, contributed to the crisis. But securitisation, in itself, has a useful role to play in markets. There were certainly far too little emphasis on measuring and pricing risk in the frantic search for return – and this was true at every level.

It is difficult to sustain the case that the crisis was caused by regulatory failure alone. The deregulation of financial markets in the 1980s, contributed to globalisation. And globalisation greatly limited the scope for national central banks/regulators to intervene by imposing quantitative limits on bank lending as a means of mitigation emerging 'asset bubbles'. Perhaps 'Moral Suasion' was not used with sufficient force but it would be difficult to go much beyond that. Equally, in retrospect the repeal in the US of the Glass–Seagal Act exacerbated the crisis. Retrospect is easy. It would be difficult to over-emphasise the fact that the regulatory environment in which the crisis took root and spread, was post-Sox. Its cornerstone was Basle II, far and away the most sophisticated framework for ensuring that banks had sufficient risk-weighted capital; and this regime operated alongside a new emphasis on market discipline on regulatory oversight. It was simply swept away albeit by a 'Black Swan' event the roots of the crisis lie deeper than any deficiency in the regulatory system.

The fragmentation of regulatory governments across markets and countries certainly compounded the problem once it had attained momentum. This fragmentation led to co ordination problems both in the UK over Northern Rock, and in the US once Wall Street began to experience serious pre-shock tremors. It was certainly evident in the lead up to the free fall of global markets in the second week of October 2008. The effects of the absence of a global financial regulator to oversee and intervene where appropriate in a co-coordinated manner were never more apparent. Markets convulsed in fear and with an unpredictable dynamic operating in real time highlighted the fact that 'co-operative arrangements' among national regulators is a reactive second–best policy instrument. It simply doesn't work efficiently in contemporary financial markets. The effects of fragmentation were entirely predictable – but they were not the root cause of the crisis.

Lightly regulated high–leveraged institutions play their part – this again was predictable (and predicted in these pages some two or three years ago) contrarians have an important role to

227

play in absorbing and transferring risk and in facilitating market efficiency. Short-term decisions based almost wholly on valuations generated by broken-back markets; trading decisions taken with little or no regard for the impact on the worth and viability of companies – and the welfare of individuals working within them – are destructive. But hedge funds were in effect trading in products which they had not themselves generated.

There is a case to be made that governments should have seen the crisis coming, albeit that they necessarily rely on regulatory authorities. The market data pointing to serious strain in the form of volatility was certainly reported by the BIS in 2006: they noted that the degree of volatility exceeded that prior to the LTCM crisis. Equally, in the Central Bank of Ireland's Whittaker lecture, the governor of the Central Bank of Italy makes much the same point. The signs were there. And the signs were there pointing to the need for 'improved risk management incapability's…[and] improving the understanding of credit risk transfer, including derivatives. That was back in 2004. Governments must have known but it has to be accepted that it is difficult for them no less than for banks to take themselves off the floor when the music is still playing. Most of us instinctively knew but allowed ourselves to be seduced and global financial institutions seemed to lack the will to break away. That's the problem with operating with a flawed and essentially nihilistic business model.

We are left with greed and power – and fear. First cousins. Markets are an indispensable element in human anthropology. They are central to the functioning of free societies. But when markets are separated from their constitutive purpose – when they are 'manipulated' and when they are prevented from functioning because of the lack of transparency of the products which are 'traded' on the markets; when they are made the measure of what is good and desirable in a community; when they are idolised by society instead of being allowed to function in the service of the community, they will bite back. By the most sober assessments – including the expressed view of the IMF managing director – they brought the global financial system to the edge of the abyss last weekend.

Economics – and therefore business and markets – are not value-free. They are inherently moral activities. They impact on the lives of individuals and communities. They are shaped by choices and motivations. No, they are not value free. The great theistic religions – with the accumulated wisdom and common sense of several millennia – are very clear regarding the morality of markets and of business. The function of all businesses is to serve the community. The community extends through the boards of companies, through legal statutes, the privilege of serving the community and responding creatively, innovatively and profitably to market demand. Profits accrue to those who do this best.

The point is that the boards of companies stand in the position of trustees of 'The Common Good'. An exceedingly wise Irish business leader, has highlighted the doctrine of 'Uberrimae Fidei' – that is, 'in utmost good faith'. This is the true test of the morality of the markets – ticking boxes, important though it is, comes some way behind obedience to the unenforceable. The argument here is that the crisis is not a technical one, nor is it primarily about regulation, important as that is. It is a moral crisis – a crisis of values, that has all but laid waste to the entire system of globalised financial markets, upon which the living standards of all countries – developed and developing – substantially depend. There are strong political resonances because there is not a huge difference between the temptations to which financial institutions succumbed and their political counter – parts which threatened fundamental political freedoms, both are about power – and it is in all of us. Leaders are just better at seeing it for what it is.

This Article appeared in Finance, November 2008.

US Fiscal Bailout a Missed Chance

The global financial crisis will get worse in the absence of fundamental reform: it is clear the Paulson rescue package is misconceived, writes Ray Kinsella.

There are two reasons why the crisis in financial markets will continue and, as a consequence, lead to a further sharp deterioration in global economic conditions. Such a prospect will, in combination with the unprecedented volatility in commodities markets, undermine budgetary projections in all developed countries, including Ireland.

This is especially the case since we have not yet experienced the full economic effects of the most recent convulsions in the markets and the knock-on effects on financial institutions.

The first reason has to do with the erosion of credibility of the regulatory authorities in large Organisation for Economic Co–operation and Development economies. Policy credibility is central to financial stability. The markets have to be convinced, and convince themselves, that the authorities are in charge. The latter have to be seen capable of reading market conditions and to steer them through the rapids to medium-term financial stability. Only to the extent that they believe this, will they buy into policy.

The market no longer believes.

The haemorrhage of trust has been evident for some time: certainly prior to the recently proposed $700 billion (€478 billion) Paulson package. This growing agnosticism on the part of markets quite desperate to believe is, for example, reflected in the increase in, and volatility of, market rates compared with official rates. The markets are fighting their own worst fears.

The defining moment, however, was the decision by the US Fed not to rescue Lehman Brothers. US treasury secretary Hank Paulson and the Fed drew a line in the sand where Lehman's had once stood. Now they have been pulled over this line.

The Paulson package takes the Fed where it did not want to go – and where it did not think it would have to go. It socialises the worst excesses of a cult that has turned banking and free markets inside out. Worse still, it perpetuates the myth that this crisis can be resolved through regulation.

History teaches otherwise. It is difficult to see anything short of fundamental reforms that will restore market confidence. There is no indication whatever that such reforms are even contemplated. It is all reactive.

The Fed. is, it has to be said, in a near-impossible position. Perhaps they should have acted earlier. There is now near-universal acceptance that the credit explosion in the US in the early part of this decade, and which happened at the nadir of the interest rate cycle, allowed the subprime/securitisation of toxic debt to take root.

It was clear, certainly to some central bankers, that this explosion in debt would be choked by rising interest rates and would eventually trigger what has been euphemistically termed a "correction". Having said that, when the crisis began to manifest itself, the Fed moved to cushion the effects of a freezing-over of interbank liquidity and the scale of the implosion of market, as well as public, confidence became evident.

The Bear Stearns rescue was an attempt to assert control over events by containing the damage that would undoubtedly have followed in the wake of a repetition of a Northern Rock-type shock.

The Fed put in place supports for the markets, even to the extent of accepting toxic debt as collateral. It bought the banks time to look to resolving their self-created problems.

When the sky fell in on Wall Street earlier this month, the Fed signalled that there was to be no rescue of Lehman. The markets were to resolve the crisis the banks had created. The banks could not: their excesses had subverted the operation of markets.

The rescue of the general insurance colossus AIG and the misconceived $700 billion Paulson package – which would vastly increase the amount of dodgy bank investments converted into real money – constitutes an unprecedented reversal of policy. The market's negative response is not primarily driven by Democratic politics or even the uncertainty over the timing of the package. It could be enacted tomorrow and it would make no difference.

It is difficult to know what else the Fed could have done. On the one hand, they could hardly have stood by while a whole new front on the market's collapse was being opened up. The collapse of AIG would have confirmed the spread of the contagion to insurance markets. It had to intervene.

On the other hand, continued intervention was creating a huge "moral hazard" – relieving financial institutions of their responsibility and encouraging them to believe that they could continue to socialise their appalling losses, recapitalise and hang out a business–as–usual sign.

The Fed cannot continue to act as lender of last resort to the US banking system. The nature of its intervention has stretched the institution's mandate while its scale has depleted its capacity to intervene. Caught between a rock and a hard place, the credibility of the Fed has been undermined, perhaps fatally. And the markets know it.

The second reason has to do with the fact that the business model according to which banks function is terminally flawed. The fact that this drama, being played out in slow motion, is occurring within the most prescriptive regulatory regime ever is compelling evidence of this reality.

There is, therefore, something depressing in listening to the UK Chancellor of the Exchequer's populist criticism of levels of remuneration in banks. This is yesterday's news. The regulators have long been aware of the yawning gap between what banks pay a small subset of their staff and the almost complete absence of responsibility on the part of recipients to deliver sustainable performance. It's what incentivises the whole rotten model.

But it's the model that's the problem – the obscene and unjustified levels of remuneration that are contrary to any concept of 'The Common Good' are a consequence of this model. Regulation will not solve this problem. It is, however, characteristic of the current regulatory mindset that it should default to a mode of "more regulation", tackling the symptoms of the problem, rather than the problem itself.

The point is this: unless, and until, the short-term shareholder value-fixated model of financial intermediation is acknowledged to be redundant, the crisis in financial markets will become progressively more acute. We no longer live in an era of capital shortage. Giving shareholders overriding primacy is contrary to common sense as well as undermining The Common Good.

It is equally the case that – until a global financial regulator is put in place which has the capacity to oversee global markets and to mitigate the effects of crisis – there can be no durable restoration of market credibility or public confidence. It is simply not tenable to entrust global financial stability to co-ordination among central banks, all of whom have different mandates, and who arrive a little breathless and a little late to crises in markets that operate in real time.

It would be dangerously naive to understate the technical and policy difficulties of migrating to a new business model and global regulatory system. There is no precedent, at least in peacetime.

The Bretton Woods conference in 1944 established the infrastructure for a new post-war international financial system. That shows it can be done. But then neither is there a precedent in modern capitalism for the kind of problems that are now sapping the financial foundations of western liberal democracies. At some stage the regulators and the institutions will have to confront the need for fundamental reform.

This Article appeared in The Irish Times, September 2008

How Should Ireland Respond to the

Global Economic Turmoil?

The Irish economy is at a turning point and so, by extension, are jobs, living standards and social solidarity. The risks confronting the global financial system, upon which Western liberal democracies rests, are enormous. The uncertainty in the global economic environment is unprecedented. For a small, trade-dependent economy like Ireland, which has enjoyed a decade and half of prosperity, the process of adjusting to a wholly new economic paradigm is daunting.

Those who wish to disengage from these realities or to dismiss them as 'talking down the economy' are in denial. That is not a good, or sensible, place to be right now.

It is possible to mitigate these effects. The Irish economy is more robust in almost every domain than it was a decade and half ago. But the scope for a further intensification of a global vicious economic circle is significant. The policy options are very limited. Our capacity as an economy and society for resilience – and humility – has never been tested as it will be over the next five years – at least.

Constraints on Economy

The Irish economy is constrained on five fronts. It was always the case that the extraordinary pace of economic expansion of the 1990s and early years of this century would inevitably abate. However, the international credit crisis, which began to manifest itself in 2006, has brought this expansion to a juddering halt. There have been previous financial crises – but nothing on this scale. The estimated total write-off's by major global financial institutions is likely to approach £1 trillion. These are just the first–order effects. The knock-on impact on international investment and trade will exacerbate these costs. What is not generally acknowledged is that this is a relatively benign scenario. Had the US Fed been less proactive in the white–heat of the crisis the outcome could well have been a 'global contagion' – a meltdown of confidence upon which financial markets ultimately depend – that could simply not be 'firewalled'.

In its Autumn 2007 *'Global Financial Stability Report',* the IMF acknowledged that the negative dynamic at the heart of the credit crisis could be further exacerbated, given the amount of 'leverage' that was built-into the financial markets insatiable demand for short-term returns from miss-priced, opaque high–risk products, and which led to the implosion.

As it is, the US is in recession. Its monetary policy – and therefore *global* policy – has been skewed. The Fed is running out of policy options. Kenneth Rogoff, Professor of Economics at Harvard and formerly Chief Economist at the IMF, has gone so far as to suggest the possible need for a coordinated global policy package to support the US economy. Nothing like this has happened before. Meanwhile, well over 2 million homes (funded by sub–prime mortgages) have been repossessed. Recent market data, as well as authoritative forecasts, point to record levels of repossession in the UK. To put this in context, the US is Ireland's largest source of Foreign Direct Investment. The UK is our largest trading partner.

A second factor has to with the precipitous fall in the value of the dollar and, also, sterling against the euro. This is putting our exporters under significant pressures. More generally, global macroeconomic policy is being undermined by the lack of alignment of policy responses to the crises by the major Central Banks. Massive injections of liquidity may be a necessary short-term palliative to unfreeze inter-bank lending – but this has entailed taking as collateral the junk-grade 'investments' that caused the problems in the first place. It's not a solution.

Nor is it a substitute for a Global Central Bank, the need for which has been highlighted by the duration, depth and severity of this crisis and the manner it which it has been transmitted, by contagion, across global markets – and which is now rolling across the 'real' economies of the developed countries including Ireland – while the poor countries are held hostage.

The mandates of the US Fed and the European Central Bank (ECB) are pulling in different directions. The former has responded to the immediate effects of recession by cutting interest rates – but at the cost of increasing medium-term inflationary pressures and of driving the dollar still further downwards. The ECB, for its part, is unambiguously focused on containing inflation, notwithstanding the seductive appeal of interest rate cuts. Global macroeconomic policy is all over the place and policy anomalies abound.

Impact on Economy

A third factor relates to how all of this impacts on Ireland. GDP growth forecasts have been cut and will be cut further. The data on the key drivers of growth are daunting. There are clear indications that retail activity has fallen significantly compared with last year. We are over-indebted and over-shopped. Personal consumption, fuelled in recent years by a range of factors including low interest rates, SSIA redemptions, through to the 'feel good' factor generated by unsustainable rises in property prices, has run out of steam. The IMF estimate that property prices in Ireland are 32 per cent over valued in relation to economic fundamentals – that is three times the corresponding figure for the US. Permissive mortgage lending criteria have 'shoehorned' a generation that has never known hard times into a *cul de sac* that, in many instances, has compromised their basic freedoms – small expensive apartments funded by 100 per cent 40-year mortgages do that, especially to young couples.

Housing, especially social housing, will continue to be of enormous importance to the economy. However, its design and financing need to be fundamentally rethought in terms of community-building, amenities, affordability and, also, a spatial strategy which takes account of massive demographic change – particularly one that encompasses the potential for growth in the western part of the country.

Public expenditure, both Current and Capital, is under sever and increasing pressure. The quarterly Exchequer Returns 'road show' used to be notable for massive fiscal surpluses, well ahead of forecasts. Not now – we are back on the brink of rising fiscal deficits, fortunately constrained by the EU Growth and Stability Pact.

Investor sentiment is inevitably negative, not alone because of much tighter lending criteria by the banks but also because of the increased uncertainty and the downturn in the global economy. In this context, inflation, partly driven by an extraordinary rise in commodity prices (notably oil and food), poses an additional threat.

Outside of Political Experience

The present, and prospective, economic environment presents challenges that are outside the realm of Ireland's recent economic experience and the experience of any Minister sitting around the Cabinet table. Essentially, there are four policy imperatives. The first two are simple and compelling. We need to maintain competitiveness at all costs. We need to maintain our present Corporation Tax regime within the EU: it is pretty well our only economic policy instrument

A fourth factor relates to an increase in a suffocating blanket of bureaucracy which has been created by every artifice known to the political process. This threatens, in a clear and present way, the enterprise sector which creates jobs and new technologies and which farms our land. There has been an extraordinary increase in the 'dead weight' of intrusion and reporting which adds nothing whatever to the quality of our lives or to economic outputs but which is, rather, wholly counterproductive. It grows by stealth and feeds on itself – the product of a mindset which is subversive of personal responsibility, initiative and even basic human freedoms. This issue cannot be addressed by dusting–down some 'anti-red tape' PR stunt. It will require, to begin with, the kind of systematic reduction in state regulation and intrusion which has been successfully implemented on a Department by Department basis in the Netherlands. It will require tenacity and leadership – but the potential gains in economic welfare and social capital are enormous.

Fifth, and most importantly, we need to maintain social solidarity. The new economic environment will, in the absence of values based leadership, exacerbate existing inequalities in Irish life, with all of the strains that this will create. The contrast between an essentially protected state sector and an enterprise sector under serious pressures will be thrown into sharp relief and may well become socially divisive.

Nowhere are inequalities more evident than in our health system. These inequalities are the product of decades of rationing, short-termism and more recently a culture of adversarialism and control that has seriously eroded Trust. With fewer resources available and a prospective intensification of recent cutbacks, Government are going to need the trust of all those involved in delivering care. Inevitably, there will be a temptation to fall back on the intensification on prescriptive intervention and ad-hoc cuts. Such initiatives wholly underestimate the leverage which Trust and Respect for those delivering care can bring to the job in hand. The very last thing they need are yet more reports, form filling and other time–wasting that distracts from the core professional duties and vocation. Where people are trusted and respected the capacity to leverage limited resources is, quite simply, enormous since they are motivated to make the commitment to go the extra mile.

There are other initiatives that can be taken to reduce inequalities in our health system. A slimmed–down HSE needs to be empowered and, in turn, be willing to delegate responsibility to those delivering care. The HSE also needs the freedom of a three year budgetary cycle. The Department of Finance may fear 'slippage' – if so, they are wrong. Ad hoc cuts, such as we continue to experience, aimed at accommodating services to a yearly budgetary cycle, are nonsense. They lead to 'mothballed' wards and urgently needed diagnostic equipment; they lead to over-pressurised staff and facilities, with all of the risk that this entails. They lead to cancellation of procedures that end up playing havoc with peoples' lives and costing a great deal more to treat in the end.

Social Solidarity

In terms of maintaining social solidarity as a framework within which to work through this unprecedented catharsis, it would be difficult to overstate the importance of supporting the Family. Writing in the Financial Times not so long ago, columnist Martin Woolf, highlighted what he called the 'war on the family'. Citing research carried out by the Institute for Economic Affairs – and whose relevance to Irish society has been highlighted by researchers such as Professor Patricia Casey and Consultant Psychiatrist Dr Sean O'Domhnaill – he went on to argue:

'It is not excessive to describe [what British politicians have done] as a "war" on the traditional family. That is what it is, as Patricia Morgan, a well known analyst in this area, argues in an excellent recent pamphlet"

The social consequences are severe. In a world in which the state replaces the father, uneducated young men are permanent adolescents, useful to father children but lacking any other valuable social role. We know that unmarried men are far less likely to work than married ones. This is partly because they are less marriageable. It is also because they have fewer incentives to work.

In current circumstances, there is little chance of restoring a strong social preference for committed marriage. But it might be possible to agree about removing the discrimination against it.'

The casualties of a society that has lost its way and the run of itself are first, and always, individual Persons. Government support for the Family is, therefore, not alone the best but also, by far, the most cost-effective way of mitigating the effects of a culture of excess that has now imploded, and of mitigating the impact of cuts in Government social expenditure.

The global economy, on which Ireland's living standards depend, is undergoing a convulsion which is the deepest and most broadly based in recent history. It may well intensify, and this carries the very real danger of compounding the risks inherent in the probability of other 'events' such as, for example, a Pandemic, which are the product of a globalised community. Much of the responsibility for this convulsion in the global economy can be laid at the door of a flawed and pernicious 'Business Model', predicated on greed and lies, and which threatens western liberal democracies. It is facile to assume that any country, let alone one such as Ireland, can insulate itself from such seismic shocks to the global economy. But the very fact that the crisis has been brought on by a subversion of values based on the dignity of the Person and of a proper understanding of 'The Common Good'– values deeply embedded in Ireland's ethos – points to the kind of changes in mindset and policies that are necessary to come through this crisis.

This Article appeared in the Irish Examiner, April 2008.

Why this Global Financial Crisis is Different

European Parliament (ALDE) Seminar on the 'International Financial Crisis' February 2008

Introduction

Western liberal democracies and the growth of international trade and investment have been built on the platform of open, innovative financial markets at the heart of which are extraordinarily efficient credit and capital markets and institutions .It would be difficult to overstate the political importance of this reality. Having acknowledged this reality, it would be foolish not to reflect on whether the pathology of the international credit crises does not indicate that all of this may now be at risk.

There has been a succession of banking and financial crises in western financial markets in recent decades: the Nordic crisis, the Russian 'default' event. Long Term Capital Management (LTCM) – which, in many ways, is a precursor of this most recent contagion? The Asian banking crisis threatened widespread contagion. On top of these, there has been a whole series of risk-management and control deficiencies within individual banks.

The present global contagion is different

- It is, by far, the largest such 'event' and its consequences are still unfolding. It has impacted on funding requirements, earnings as well as capital positions of banks and the wider credit markets. It has impacted on market confidence and Trust. When we reflect on the component parts of what was a 'new' credit market landscape – the sub-prime mortgage market loans and their infection of the Asset Backed Commercial Paper market (ABCP) market, the kind of junk that was being securitised; the off-balance sheet Special Investment Vehicles (SIV's) and 'Conduits, the impairment of the wider markets and the 'final' costs – a trillion or so...it makes you think.

- We **know** the combination of circumstances – global savings/excessive liquidity and a scramble for 'yield' against the background of what the market **knew** had to be unsustainably low interest rates – which was the 'seedbed' of the crisis which finally ignited in mid-2007,but which was evident well before then.

- We **know** that it took root and developed within the *most prescriptive regulatory* regime in advanced monetised economies.

- We **know** that it was – and still is being – transmitted across markets which have been considerably strengthened by such initiatives as Basle II and new accounting and auditing standards, as well as by initiatives within the major banks
- It still happened. The injection of liquidity by major Central Banks hasn't solved the underlying flaws. It has simply bought time.

What we also **should know** by now is that 'band-aid' in the form of 'policy-speak' initiatives such as 'intensification of cooperation' and 'concerted action', do not begin to address the underlying issues that have brought us one, perhaps two, steps from the unthinkable: a major fault-line emerging across western financial markets. It is important to stress that the absolute magnitudes of existing and even prospective losses/write-downs are small compared with the total stock of wealth encompassed in one form or another within the markets.

That's not the point. It's the innate dysfunctional nature of such a highly leveraged set of markets that has experienced a crisis of confidence and of Trust that is of most concern.

There are three issues which go to the heart of **global contagion** and which need to be addressed:

1. The Effects of Contagion:

The effects of Contagion cannot be measured solely by its impact on the balance sheet of financial institutions, or even, the functioning of credit markets – even though these are unprecedented in terms of their scale since the first public acknowledgement of the crises in mid 2007.These effects are summarised in the boxes set out below.

Contagion creates a virus like pathology in the heart of households and in the social economy. It impacts on individuals and families (an estimated 2 million in the U.S will lose their homes). It impacts on *lives*, *living standards* and on *relationships.*

"Caveat emptor", is not an adequate response to a malign dynamic that generated this Contagion. Moreover, the burden is primarily born by those less able to either understand, or to cope, with its effects.

2. The Business Model:

Western mainstream financial innovation is based upon maximising short-term Shareholder Value. This is fundamentally flawed. The scarce factor of production today is not capital but *intellectual capital.* This should be evident from what is driving the pace of technological and financial innovation within the markets; namely People.

This Business Model gives overriding priority to shareholders, is configured to optimise next quarter's earnings and is driven by perverse incentives; is not just flawed – it is a dead man walking.

We need to rethink this 'Business Model' upon which banks and the western financial markets – with all of the benefits which they have brought – are based .At the heart of all economic, political and social 'constructs' is the Human Person. What is it all for – or about – if not to serve the substantive interests of the Human Person?

How much time and effort do banks invest in reflecting on the Human Person, compared with what is invested in generating the latest algorithm or the most effective marketing 'strategy' to increase 'share of the wallet'.

The banks, *as corporate entities,* have an almost wholly dehumanised view of their business, their employees, their clients and, in general, society. They are ignorant of and/or have 'crowded out' the single most important issue and it is this which is at the heart of the increasing fragility of an exponentially expanding set of interlocking markets. Hijacking the term 'Ethics', or embracing CSR, are not adequate substitutes.

At another level, the integrity and efficiency of markets themselves are being subverted by systematic deficiencies (such as failures in risk pricing) and in the separation of markets from their original constitutive purpose. The monumental Compendium of Social Teaching (2006) makes the enormously important point that:

"The Financial Sector, which has seen the value of financial Transactions far surpass that of real transactions, runs the Risk of developing according to a mentality that has only itself as a point of reference, without being connected to the real foundations of the economy."

"A financial economy that is an end in itself, is destined to contradict its goal, since it is no longer in touch with its roots...it has abandoned its original and essential role of contributing to the development of people and the human community"[48].

It would be facile to make this point without acknowledging that addressing these deficiencies represents formidable challenges: we confront the need for a 'Kuhnian' paradigm shift in our way of thinking about money and markets. On the other hand, there *are* alternative paradigms based, for example, on the Judeo–Christian teachings – which have much to say of money and markets, Trust and integrity.

3. No one is in charge

The present regulatory structures underpinning Financial Stability are simply incapable of keeping pace with market innovation – and this market innovation, remember, is driven by a dynamic that is almost wholly at odds with concepts such as 'The Common Good' and Social Solidarity which are at the heart of the political model which we in Ireland and the wider EU ostensibly embrace as representative of our values.

---

[48] JPII to Pontifical Academy of Social Sciences (1997), see Compendium

*The fragmentation of regulatory governance, in a world of 24/7 global financial flows embodying quite enormous **'leverage'**, represents a 'Black Hole' that threatens to swamp global Financial Stability. It means that there is no single body, with the mandate, technical capability and resources to proactively engage with market innovation and to intervene, when necessary, in the interest of Financial Stability.*

The difficulty here is that in the EU and the wider G–7, national regulators operate to different mandates. As crises succeed crises, they have arrived 'a little breathless and a little late' and tend to trip over each other, in *reactively* addressing the problem of global contagion and its underlying causes.

We need a global Central Bank aligned to the reality that financial markets and institutions now operate in a global environment. Financial instability will inevitably spread across borders, with all of the dangers of contagion .The focus of a global Central Bank would be to oversee and where necessary intervene to maintain financial stability and to mitigate the effects on global monetary and macro-economic policy. 'Cooperation' among major Central Banks with different mandates and capabilities is a 'second best' approach, as the international credit crisis demonstrated. The technical and political difficulties which this raises are trivial compared with the vulnerability which western financial markets and economies – and those economies dependent upon them – are faced with in the absence of a failure to act on this imperative.

4. A Way Forward:

It's worth pointing out that recent theoretical work demonstrates that contagion, as presently understood, understates the severity of macroeconomic impacts by ignoring 'second order' micro-linkages among companies within banks credit portfolios especially Large Complex Banking Groups(LCBG)

Wars happen. So too do global financial crises. What is at issue here is not whether there will be another such event: it is instead the form, nature and scale of such an event and the prospective damage to both financial and political structures.

We should, as already pointed out, be concerned not alone about the major monetised countries – which drive global markets and economic growth, but also about the consequences for smaller countries and more especially developing countries which are effectively held hostage to our capacity to get to grips with the underlying causes of global contagion and to put in place an appropriate global regulatory structure,

Within the EU at present there are competing national, regulatory agendas – sometimes within a single country. We need to be very clear that, unless the EU rises above these differences, the prospective outlook for Europe and for the global community are extremely grave.

More specifically:

- Europe will be unprepared for the next 'structural' event, whatever form it takes and for its impact on European living standards.
- Europe will cede a leadership role to the US with all of the consequent dangers of 'regulatory imperialism', which were so evident in SOX.
- The work of the EU Commission and ECOFIN, in partnership with the Parliament, provides a robust basis for taking the discussion forward as a global initiative, initially within the G7 and, later this year, at the IMF/ World Bank meetings with the participation of the BIS. National and international banking and financial services representative bodies need to participate proactively in these discussions.

This was presented to the Financial Services Club, Herbert Park Hotel 6th of March 2008.

An earlier form of this paper was presented as an Opinion piece in the Irish Times, February 2008.

Global Central Bank is Needed

The scale of the global financial crisis is still unknown, writes Ray Kinsella. What we do know is that global leadership to deal with it is absent.

There have been market collapses on previous occasions, though by any standards the carnage on global equity markets which began on Monday is exceptional.

Markets have adjusted to previous crises – it's what markets do. This time may be different. While the immediate cause of the dramatic falls in market indices appears to be the acknowledgment of a recession in the United States, it comes on the back of a full-blown contagion such as has not been seen before since the breakdown of the international system in the early 1970s.

What is equally disturbing is the panicked response by the US Fed to the collapse.

This point needs to be made: the still evolving sub–prime crisis in the US, has generated unprecedented write-offs by major financial institutions and has induced a quasi-paralysis within and across markets, the full scale of which is still not evident.

What we are observing now is a global problem. What is demonstrably missing is global leadership, commensurate with the scale and nature of the problem.

This is not, it should be said, simply about macroeconomic imbalances. Nor is it about the very real pain and suffering that will be inflicted on individuals and households, as well as on the corporate sector, by a failure of leadership. This is about massive uncertainty, and even fear, in the face of a systemic crisis in global financial markets and a shambolic response on the part of global central bankers and policy makers.

A sense of proportion is always important. In the last two decades, there have been a number of catharses in the global economy and there have, as the European Central Bank has demonstrated, been a succession of individual bank failures.

What confronts us now is something of a different order. The global Western markets are under threat from the fundamental flaws in the business model upon which it is based and in the failure to develop a system of global financial governance which matches the explosive growth and pervasive importance of international financial markets.

Following a succession of tremors, this latest shock to the system ranks very high on the Richter scale.

Western mainstream financial institutions are based on a business model aimed at maximising shareholder value (SV). This model subjugates The Common Good to the interests of the owners of capital. This is a model well past its sell–by date. In a knowledge-based economy, capital is no longer the key factor of production. This alone argues against the over-riding priority of the business being to maximise shareholder value. This fallacy has been compounded by the short-termism embedded within the model – the fixation of management, and of the whole organisation, on the next set of quarterly earnings.

The consequences of this mindset should have been obvious from the events of the 1990s and early 2000s, for which Enron stands as the defining metaphor. But the lessons were not learned. Some initiatives – notably international standard-setting in accounting and auditing – were eminently sensible and did not require a prior justification. However, some attempts to fix a terminally flawed model were downright counter–productive – for example, the US Sarbanes Oxley Act (SOX), which is in reality an over–prescriptive form of regulatory imperialism. The term "ethics" was hijacked and pressed into service in various domains across financial market activity, without any evident understanding of what ethics actually involves, especially in regard to respect for the person.

Notwithstanding this, the SV model – an antiquated construct and a time–bomb waiting to detonate – began ticking in the low interest rate environment of the early years of this decade.

The term "sub-prime" is an exotic euphemism for what were high–risk mortgage loans to vulnerable individuals and families. The exponential growth in this market was driven by the insatiable demands of the SV business model to generate more and more earnings, irrespective of developments in the monetary environment and the knock–on impact on the real economy over the median term. The search for yield, for ever higher returns, albeit at the costs of taking on excessive risks, within new exotic and opaque financing structures, contributed to increasing volatility in international financial markets. This reached alarming dimensions by mid-2006.

The more than doubling of interest rates by 2006 provided the inevitable reality check. It precipitated a crisis in the sub-prime market, a collapse in balance-sheet valuations of institutions which had invested in mortgage-backed securities.

This was then transmuted into a generalised crisis of confidence. Institutions in highly interlocked markets finally realised that what they had thought was a very clever game of generating higher returns from dodgy investments was, in effect, more like "pass the parcel" of high–risk illiquid investments. Catastrophic multibillion-dollar losses were recorded by major financial institutions and, within an environment characterised by an erosion of trust, which is central to the functioning of the markets, there was a freezing-up of international credit markets.

It should not have happened and the primary reason it actually did happen is that financial institutions and intermediaries remained – notwithstanding the Enron experience – fixated on earnings and profits and levels of compensation, to the exclusion of sustainability and 'The Common Good'.

In terms of regulation and governance, there was an almost total lack of coherence in the response at a national and global level to the "sub-prime" crisis and to its effects across the markets. This was encapsulated in the reaction by the UK authorities to the near meltdown of the Northern Rock model for funding its mortgage book.

For all that has been written on this event, the single most compelling point is this – there is hardly a single monetary economist in these islands who believed they would witness a full-scale "run" on a major financial institution in a highly monetised society.

Issues of politics, monetary policy and financial stability ebbed and flowed across the corridors of Whitehall, reflecting the fragmentation of regulatory authority. There were problems of co-ordination and alignment of the different objectives of the Treasury, the Bank of England and the Financial Services Authority, as they struggled to respond. The instincts of depositors, who queued, in the teeth of official reassurances, were right – this has severed the umbilical cord of trust on which both markets and regulators depend. It will be even more difficult for the authorities to hold the line next time.

The response of the authorities was belated and reactive. Responsibility for managing the effects of the Northern Rock debacle has passed from the boardroom to the Treasury. It's not clear whether it will be nationalised or sold. The proposals recently announced by the Chancellor of the Exchequer amount to yet more regulation. The UK experience is a microcosm of the fragmentation of regulation and governance at a global level.

The global credit crunch – of which Northern Rock was a predictable victim – was a manifestation of a contagion: the phenomenon whereby market failure spreads, virus-like within, and across, financial markets. It is what keeps central bankers awake at night. It was the prospect of contagion which prompted the intervention, in September 2007, by the US Fed, the Central Bank of Canada, the Bank of England and the ECB. Acting as de-facto lenders of last resort to global (basically western) financial markets, they signalled their willingness to make available funds to the credit markets against a wide range of collateral (some of which had been infected by the sub-prime crisis) at non-penal rates.

This intervention came late in the day and merely papered over cracks. There is no evidence that the key lesson of the near–collapse of Long Term Capital Management (LTCM) in 1998 had been learned. LTCM and the contagion which it threatened to unleash were stopped in its tracks only by the purely fortuitous and courageous intervention by the former president of the New York Fed. This is not the NY Fed's job.

There is no one in charge in the event of a future full–blown crisis in global financial markets – not the IMF, not the Bank for International Settlements, not the OECD, not the ECB. Attempting to co-ordinate a set of regulators in enormously large and complex financial markets is a wholly inadequate response to the very real prospect of future contagion. This co-ordination problem will become progressively greater, not alone because of, for example, the prospectively greater role of China in the international financial system, but also because technological innovation will leave central banks behind.

The problem does not lie in markets or money or in profits: it lies in the idolatry of markets which is at the heart of Western mainstream finance and which, in reality, serves only to subvert and skew the operation of markets. The SV business model has, effectively, separated markets from their constitutive purpose of enhancing economic efficiency and thereby promoting The Common Good.

There are alternative paradigms. The principles of Islamic finance provide one pointer. The Judaeo-Christian ethos provides the most sensible guidance to ethical business behaviour within highly monetised market-based institutions.

If – more likely when – a structural fault-line opens up across western financial markets as a consequence of this business model, it may well prove impossible to contain the effects in the absence of a single, global monetary authority whose mandate and capabilities are aligned with the scale and complexity of financial markets. This will, almost inevitably, precipitate the transition to a new paradigm which will be traumatic and costly.

We need to begin a debate on moving to a new business model, governed by a sustainable ethos which transcends a purely prescriptive regulatory regime. The EU, and specifically the ECB, has no greater priority than leading such a debate and, at a global level pressing for a fundamental reform of the BIS/IMF into a genuinely global central bank.

This Article appeared in The Irish Times, January 2008.

Heading Off Global Financial Collapse – Lessons from the 2007 Credit Crunch

2008 brings closer the prospect of a major structural crisis in global financial market, writes Ray Kinsella.

A tear in the fabric of international financial markets would have incalculable consequences for the global economy. Such an 'event' is increasingly likely. Developments in financial markets in 2007 – at the heart of which was the global 'credit crunch' – increased the probability of such an event. However, the weaknesses have been evident for the past two decades.

Two factors will appear in retrospect to have been glaringly obvious pointers to the crisis. The 'Business Model' which dominates global financial institutions and markets is one. The second is the vulnerability of this structurally flawed Business Model arising from the fragmentation of international regulatory governance. No one is in charge. This fragmentation – as was blindingly obvious in 2007 – constrains the scope for responding in a timely and proportionate manner to systemic disturbances in the financial markets and, more importantly, to address the root causes.

Western mainstream financial institutions are based on a business model aimed at maximising Shareholder Value (SV). This model subjugates The Common Good to the interests of the owners of capital. This is a model well passed its sell-by date. In a knowledge-based economy capital is no longer the key factor of production. This alone argues against the over–riding priority of the business being to maximise shareholder value. This fallacy has been compounded by the 'short-termism' embedded within the model – the fixation of management, and of the whole organisation, on the next set of quarterly earnings.

The consequences of this mindset should have been obvious from the events of the 1990s and early 2000s, for which 'Enron' stems as the defining metaphor. But the lessons were not learned. There was, instead, a concerted attempt to salvage this Paradigm, precisely as Kuhn (who coined the term) predicted. Some of the initiatives – notably international standard–setting in accounting and auditing – were eminently sensible and did not require a prior justification. However, some attempts to fix a terminally flawed model were downright counter–productive – for example, the US Sarbanes Oxley Act (SOX), which is in reality an over–prescriptive form of regulatory imperialism. The term 'ethics' was hi-jacked and pressed into service in various domains across financial market activity, without any evident understanding of what ethics actually involves, especially in regard to respect for the Person.

Notwithstanding the SV model remains at the heart of western financial markets – an antiquated construct and a time-bomb waiting to detonate. It began ticking in the low interest rate environment of the early years of this decade.

The term 'Sub-Prime' is an exotic euphemism for what were high-risk mortgage loans to vulnerable individuals and families. The exponential growth in this market was driven by the insatiable demands of the SV business model to generate more and more earnings, irrespective of developments in the monetary environment and the knock-on impact on real economy over the median term. The 'search for yield' – for ever higher returns, *albeit* at the costs of taking on excessive risks, within new exotic and opaque financing structures, contributed to increasing volatility in international financial markets. This reached alarming dimensions by mid-2006.

The more than doubling of interest rates by 2006 provided the inevitable reality check. It precipitated a crisis in the sub-prime market, a collapse in balance sheet valuations of institutions which had had invested in mortgage-backed securities. This was then transmuted into a generalised crisis of confidence. Institutions in highly interlocked markets finally realised that what they had thought was a very clever game of generating higher returns from dodgy investments was, in effect, more like 'pass the parcel' of high risk illiquid investments. Catastrophic multi-billion dollar losses were recorded by major financial institutions and, within an environment characterised by an erosion of Trust which is central to the functioning of the markets, there was a freezing up of international credit markets.

It should not have happened. Credit–scoring models are highly sophisticated and the balance sheets of banks are closely monitored by national regulators. 'Stress testing' is mandatory. There are very rigorous liquidity criteria applied by these same regulators. A new, more risk sensitive, capital adequacy regime was fortuitously being implemented.

The primary reason it actually did happen is that financial institutions and intermediaries remained – notwithstanding the 'Enron' experience – fixated on earnings and profits and levels of compensation, to the exclusion of sustainability and The Common Good.

In terms of regulation and governance, there was an almost total lack of coherence in the response at a national and global level to the 'sub-prime' crisis and to its effects across the markets. This was encapsulated in the reaction by the UK authorities to the near meltdown of the Northern Rock model for funding its mortgage book. What began as acute pressure on its liquidity very quickly morphed into a full-blown solvency crisis For all that has been written on this event, the single most compelling point is this – there is hardly a single monetary economist in these Islands that believed they would witness a full scale 'run' on a major financial institution in a highly monetized.

Issues of politics, monetary policy and Financial Stability ebbed and flowed across the corridors of Whitehall reflecting the fragmentation of regulatory authority. There were problems of co-ordination and alignment of the different objectives of the Treasury, the Bank of England, and the Financial Services Authority, as they struggled to respond to an unfolding and unprecedented crisis of confidence in the full gaze of the media. The instincts of depositors, who queued, in the teeth of official reassurances, were right – this has severed the umbilical cord of trust on which both markets and regulators depend. It will be even more difficult for the authorities to hold the line next time.

The response of the authorities was belated and reactive. Responsibility for managing the effects of the Northern Rock debacle has passed from the Boardroom to the Treasury. It's not clear whether it will be nationalised or sold – whichever it is, the cost will be enormous and will be borne by the public sector rather than by shareholders. The proposals recently announced by the Chancellor of the Exchequer amount to yet more regulation the UK experience is a microcosm of the fragmentation of regulation and governance at a global level.

The global 'credit crunch' – of which Northern Rock was a predictable victim – was a manifestation of a 'contagion': the phenomenon whereby 'market failure' spreads, virus–like within, and across, financial markets. It is what keeps Central Bankers awake at night. It was the prospect of contagion which prompted the intervention, in September 2007, by the US Fed, the Central Bank of Canada, the Bank of England, and the ECB. Acting as *de–facto* 'lenders of last resort' to global (basically Western) financial markets, they signalled their willingness to make available funds to the credit markets against a wide range of collateral (some of which had been infected by the Sub–Prime crisis) at non-penal rates.

This intervention came late in the day. It was ad-hoc. It papered over cracks regarding, for example, whether or not to cut interest rates. It is not clear how far it will mitigate the real business costs of contagion – the full impact of which will only be evident later this year. There is no evidence that the key lesson of the near-collapse of Long Term Capital Management in 1998 had been learned. LTCM – and the contagion which it threatened to unleash – were stopped in its tracks only by the purely fortuitous and courageous intervention by the former President of the New York Fed. This is not, however, the NY Fed's job.

There is no one in charge in the event of a future full-blown crisis in global financial markets – not the IMF, not the BIS, not the OECD. Even within the EU, National Regulators are reluctant to cede further responsibility for Financial Stability to the ECB. Attempting to co-ordinate a set of regulators in enormously large and complex financial markets is a wholly inadequate response to the very real prospect of future contagion. This co-ordination problem will become progressively greater, not alone because of, for example, the prospectively greater role of China in the international financial system, but also, as Browne and Cronin have pointed out, the capacity of Central Banks to influence monetary developments will be constrained by technological innovation.

The problem does not lie in markets or money or in profits: it lies in the 'idolatry of markets' which is at the heart of Western mainstream finance and which, in reality, serves only to subvert and skew the operation of markets. The SV business model has, effectively, separated markets from their constitutive purpose of enhancing economic efficiency and thereby promoting The Common Good.

There are alternative paradigms. The principles of Islamic finance provide one pointer. The Judaea-Christian ethos provides the most sensible and incisive guidance to ethical business behaviour within highly monetised market-based institutions.

If – more likely when – a structural fault-line opens up across Western financial markets as a consequence of this business model, it may well prove impossible to contain the effects in the absence of a single, global, monetary authority whose mandate and capabilities are aligned with the scale and complexity of financial markets. This will, almost inevitably, precipitate the transition to a new Paradigm. The transition will be traumatic and costly, especially for poorer countries whose welfare is inextricably bound up with the Financial Stability of the Western Monetary system.

We need to begin a debate on moving to a new business model, governed by a sustainable ethos which transcends a purely prescriptive regulatory regime. The EU, and specifically the ECB, has no greater priority than leading such a debate and, at a global level pressing for a fundamental reform of the BIS/IMF into a genuinely global Central Bank.

This Article appeared in the Irish Times, December 2007.

Developments in Hedge Funds and Global Systemic Stability:

The Case for Regulation

The accompanying article sets out the nature and dynamic of the Alternative Investment Markets (AIM), and the kind of regulatory system which the industry believes is appropriate, particularly in respect of Hedge–Funds. The perspective provided here is rather different. It argues in favour of a normative and rigorous Principles-based regulatory system, for two reasons. Firstly, on the grounds of the latent instability of Hedge-Fund, arising from their enormous leverage as well as developments in Hedge-Fund markets in recent years. The second reason has to do with a more philosophical, but nonetheless important point, which relates to an emerging fracture between increasingly complex markets and their relationship to the real macro–economy.

The EU Commission will shortly publish a White Paper on Investment Funds, including the future regulation of Hedge Funds. The Commission has consulted widely with the Industry. It has also had input from two Expert Groups – on Hedge Funds and on Market Efficiency – which were set up following the earlier publication of a Green Paper. Notwithstanding the consultation process, the White Paper proposals will initiate a debate direct of fundamental importance to global financial services, and to financial stability, over the medium-term. Three base–line issues stand out as being of particular importance:

- What is the probability of a global systemic crisis?
- What reasons are there for believing that Hedge Funds, and developments in Hedge Fund-related markets, are more likely to play a' trigger' role in the transmission of instability than are mainstream markets?
- What form of regulation is most appropriate for Hedge Funds going forward?

The Need for Normative Regulation

These questions are, of course, clearly inter-related. The near failure of Long-term Capital Management (LTCM) was an 'event' which could, very easily, have triggered a wider market catharsis and liquidity crises than, in fact, it did. Importantly, they are not alarmist. While the possibility of global crises is discussed a good deal in the academic literature, as well as among Central Bankers, it is generally regarded as 'sensationalist' and not quite 'good form' to raise the matter within the public arena.

This is misconceived. There is positive probability of a systemic crisis, despite official and private-sector risk mitigating initiatives in recent years. The Hedge Fund industry, because of its size and its capacity, through leverage, to move asset prices, requires a rigorous regulatory framework, which recognizes <u>both</u> its positive and innovative nature in commoditizing risk <u>*and*</u> its unique potential to generate and transmit contagion across markets.

It is difficult to imagine a systemic crisis originating in, and being propagated through, retail financial services .Contemporary analogies of, say, Herstatt, Continental Illinois or even BCCI, would be localized 'events', where the impact could be mitigated by local and cross-border regulatory action. Yet retail financial services operate under an enormous compliance burden that can only be partially explained by the (proper) emphasis in recent years on consumer protection. The fact is that retail financial services, from the authority's perspective, are easy to regulate.

Not so Hedge Funds. The aggregate savings of pensioners are, for example, a major source of funding for Pension Funds. Informational asymmetries between, on the one hand, Hedge Funds Managers strategies and, on the other hand, pensioners at the far end of the investment 'food chain', are enormous. More generally, the potential for volatility and, possibly, contagion, arising from an 'event' within the Hedge Fund sector, is significantly greater than within retail financial services. The temptation to trust to market discipline rather than normative regulation is understandable – but fraught with dangers to global financial stability

Lessons from market 'events'

There have been a number of major financial market 'events' over the last decade or so. The Russian currency crisis in early 1998 arose from the decision to at least partially default on domestic government debt There was a major impact on both credit and capital markets. More importantly, however, the Russian crisis overlapped, and exacerbated, the effects of the near– meltdown LTCM that autumn. That was something new.

Two points in particular stand out. Firstly, the exposure of BIS–area banks to Russia was very limited – less than 5 per cent of their total foreign currency claims. So, the immediate balance-effects, in terms of capital, were not an issue. However, there was, as a recent Bank of England analysis points out 'a generalized reassessment of credit risk in emerging and mature markets', precipitating a 'flight to quality'. Highly leveraged institutions, notably Hedge Funds, were forced to sell assets. There was a concomitant effect on trading strategies within investment banks. The resultant volatility – a point to which we return below – triggered a 'programmed selling' type scenario by investors. The key point is that the impact was transmitted not through *direct* effects on the capital of major banks but, rather, through *indirect* effects on volatility and movements in, and prices unrelated to, market fundamentals.

The LTCM crises occurred within an already brittle market that was in shock. In retrospect, two points stand out. Firstly, in the absence of official intervention, LTCM would have failed and, in so doing, triggered a crisis not alone amongst creditors and counterparties but diffused, through different channels, across the markets, impacting in a very real way on all countries and on the Household and Corporate sectors within these countries.

Secondly, the €3.6 billion intervention by private sector institutions that stemmed the crises and stabilized LTCM was fortuitous. It might well not have happened. To put this another way, the effectiveness of the intervention owed everything to the character and credibility of the (then) chairman of the New York Fed. And, also, to the fact that he just happened to be around when the crisis finally broke. Another Chairman, another set of circumstances – a very different outcome. As it was, he moved swiftly, clearly signalled that there would be no official 'bail-out' [which took some courage] and knocked heads of major banks together, thereby 'fire walling' the crises. This initiative was no part of the Feds mandate. It owed nothing to international regulatory policy or 'Global Financial Architecture.

The third event was 9/11. In the penumbra of human tragedy, one fact stands out. In terms of risk modelling and risk mitigation – and therefore regulation – 9/11 was less of an 'event' than a 'singularity'. Its impact continues to reverberate across the global politico-economic landscape; certainly more risky but also a great deal more uncertain

There was a necessary emphasis on terrorism-related financial regulation. But global authorities also paid less attention than was justified in this new environment to the risk of global instability and on the need to take commensurate global regulatory initiatives. This has left the financial system vulnerable – within a reactive global political environment, lacking any moral credibility or leadership.

By definition, it is not possible to foresee the next global 'event' and whether – and if so how – its effects can best be mitigated. It is, however, possible to infer two points from what has been said. Firstly, there *will* be such an event. Financial history is not about to stop in 2007. Secondly, it is unlikely to be a single 'event. Instead, what is likely is a "trigger" event, whose impact will be amplified by contemporaneous events across asset markets, including relatively illiquid Alternative Investment Markets, with 'impact and feedback' effects on the global macro-economy.

Developments in Hedge Funds as a 'trigger event'

Hedge Funds and FOHF continue to expand rapidly in depth and sophistication. There is currently in excess of €2.5 trillion under management. That represents a lot of leverage, especially in the wider context of their role in the Alternative Investment Markets.

The issue is not whether Hedge Funds have an important role to play. They obvious do. The question is whether there is an adequate global regulatory system in place to regulate and to monitor Hedge Funds – and whether initiatives aimed at market efficiency are sufficient to guarantee an easy night's sleep to regulators and pensioners. There are reasons for believing that this may not be the case.

The ECB's most recent Financial Stability Report points out that persistent low interest rates and an increased appetite for risk in mainstream markets has contributed to an expansion in the AIM's. Even with recent interest rate changes, the search for yield has provided powerful impetus to the growth of AIMs, which are subject to bouts of discontinuities and illiquidity. Hedge Funds are at the heart of these markets. In particular, the ECB analysis points to:

- An increase in absolute and relative allocations by Institutional Investors to Hedge Funds.

- An increase in market concentration of under management, especially in FOHF.

- Evidence of lower Hedge Fund returns relative to longer-term averages ;these diminishing returns reflecting in part a reduction in perceived arbitrage opportunities, and crucially.

- Higher correlation of returns across Hedge Fund strategies, reaching levels in late 2005 that exceeded those that prevailed just prior to the LTCM crises.

More generally, the ECB made the point that "The fact that correlations are trending higher not only within some strategies but among strategies, raises concerns that a triggering event could lead to highly correlated exits across large parts of the Hedge Fund industry". This highlights, in the starkest terms, the questions: Who would be charge in these circumstances, what regulatory framework would they operate within, and what instruments and resources would they have at their disposal to mitigate a crisis?

Financial innovation and the constitutive purpose of markets

There is another largely ignored dimension of Hedge Funds that bears directly on the need for regulation and the fact that ideas of a 'light regulatory touch' are simply misconceived. It relates to the constitutive purpose of markets.

Professionals, up close and personal with a market that even regulators – let alone ordinary savers and pensioners (who provide a key part of the funding) – find it hard to comprehend, seldom find time to reflect on this matter. Yet it is central to the whole issue of regulation– and the kind of regulation that is appropriate for Hedge Fund-related market. The point is that markets are an essential economic and social artefact–but they are a means to an end. Their whole *raison d'etre* is to serve the real economy: In this context, the Compendium issued by the ISCJ notes:

A financial economy that is an end unto itself is destined to contradict its goals since it is no longer in touch with its roots and has lost sight of its constitutive purpose, In other words, it has abandoned its original and essential role of serving the real economy and ultimately of contributing to the development of people and the human community"

In a world of the financial exotica – of algorithms and arbitrage – it is easy to lose touch with what it's all about – and the potentially catastrophic consequences and spill over effects in the wider system if something goes wrong. Regulation is there to see to this – and to leave regulation of such opaque and pivotally important markets primarily in the hands of the industry is both unrealistic and irresponsible. This does not exclude a role for the industry in relation to market efficiency – quite the contrary.

System-strengthening initiatives and the global 'regulatory-gap

There are a number of factors which make full-blown systemic crises less likely than, say, ten years ago – but do not change its probable locus. Financial Stability has emerged as a specific discipline within the domain of Central Banking. There is greater understanding of the propagation of 'events 'across markets. Basle II [and its counterpart in Insurance] has impelled institutions towards a greater understanding of Risk – and the reality of emerging risks (e.g. 'crowded trades') in potentially volatile and brittle markets – but there is a limit to what better risk adjusted capital allocation can achieve.

There has significant investment in systems to minimize counterpart /collateral risk. All institutions carry out 'stress-testing' and, at an aggregate level, so do Central Banks. There is increased cooperation amongst market regulators. The IMF plays a role in market surveillance and the BIS continues to play a key role as a developed countries Stability Club, as well as producing the most incisive and elegant reports in the business. *But no one is in charge*. LTCM proved that.

At the same time, the reality is that the scale, and the potential volatility of Alternative Investment Markets – and indeed the wider set of markets, of which they are a sub-set – is highly fragmented. Within a global financial markets domain, there is no single global financial authority, combining the roles of surveillance, fostering market discipline, and providing of liquidity in the event of 'spill-over' effects in major market events. This has evolved, not through any conscious decision in favour of an evidenced-based 'decentralized' global financial architecture. It's happened by default, and through cooperative 'ad-hocery'.

SOX has highlighted the dangers of regulatory imperialism and ad-hocery. Whether, or not, SOX was a measured and proportionate regulatory response to deficiencies in auditing, accounting and internal controls, especially as regards the governance of global banks, is open to question. Leadership *does* have a role to play, as was all too evident in the case of LTCM. But SOX also highlighted the equally pressing problems of 'regulatory unilateralism'. Its *de facto* global roll–out took little account of alternative   approaches. The iterative consultation-based approach taken in developing the EU Eight Directive – which incorporated the principal of Subsidiary in regard to national standard-setting over and above 'core' provisions – leads to more informed and balanced outcomes.

The key point is that in a *global* commercial, including financial, environment characterized by integration, linkages as well as multiple – transmission mechanisms for propagating 'contagion' across markets' fundamentally different regulatory models, let alone provisions is an indulgence that puts the entire system at risk. Unilateralism cannot   be the answer. In the case of SOX *ex post* consultations between the US and the EU were very much a second-best means of achieving a global regulatory 'level playing field'.

It is equally the case that financial regulation in the US is not alone fragmented – but it's also highly politicized. This is a reality – and it's not conducive to achieving global Financial Stability, in the face of very real prospective threats.

Against this background – where the US de facto sets the tone and substance of global regulation – the absence of a single global regulator which has both a mandate and instruments to deal with a future systemic event, is disturbing. And it reinforces the argument that those sectors of the market – notably Hedge-Funds – which are particularly sensitive to, as well as being a potential transmission mechanism for shocks, simply cannot be left to the industry or to the markets to regulate.

Developments in Hedge Fund Markets as a Trigger Event

The Expert Groups set up by the EU Commission on Hedge-Funds and, also on the key issue of Market Efficiency, set out a wide range of important initiatives. But the underlying theme, that what is needed is a light regulatory touch, is wrong. In fact, *the possibility* of it being wrong is, in itself, a sufficient reason for a risk-averse regulatory approach. Insipient strains in Alternative Investment Markets – within which Hedge-Funds play a pivotal role – reinforce this argument. There is increasing pressure to generate returns which are not possible within mainstream markets. The unrealistic burden of investor expectations is itself a latent source of instability. The efficiency of Hedge-Funds, using derivative-type products, has to be set against new forms of risk and the volatility associated with factors set-out above.

Equally, the issue of whether, or not, Hedge-Funds are losing touch with their constitutive purpose has to be at least debated. Severing the umbilical cord between highly exotic and increasingly zero-sum game markets, and the real economy – (especially the economies of developing countries which do not benefit from financial innovation, but which are highly exposed to the negative effects of 'event shocks') – creates both the preconditions for a systemic crises, as well as pointing to the obvious need for a 'Global Sheriff'.

No one – especially those with a vested interest in the status-quo ever anticipate catastrophe – but it happens. In these circumstances, there are compelling arguments for a normative, Principles-based Framework for the monitoring and regulation of Hedge-Funds. The EU White Paper provides an ideal opportunity for the EU to play a leadership role both in regard to the need for regulation that *"will protect the stability of the financial system in all its intricate expressions, foster competition between intermediaries, and ensure the greatest transparency to the benefit of investors"* (Compendium , paragraph 369).

Particular reference is made in this article to: Bank of England's 'Financial Stability Report, Issue 20 (2000); The European Central Bank, "Financial Stability Review", (June 2006), Finance Dublin, Fiona Redden "Expert Groups give Opinion on Future Direction of the European Funds Markets", (July 2006), ICSJ Compendium of Social Teaching.

This Article appeared in Finance, November 2006.

New Insurance Behemoths Scoop up Business Globally

Global concentration of insurance has a direct effect on the Irish market and points to risks for market stability which must be addressed, writes Ray Kinsella.

It is a big – a very big – deal. The combined CGU/Norwich Union merger will create a global insurance giant, with a market capital of £18 billion, gross premium income of £25 billion, and Funds under management in excess of £200 billion.

The merger is the latest stage in a process of acquisition-driven consolidation that is transforming the global insurance market place. The Irish insurance market is being caught in the slip steam. It is not over yet – there is still a long way to go. Nor are the strategic implications – for banks, amongst others – clear. The very nature of Insurance – the pricing and transfer of Risk – is being worked over, as Alternative Risk Transfer (ART) rapidly develops outside of the traditional insurance paradigm.

The topography of the insurance market place is visibly changing. So, too is the way in which insurance providers engage with customers. So, the CGU/Norwich Union merger is important in itself; in what it signifies about what's happening in the industry and, equally important, in the response that it is likely to evoke amongst its new peer group.

The global market

There is now a 'Premier League' of global insurers.

The figures understate, if anything, the market reach and financial muscle of these behemoths – and especially the latent scope for change – through acquisition, diversification and organic growth – embedded in their balance sheets.

Two factors are likely to add additional momentum to the consolidation process. Firstly, recent changes in the capital gains regime in Germany will allow the world No.1, Allianz, to divest itself of the substantial investments in non–core sectors. These resources will be put to work. Royal and Sun Alliance – which is represented in Ireland – is now directly in the firing line. Such an acquisition would facilitate Allianz entry into the important US market. Equally, of course, AXA – which has grown enormously quickly through acquisition – has the capacity to make such a bid.

Impact on the Irish market

The merger reinforces the consolidation that has transformed the face of Irish insurance market over the last five years. What is also apparent is that the non-life market has changed. It really is a quite unprecedented transformation. And it is set to continue. There are also further indications that the market share position in terms of gross pensions annual premium income for the top six players in the Irish insurance industry.

What we are essentially looking at are three major players: Allianz (Church & General), Cornhill and Irish Insurance Corporation); AXA (Guardian/PMPA) and, now, CGNU (General Accident, Hibernian, Norwich Union).

CGNU's pre-merger decision to retain the Hibernian brand following its acquisition last year is a key outcome of the shake-up. Hibernian's strong position in the non-life market will provide very considerable leverage to Norwich Union's motor and casualty book.

The impact on the life side is, if anything, even more far-reaching. This is hardly surprising. The whole global and UK logic of the CGU/Norwich merger is precisely to strengthen the combined group's position in the life/long-term savings market. This resonates with the likely impact of the merger in the Irish market.

Norwich's strengths lie in the life and pensions products and will complement and broaden Hibernian's suite of products. There will eventually be some rationalisation with the inevitable human resource causalities this will entail. The net effect in purely market terms will be to strengthen Hibernian's position as a major composite insurer.

Further change is inevitable. To begin with, at the global level, attention has as noted, shifted to Royal Sun and Alliance – who are, of course, established in Ireland, as a likely acquisition target. Allianz is the probable predator. This would further reinforce the presence of Allianz Church and General in the Irish market. Recent and prospective developments are likely to fire AXA into strengthening its own position. The Irish banks, especially through their respective life and pensions subsidiaries, will face increased competition, albeit in a dynamic and growing market.

And in the longer run...

Firstly, the insurance market has become more concentrated. Concentration will rise further. The important point here is that, previously, this would have raised anti-competitive concerns. In practice, because of increased global consolidation – which is inevitably reflected in national markets – both national and EU competition authorities now have to take a broader view of increased market concentration and its possible impact on competition. New distribution channels and the growth of bank assurance, together with the increased contestability of the financial markets generally arising from technology, have diffused the latent adverse effects of concentration on competition.

Secondly, the new global insurers are driven by the imperative of generating shareholder value. It is this that will decide the allocation of capital to national markets and to specific businesses within these markets. Insurers are likely to require a minimum return on capital of at least 15 per cent. What this, in turn, means is that for a given market to be competitive –

that is, to be open in practice to new entrants – will require that these entrants can achieve at least this rate of return.

Competition and competitive markets do not exist in a vacuum: they need participants – especially global participants, with all that they bring to the market place. To take the Irish PMI market as an example, the government's goal of a 'competitive PMI market' cannot effectively exist where artefacts such as 'risk equalisation' effectively precludes new entrants – because, quite simply they make it well neigh impossible for such entrants to generate the required rate of return on their capital.

What is in prospect, therefore, is a lessening of national authorities' control over national insurance markets and a more demanding commercial regime. In principle, this should bring benefits – in terms of cost and product innovation – to customers. Having said that, businesses which do not generate sufficient shareholder value, which are under-priced, will be re-priced. Motor business is a case in point. The ultimate effect will depend on how lower-cost access and competition offsets the irresistible upward pressure for full economic pricing so as to generate an acceptable return on capital.

Impact on regulation

Thirdly, there are regulatory and market stability issues which arise from the impact of global consolidation in the insurance market. There has, of course, been considerable EU harmonization as well as the development of 'core principles' and 'standard-setting'. But the fact is that the nature of insurance is being redefined. Risk is migrating to the capital markets, where it means a quite different thing to traditional underwriting risk.

Moreover, insurance now encompasses banking and Fund management. There is considerable locational arbitrage, especially in the reinsurance sector. The point is that voluntary cooperation, through the International Association of Insurance Supervisors (IAIS) – which has a permanent staff of 5 people – means that effective, proactive supervision is lagging further and further behind the momentum of market change. It would be facile to say that there is an easy answer. There is not. It would be equally facile to claim that there are not systemic risks. There are. In the case of Ireland, these developments highlight the clear and present risk of diluting, within a Single Regulatory Authority for financial services, responsibility for market stability, by folding it in with consumer protection, which has a quite different focus.

Banks under pressure

Finally, there are the implications for the banking sector. Now, it is true to say that banks have proved strategically adept at adapting to the new environment. They are more robust today than, say, a decade ago. In Ireland, the major banks have been markedly successful in leveraging their advantages by diversifying – through ARK Life and Lifetime – into the life and pensions business. The development of Irish Life and Permanent is a perfect case study in market adaptation. But specifically in relation to banking, there are longer-term forces that cannot be gainsaid. And the consolidation of global insurance, and the emergence of global leaders such as Allianz, can only serve to accentuate these forces. Just a word on these.

The value of the banking franchise is under pressure and is being eroded. This has to do with the increased contestability of the market. It has to do with disintermediation – the progressive crowding out of banks by the securities markets, notably in the US, but increasingly in the EU (as recent European Central Bank studies demonstrate). The process of adverse selection – where banks, in effect, progressively are left with less attractive riskier corporate customers, as more robust companies access the securities/capital markets – accentuates these difficulties. Bouyant economic conditions may disguise – but cannot reverse – this difficulty within the traditional banking template.

Net interest margins are contracting under the twin–pressures of competition and a secular decline in interest rates. This decline has demolished the attractiveness of traditional bank savings products. Banks have been impelled to develop 'shareholder value' strategies around fee generation and capital–market based products. These strategies include bank assurance and fund management.

New battleground

Effectively, the centre of gravity in banking is shifting away from traditional intermediation and precisely towards the battleground being staked out by the new (re) insurance giants, like Allianz, Swiss Re, and prospectively CGU/Norwich Union. This market is dynamic, with considerable growth potential. But banks will need to re-think their whole rationale and strategy to be competitive. The capital market-based (re) insurers have enormous balance sheet capacity as well as strategic options that they have not, as yet, exploited. A case in point is the possible scope for Allianz to use as holdings in Dresdner Bank to build a global 'citibank' – type capability.

These are the big change-drivers. But such is the scale and pace of change that the more important ones may not yet be evident. What is clear, however, is that the art of managing under uncertainty is now the single most important competency. And for national and international regulation authorities, the words of Brian Quinn, formerly in charge of banking supervision at the Bank of England may not yet find a resonance: 'Each night I say a prayer: please Lord send me a small – orderly – collapse' (Princeton, 1990).

This Article appeared in Finance, April 2000.